Shotokan's Secret
The Hidden Truth Behind Karate's Fighting Origins

by Bruce D. Clayton, Ph.D.

Edited by Raymond Horwitz
and Edward Pollard
Graphic Design by John Bodine

©2004 Black Belt Communications LLC
All Rights Reserved
Printed in the United States of America
Library of Congress Control Number: 2004093398

ISBN-10: 0-89750-144-6
ISBN-13: 978-0-89750-144-6

Sixth printing 2006

BLACK BELT BOOKS
A Division of **OHARA PUBLICATIONS, INC.**
World Leader in Martial Arts Publications

Karate is the most difficult martial art.

Kata is the most difficult part of karate.

Bunkai is the most difficult part of kata.

Vision is the most difficult part of bunkai.

Silence is the most difficult part of vision.

Self is the most difficult part of silence.

Silence reveals the answers.

Answers contain the vision.

Vision teaches bunkai.

Bunkai inspires kata.

Kata makes karate real.

Karate teaches us to live.

Only self bars the way.

Set self aside, and listen to the silence.

Bruce D. Clayton

Acknowledgments

I want to thank Hanshi Vincent Cruz and the senior instructors of the International San Ten Karate Association (the San Ten Sensei), who are my instructors, colleagues and friends. Rick Llewelyn of Benicia, California, Armando Jemmott of Riverside, California, and Randhir Bains of Modesto, California, helped with bunkai suggestions and photographs. Jerry Fitzpatrick of Sacramento, California, has been a solid source of hard technique and common sense. Robert Stevenson of Fresno, California, serves as a constant reminder that hard style means hard training. If this book earns any praise, they deserve part of the credit.

Other friends have also made valuable contributions. Gary Simpson of Perth, Australia, was a typhoon of bunkai. Liu Haixiang of Beijing helped me make simultaneous sense of Japanese, Okinawan, Chinese and Korean karate terminology. Eri Takase, our Japanese interpreter and calligrapher, has been patient and helpful throughout. David LaVerne taught me the difference between *honne* and *tatemae*. Rafael Malabanan gave permission to publish a portion of his computer-generated Shuri Castle map. Beth Waldow, Jennifer Clayton and Alex Jones, my black belt assistants at the Claw of the Dragon *dojo* in Mariposa, California, have suffered through many painful experiments. Some of the experiments have left permanent scars, on them and on me. Karate isn't for sissies.

Special thanks to the San Ten photographic models: Sam Anderson, Penny Arnold, Christopher Arredondo, Randhir Singh Bains, Brett Banning, Russell, Nathan and Carly Bryson, Nick Busse, Manuel Carrillo, Jennifer Clayton, Marcelino Cortez, Jr., Dan Durun, Lisa Feller, Cheryl De Friez, Jerry Fitzpatrick, Arlene T. Gan, John Harlan, Alex C. Huichapan, Armando Jemmott, Alex Jones, Luke Julian, John and Anisa Kinsey, Arthur H. Kinsey IV, David and Dianne LaVerne, John Leggett, Ricardo Llewelyn, Candis, Remy, Brett and Matt Mason, John M. Morris, Daniel Nemiroff, Jeanna Phillips, Mark Radanovich, Robert Stevenson, Beth Waldow, Jenny Williams and Jim Wooles. They had not read the book when they posed for the pictures, and I appreciate their trust in me. Thanks also to Ira Estin for the composite photo of hanshi Cruz and the San Ten Sensei. Special appreciation to George Alexander and Patrick McCarthy regarding the issue of the Okinawan portraits.

Every single person I know has taught me something important— my wife, Jeannie, most of all. I appreciate her trust in me, too.

About the Author

Bruce Clayton received his Ph.D. in ecology from the University of Montana in 1978 after earning his bachelor's degree in zoology and botany from UCLA in 1972. While studying at UCLA, he began his martial arts career as a protégé of Briggs Hunt, a scrappy wrestling coach who loved dirty fighting. Clayton was introduced to *shotokan* karate in 1973.

Today Dr. Clayton is a fifth-degree black belt instructor in shotokan karate, under the direction of hanshi Vincent Cruz and the San Ten Sensei. Dr. Clayton gives lively seminars on self-defense, vital points, expedient weapons and karate bunkai.

Figure A: Sensei Clayton practicing beside a Sierra stream at the San Ten 2002 Sierra Camp weekend.

Clayton is also a well-known survival expert, author of *Life After Doomsday*, *Fallout Survival*, and *Thinking About Survival*, as well as co-author of *Survival Books* and *Urban Alert*. His most recent survival book is *Life After Terrorism* from Paladin Press (2002).

He has been interviewed as a survival expert by several national television programs, including *The CBS Evening News*, *The Tomorrow Show*, *Today*, and *60 Minutes*, and has appeared on many local radio programs in the United States, Great Britain, Canada and Australia.

For the record, Dr. Clayton has never been a member of *any* political party, any religious organization, or any group that is based on animosity or intolerance.

The San Ten Sensei

"A black belt is just a white belt who never quits."
— Hanshi Vincent Cruz

Sensei Clayton is part of a faculty of senior shotokan instructors under the direction of hanshi Vincent Cruz. These teachers are known as the San Ten Sensei. They are the senior instructors of the International San Ten Karate Association (ISKA), founded by Cruz in 1979.

Figure B: Hanshi Vincent Cruz and (some of) the San Ten Sensei. Left to right: Bruce Clayton, Randhir Bains, Robert Stevenson, Ricardo Llewelyn, Jerry Fitzpatrick and Armando Jemmott.

This team is dedicated to researching and promoting the basic principles of linear karate power, which have all but disappeared in the sport karate world. This work is based on the lifelong research of Master Hidetaka Nishiyama, a karate legend in his own lifetime and Cruz's teacher for the last 50 years.

For more information on the activities sponsored by the International San Ten Karate Association, visit our Web site at http://www.santenkarate.com.

Table of Contents

Introduction

Shotokan's Secret asks and answers a number of important questions about the past and future of hard-style karate. The first question is: *How did this book come to be written?*

This book began as an innocent quest for a picture of Yasutsune Azato, who was shotokan Master Gichin Funakoshi's first teacher. Karate historians say that there is no known picture of Azato, but I wanted one to put on the wall of my shotokan dojo. I could not believe that no one had ever made a picture of Azato. I made a two-year hobby of searching for this picture.

Azato was a member of the court of King Sho Tai at Shuri Castle in Okinawa, whose reign began just before the American Civil War. Surely, I reasoned, *somebody* had taken a daguerreotype photograph of the king and his advisors during some important ceremony. There must have been a coronation or a wedding or some other event worthy of a photograph. I searched for this photo. I studied books on the history of Japan and Okinawa. I dug for original sources. I sent e-mail to experts. I bid on rare Japanese books at auction. I scoured the Internet looking for clues. I even learned to interpret *kanji* symbols into English so I could painfully translate the captions in the Japanese books. In the end, Azato remained as sadly elusive as before, but along the way I discovered a remarkable window into the early history of karate.

For over a thousand years, Okinawa imported unarmed martial technique from China, with no particular evolution of the art. The Okinawans seemed content to use the imported skills while making only minor modifications to their own. Then suddenly, in the middle 1800s, a group of Okinawan lords set aside their traditional Chinese fighting skills and began to practice a new and highly lethal form of unarmed combat.

The new art, called *Shuri-te*, was fundamentally different from traditional *chuan fa*.[1] Compared to Chinese fighting, the new art was shockingly ruthless. The new style made no attempt to subdue the opponent through painful nerve strikes or immobilizing joint locks.

---

[1] I am using "chuan fa" as the equivalent of the American term "kung fu." There is endless debate about the proper use of these terms. In this book they both mean "Chinese boxing" in a general sense.

Instead, every element of the new art emphasized destroying the opponent completely in one or two seconds. We recognize this art today as the first emergence of hard-style, linear karate.

Shuri-te was based on overwhelming impact, and largely ignored the grappling and submission skills of traditional chuan fa. This was not just a natural evolution of chuan fa based on an accumulation of small differences over time. It was a sudden revolution in the early 1800s that requires an explanation.

Karate historians have done an impressive job of collecting random facts, stories, legends and surmises about the early masters of Shuri-te karate. They have shown us a picture of formidable men pounding their *makiwara* posts secretly in the dead of night. The historians have dug diligently, comparing techniques and records with legends and rumors, searching for the origin of each individual piece of modern karate. They have done an outstanding job of collecting the minute fragments of the karate puzzle.

I respect them deeply, but I think they missed something. We already knew what the Shuri-te masters did at night. The unasked question is: *What did they do in the daytime?*

When you read about karate history, you quickly learn that karate arose on the tiny island of Okinawa in the East China Sea. As you read more deeply, you realize that hard-style karate arose in Shuri, the capital of Okinawa. A little more reading reveals that the Shuri masters were all knights and nobles, the lords of Okinawan society. After studying the history of Okinawa itself, it gradually becomes clear that the masters were not just idle gentry, as we would naïvely expect. They were, in fact, hard-working employees of the Shuri national government.

The seat of Okinawan government was a small cluster of buildings in the center of Shuri Castle. The castle is not a very large place, and most of the office space was in four wooden buildings surrounding a central square. One building in particular, the Seiden, was the king's office complex and throne room. On a typical business day in the 1850s, the Seiden and adjacent buildings were full of famous karate masters working diligently to administer the government of Okinawa.

The Shuri masters performed routine government functions in offices only a few yards from the throne room. In modern terms, they were coworkers. They worked together every day, with some of them walking to work together in the morning and strolling home together in the evening. They planned and executed government projects, ate lunch, and confronted and solved national problems, advised the king and ran the country together.

And in the middle 1800s, they invented linear karate—together.

Shuri was not a tranquil place in the 1800s. The national interests of Japan, China, Europe and America collided fatally in 19th century Shuri, with consequences that changed Okinawa and Japan forever. The Shuri ministers were in real physical danger during this period, but they didn't have a single weapon to use in their own defense. All they had was their bare hands. This is the situation I call the "Shuri Crucible."

At the center of this storm stood Sokon "Bushi" Matsumura, a brilliant fanatic whose commitment to the martial arts bordered on madness. For 50 years, Matsumura was the military officer responsible for the safety of Okinawa's royal family and the Shuri ministers. During this time, Matsumura confronted many groups of angry, armed adversaries. Under the intolerable pressure of the Shuri Crucible, Matsumura changed the soft techniques of Chinese chuan fa into a new kind of unarmed fighting in which a single blow could be as decisive as a pistol shot.

This book is founded on historical fact and detailed in more than 250 footnotes. The background information about the people, the dates, and the geopolitical events cannot be seriously challenged. We are forced to rely on anecdotal information and oral tradition to fill in personalities. While anecdotes are instructive, undoubtedly some of this information has been exaggerated, altered, misunderstood, suppressed or even invented. At a certain point, both fact and oral tradition fail us, and we must fill in the gaps guided by our own martial experience and common sense. The historical context, however, defines Matsumura's tactical problem quite clearly. It is easy for us to recognize his solution to the problem, because linear karate fits the tactical problem like a key fits a lock.

There are overlooked documents that show us the Shuri Crucible in action. One is the two-volume narrative of U.S. Navy Commodore Matthew Perry's expedition to Japan in 1853. Another is Perry's personal diary that he kept during this expedition, which was not published until 100 years after his death. Perry negotiated with the Okinawan ministers and was not happy with the results. He forcibly led 200 U.S. Marines into Shuri Castle to express his displeasure. In Perry's narratives of this event we get to see something truly special: We see what the Shuri karate masters did in the daytime. Seeing them at work explains, once and for all, why they stayed up late every night learning how to kill with their bare hands.

Matsumura's tactical problem was unique, and has never been duplicated anywhere in the world. He faced opponents and weapons that will surprise you. His tactical applications were vicious and practical, even for today's street scenarios. It is a small wonder that a unique martial art was born from it. The Shuri Crucible opens whole new avenues for interpreting the shotokan kata (and kata of many related styles of karate).

I started out looking for a picture of Azato, and ended with a completely new view of hard-style history and bunkai. I uncovered many interesting things along the way that have greatly enriched my own shotokan classes. Even if you don't agree with my conclusions, I promise that you *will* enjoy reading this book. I certainly enjoyed writing it. And when you finish, you will know a lot more about karate and shotokan bunkai than you did when you started. *Shotokan's Secret* brings karate to life. The reward is worth the effort.

I never found that picture of Azato, but I came very close.

Bruce D. Clayton, Ph.D.
April 2004

Chapter 1

The Place
and the Time

Shotokan's Secret: Hard-style karate was invented in the mid-1800s by the bodyguards to the king of Okinawa. These unarmed guards were often outnumbered by armed and aggressive enemies. To defend themselves and the royal family, they were forced to turn their bodies into lethal weapons.

To make this argument, I need to take you back to 19th century Okinawa so you can see for yourself how this came about. In this opening chapter we will set the stage for our drama. The material may seem familiar at first, but within a few pages we'll be exploring paths you haven't seen before in a karate history book.

The problem with published karate history is that there is too little information about things that made a difference, and too much about things that did not. In particular, karate historians have entirely overlooked the enormous political pressures that shaped and then destroyed the Okinawan way of life in the 1800s. To understand the men who invented linear karate, we have to understand the danger they were in.

There is a dramatic story behind the birth of karate, but we must assemble it from tiny fragments scattered among a plethora of truly irrelevant information. Leafing through karate history, one feels like an archeologist sifting through tons of dirt for a few fragments of broken pots. This chapter and the next present the few fragments that matter, and place them in context so we can see what they mean.

Island of Conflict

The Shuri Crucible was born out of simple geography. The island of Okinawa is one of those unfortunate places that will always be a battleground. There are half a dozen places like this in the world, where great powers come into conflict.

Okinawa is a semi-tropical island similar to Hawaii. It is the largest island in the Ryukyu (or "Lew Chew") archipelago, which stretches from Japan on the north to Taiwan on the south. Okinawa has sugar cane fields, beautiful beaches and palm trees. The waters off Okinawa are rich with ocean life, including a large population of humpback whales. These whales, oddly enough, played a significant role in the history of karate.

The island is large enough to have a solid population of tax-paying farmers and fishermen, but too small to support a standing army. It

Figure 1-1: Okinawa in 1853. Tomari is the village on the near side of the Asato River; Naha lies in the distance. U.S. warships ride at anchor in Naha bay. The Okinawans with bare legs are peasants. Figures in floor-length *hoari* coats are keimochi nobles.[2]

has the misfortune to sit halfway between Japan and China, and it has a very attractive harbor at Naha. Throughout history, the Okinawans have had China looming on one side and Japan on the other. Okinawa could neither run nor hide, and was not strong enough to resist invaders. Naturally, the island has been conquered by both powerful neighbors.

The Okinawans are a long-suffering people. Their name for themselves is the *Uchinanchu*.[3] They have their own language, *uchina guchi*, which is distantly related to Japanese and Chinese in the sense

---

[2] Some of the pictures reproduced here look like fabulously detailed paintings, but they are actually *lithographs*. A lithograph is an etching made on a sheet of limestone by tracing a photograph. The etched stone was used to print high-quality copies of the picture. In the 1850s there was no other way to print a photograph in a book. I obtained some of the original lithographs from the 150 year old narrative of the Perry expedition, and scanned them for these illustrations. See Perry, M.C., *Narrative of the Expedition to the China Seas and Japan*, 1852-1854, reprinted by Dover Press, 2000.

[3] McCarthy, Patrick, *Ancient Okinawan Martial Arts: Korryu Uchinadi*, Volume 1, Tuttle, 1999a, p. 104. Karate historians fight a continous battle to sort out the original Okinawan terminology. Very few people still understand *uchina guchi*.

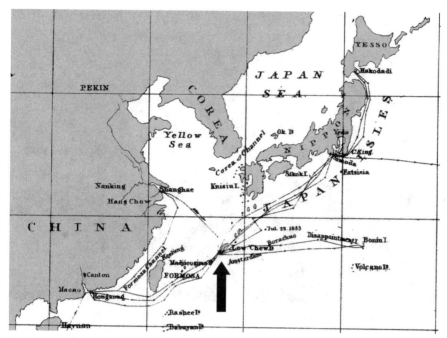

Figure 1-2: Vicinity of Okinawa, showing a tiny island trapped between China and Japan. This is the map of Commodore Perry's voyages in 1852-54. Okinawa was called "Lew Chew" by Perry's Chinese translators (see arrow).[4]

that English is distantly related to French and German.[5] A person who grew up on Okinawa in the 1800s could not make himself understood in either China or Japan, yet all three languages (and Korean) are written using the same kanji characters. Since Okinawa was halfway between Japan and China, they had, and still have, a constant need for translators.

Shuri, Naha and Tomari

At the local level, the development of linear karate occurred mainly in Shuri, the capital of Okinawa, in and around Shuri Castle. People also speak of famous karate masters who lived in the nearby seaport villages of Naha and Tomari, and one prominent figure lived in Asato

---

[4] Perry, 2000, p. 513.

[5] Sells, John, *Unante, The Secrets of Karate,* 2nd Edition, W.M. Hawley, 2000, p. xvi. Sells points out that karate books often identify the Okinawan language as "Hogen," which is simply the Japanese word for "dialect."

village, on the road from Tomari to Shuri. Every history of karate mentions these famous landmarks.

In the 1920s there arose a karate myth that these three communities were somehow isolated from one another, and that different kinds of karate "developed" separately in the three locations. This story served the needs of the time, but it has no historical basis. It is important to realize that these "villages" are all part of the same small community. The whole Shuri/Naha/Tomari triangle is about the same size as Golden Gate Park in San Francisco or Central Park in New York City. If you wanted to fly from Shuri to Naha, you'd just taxi the airliner to the far end of the runway and get off.

The men who invented linear karate spent their *entire lives* in this limited area. It is very hard to justify the idea that a martial artist who grew up on the streets of this small community was significantly "isolated" from anyone else who lived there. Let's set that myth aside and look a little harder for the truth.

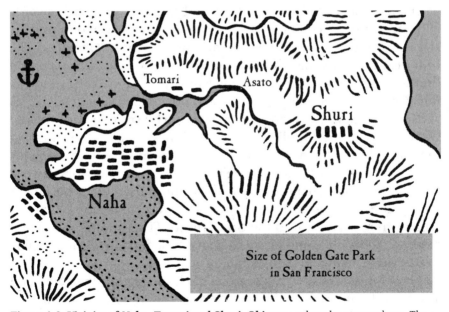

Figure 1-3: Vicinity of Naha, Tomari and Shuri, Okinawa, where karate was born. The anchor shows where visiting ships could anchor safely. Compare with Figure 1-1, which was taken from the ridge above Tomari, facing southwest.[6] The coast near Naha was lined with salt flats, and there were reefs, shoals and rocks just offshore. It is a three-mile walk from Naha to Shuri.

---

[6] This map is based on Perry, 2000, p. 184.

Second Sho Dynasty

Okinawa has been populated since the end of the last ice age, but the period we are interested in is known as the Second Sho Dynasty. This dynasty was founded when an ambitious accountant saw a chance and took it in 1477, declaring himself Sho En, King of Okinawa. The island had nominally been the property of China since the Chinese conquest in the seventh century. Okinawan kings have always ruled under a license from the Ming Emperor in China. Sho En petitioned the Emperor for a charter to be King of Okinawa, and was approved. Reading about Sho En, there is no doubt that money changed hands. He was an unprincipled rascal.

This would not concern us except that his son, Sho Shin, was one of the great kings of Oriental history. In his 30 year reign, Sho Shin transformed Okinawa from a collection of bickering warlords to one nation under a strong central government. He built a palace on a hill at Shuri, moved the scattered Okinawan warlords into nearby townhouses where he could keep an eye on them, and collected all of their swords in a warehouse. His building projects stimulated the economy and for about a century there was peace and prosperity in Okinawa. The historical accounts may be exaggerated, but you get the impression that Sho Shin was a genuine benevolent dictator. He turned his impoverished island into a peaceful and prosperous kingdom.

Having taken away civil war as the primary diversion of the Okinawan samurai families (the *keimochi*), Sho Shin wisely drafted them into his new government and established hereditary stipends for various government offices. He put the disarmed warriors to work by creating a bureaucratic ruling class who staffed the government offices at Shuri Castle. Every family had perpetual job security as long as they were loyal to the Sho dynasty. (There were less than a hundred keimochi families, so the government could easily employ two or three members of each family at a time.)

Sho Shin established a hierarchy of classes within the keimochi. The royal family was at the top of the pyramid, of course, and the former warlord families formed a princely second layer. The third layer was devoted to the ministers, who were the powerful department heads of the government. After that came four ranks of keimochi who were government employees (not unlike the system of GS salary ranks used in the U.S. government today.) These nobles were granted the special title of *Peichin*, which was similar to being a knight. Saying "Peichin Takahara" was like saying "Sir Takahara."

The Peichin nobles were assigned jobs in government service, such as tax accounting, law enforcement, map making, diplomatic relations, translation, warehousing rice (their version of banking), and keeping official track of Okinawa's complex family genealogies.

Since these knights could not carry swords, they needed some other outward sign of their noble status. They adopted a unique, turban-like hat, the *hachimaki*,[7] as the badge of their high rank. (See Figure 3-5.) The color of the hat declared the wearer's exact status. They also wore their hair in a tight bun, or topknot. A special silver pin, stuck through the topknot, served as a second method of declaring rank. The size and design of the pin served as a form of heraldry to declare a family's exact status.[8] Other signs of high keimochi status included the *haori* topcoat with its floor-length skirts and enormous belled sleeves, and *tabi*, the split-toed socks one wears with *zori* sandals.[9] Peasants were not allowed to dress so ostentatiously. Peasants wore a pullover smock and little else.

Disarming the warlords established an Okinawan tradition of life without visible weapons, a tradition reinforced and continued by subsequent historical events. This stopped the petty wars but proved somewhat short-sighted in the end. The absence of weapons made Okinawa a little too vulnerable.

Shogun Ieyasu Tokugawa

One of the important factors that led to the invention of karate was the genius of Ieyasu Tokugawa, the warlord who took control of Japan away from the imperial family in a series of battles and intrigues at the beginning of the 17th century.[10] Tokugawa was not a benevolent dictator. He was a ruthless tyrant with a genius for enslaving people. Once he had declared himself *shogun*, or military dictator of Japan,

---

[7] Kerr, 2000, p. 95, and others, use *hachimaki* to refer to this headgear, meaning it looked like a turban. The familiar Japanese headband is a very *minimal* turban.

[8] Sells, 2000, p. 5-10.

[9] McCarthy, Patrick, *The Bible of Karate: Bubishi*, Tuttle, 1995, p. 48.

[10] James Clavel's novel, *Shogun*, presents the story of Tokugawa's rise to power. Clavel, James, *Shogun*, Dell, 1976.

he set about establishing a dynasty. To secure the *shogunate* for his family, Tokugawa issued a series of proclamations designed to make revolution against him impossible. Tokugawa created a strictly-regulated society in which freedom, innovation and new ideas were not only forbidden, but were regarded as dangerous. The punishment for the slightest infraction was torture and death.[11]

The Tokugawa edicts allocated land to specific friends of the regime. The land grants made Tokugawa's samurai allies wealthy (but not wealthy enough for any one samurai to build an army as big as Tokugawa's). In return for their wealth, the samurai families were required to administer the economy and taxes of the nation, and to ruthlessly enforce the rules of correct behavior.

If you had lived during the Tokugawa dynasty, you would have found that every aspect of your life was regulated and spied upon. Every profession had a list of rules to follow. These rules controlled how you did business, what clothes you could wear, what kind of house you could live in, what kind of person you could marry, what kind of gifts you could give your children on their birthdays, where you could build your outhouse, and the exact limits of where you could go and what you could do without explicit overlord permission. Any sign of independent thought was evidence of rude behavior, and death followed swiftly.

It is hard for us to imagine the severity of punishments in Tokugawa's Japan. Crucifixion was common, for crimes as small as the theft of a radish. Mothers were crucified with their babies strapped to their chests, so the mother had to watch her baby die of thirst before succumbing herself. The samurai showed great ingenuity in devising other novel forms of execution, such as boiling victims to death in volcanic hot springs, or beheading them with a saw instead of a sword.

A criminal could be certain of execution, but often his family died too, and sometimes the punishment included neighbors, friends and entire villages. In one situation, 35,000 people were put to the sword— one throat at a time—to purge a province that had become too tolerant of Christians.[12]

---

[11] Henshall, Kenneth, *A History of Japan from Stone Age to Superpower,* St. Martin's Press, 1999, p. 48-69.

[12] Henshall, 1999, p. 55.

It is no wonder that the Japanese people developed a culture where the greatest virtue was to follow the rules and behave *exactly* like everyone else. This was the only way to protect one's family and friends from accusations and retribution. The fear of being different even forced left-handed people to pretend to be right-handed. In ancient Japan, a man who discovered that his wife was left-handed had legal grounds for divorce.[13]

The people memorized the rules of behavior by creating kata, which were rituals that exactly prescribed how to perform everyday activities like dressing, bowing and cooking. If you followed the kata exactly, you were following the rules and your family was safe.[14] The Japanese tea ceremony is an example of kata taken to a high art, as is the ceremony of sword-making.

Since all questions had been answered in advance by the shogun's edicts, anyone who raised his voice to ask questions was a dangerous freethinker. Such a person would be punished for being inquisitive, and punishments were harsh.[15]

Tokugawa's conquest of Japan in 1600 had been assisted by a stranded English sea captain named Will Adams.[16] Adams helped Tokugawa by building ships and forging cannons for the dictator. Tokugawa took a lesson from this experience: new foreign ideas and new foreign technology could be a threat to his heirs. He issued orders to *seal the borders of Japan*, and allowed no commerce with western societies.[17] As a society, Japan went into suspended animation. This edict applied to the home islands, but was also enforced on outlying provinces such as Okinawa. Contact with the West was prohibited, avoided, strictly regulated, and sometimes severely punished for the next two and a half centuries.

---

[13] This is from a Web site for left-handed people. It might be apocryphal, but it fits. http://www.ac2w.com/en_anecdotes.htm.

[14] De Mente, B. L., *Behind the Japanese Bow*, Passport Books, 1993, p. 47.

[15] *Deru kui wa utareru.* "The nail that sticks up gets hammered down." Japanese proverb.

[16] Alexander, George, *An Analysis of Medieval Japanese Warrior Culture and Samurai Thought as Applied to the Strategy and Dynamics of Japan's Twentieth Century Era of Warfare*, doctoral dissertation, Western Pacific University, 2001, p. 37.

[17] Henshall, 1999, p. 56. The Dutch were allowed to dock at one seaport, and there was continuing costal trade with China and Korea. Other than that, it was a shutout.

The Tokugawa shogunate lasted from 1603 to 1867. The policy of isolation was successful until 1853, when U.S. Navy Commodore Matthew Perry sailed a squadron of warships into Tokyo harbor and demanded at gunpoint that Japan open her doors. By that time, Japan was so far behind the industrial West that she couldn't really refuse.

Tokugawa had been right. His dynasty lasted only as long as Western ideas could be locked out. The Tokugawa regime lost face, and within 15 years lost everything. Revolution ensued. The shogun's dynasty ended. The Japanese imperial family resumed control of the nation in the Meiji restoration of 1868. Japan began a program of ambitious industrial modernization that led directly to a series of wars with Russia, Korea, China and, ultimately the United States.

Tokugawa's influence is still very evident in modern Japan, and also in our formal karate classes. We have Tokugawa to thank for the fact that students line up, sit down, and stand up strictly by rank, must all wear identical clothing, and must all tie their belts in exactly the same way.

In many karate schools it is considered rude and disrespectful to ask questions of the master. Your next promotion might be deferred by a year to teach you humility. This makes an important point about karate history. You can learn the techniques and kata by imitating the teacher, but you can't learn about history that way. You have to ask questions. In most karate organizations, the seniors are distant, unapproachable and do not tolerate an inquisitive attitude. As a result, the seniors themselves never learned very much about karate history. They *can't* answer our questions. They don't know.

Ieyasu Tokugawa is still very much with us. For the purposes of this book, the important thing is that he created a police state in which subjugated people could not own weapons, and contact with the west was absolutely forbidden. This proved to be a deadly diplomatic problem for a small, disarmed island with a strategic seaport.

Tokugawa's tomb is the original source of those three famous monkeys who advise "Hear no evil, see no evil, speak no evil." This is an appropriate parting thought from the man who imposed mind control on an entire culture.

Satsuma Invasion

In 1609, with the blessing of the new shogun Ieyasu Tokugawa, Lord Shimasu of Japan's southern Satsuma province sent 3,000 soldiers to Okinawa with ambitions of conquest that were quickly realized. The battle for the island was fierce but brief. The Japanese invaders lost 57 men. They killed 539 Okinawan fighters, who were hurriedly armed and ill-trained for the conflict. That's what happens when the invaders have firearms and the defenders have never used their grandfathers' rusty old swords.[18] The Satsuma victors liked the idea that Okinawa was unarmed, and suggested pointedly that this policy should continue. This order remained in force for the next two and a half centuries.

After 1609, Okinawa was in fact a colony of Japan, even though it

Figure 1-4: Satsuma overlords. A party of Satsuma samurai examining a map in the 1860s. These were the evil puppetmasters who controlled the kings of Okinawa. Note the ostentatious display of weapons.[19]

---

[18] Hokama, Tetsuhiro, *History and Traditions of Okinawan Karate*, Masters Publications, 2000, p. 24. Also Cook, Harry, *Shotokan Karate, A Precise History*, (no publisher), 2001, p. 6.

[19] Bennett, Tony, *Early Japanese Images*, Tuttle, 1996, p. 82. Photo by pioneer photographer Felice Beato. Courtesy of the Old Japan Picture Library.

did not suit the shogun to admit it. Okinawa continued to be a nominal province of China while actually being controlled by Japan, a bizarre situation the historians refer to as "dual subordination." The long-suffering Okinawans paid taxes to *both* neighboring nations. To facilitate this delicate diplomatic situation, the Second Sho Dynasty spent 250 years as a puppet government. They faced the world as the rulers of Okinawa, but in fact had no independent authority. The puppeteers watched from the shadows, fingering their swords.

The Satsuma officials wielded the full, despotic authority of the shogunate. They ordered the Shuri officials to conceal and deny their relationship with Japan, to the extent that it was forbidden to speak Japanese or wear Japanese clothing in the presence of foreign visitors.[20]

The Chinese knew perfectly well what was going on, but they didn't want a war, either. They were still getting their tribute ship every year. Why rock the boat? They took their money and looked the other way.

This created a unique situation that bears forcefully on the history of karate. The Sho kings were not allowed to keep military forces. In fact, even the king had no right to own or carry weapons. The king had no authority to make treaties or agreements with foreign powers. He had to *pretend* to be a head of state, but in fact he had only enough power to collect taxes and enforce local laws. If his men made a mistake, he paid for it personally.

Life under Japanese domination was brutal but stable during the 1600s and 1700s. The 1800s were a more turbulent time. The last three kings of Okinawa played roles in the creation of linear karate. King Sho Ko reigned from 1804 to 1827 when he was deemed unreliable by his Japanese minders and was forced to give up the throne.[21] His son Sho Iku reigned from 1828 until 1847, when he was arrested and taken to Tokyo.[22] This put the last king of Okinawa, Sho Tai, on the throne in 1847 at the age of seven. (Most of the story of karate takes place during the reign of Sho Tai.)

In 1879, the office of king was abolished. Sho Tai was deposed by Imperial Japanese decree and forced to live as a hostage in Tokyo, along with many of his family and court retainers. Sho Tai died in

---

[20] Kerr, 2000, p. 247. Also Sells, 2000, p. 21.

[21] Kerr, 2000, p. 244.

[22] Kim, 1974, p. 51.

exile in 1901. These three kings did not die in office. They were all fired and placed under house arrest. The fact that a king could be fired shows just how bizarre this situation really was.

All of these facts are missing pieces to the puzzle of linear karate. We'll touch again on each of them as our story develops.

Peasants, Lords and Overlords

The Okinawan karate stories are somewhat confusing in terms of unexpected class distinctions, which make it hard for modern readers to interpret the Okinawan legends. It is critical to understand that there were two different types of samurai involved: the disarmed Okinawan keimochi and the armed Satsuma overlords. The critical conflicts arose between Okinawan and Japanese samurai, not between nobles and peasants.

Figure 1-5: Okinawan peasants, working a field barefoot, ungroomed and nearly naked.[23]

---

[23] Perry, 2000, p. 157.

In general, there were five classes of people walking the forested lanes of Naha/Shuri in the 1800s:

- **Okinawan keimochi:** Disarmed for two centuries, these were the traditional island nobility. This class includes all of the famous Shuri masters, including Funakoshi. Linear karate and *kobudo* arose among this class, not among the peasants.

- **Police:** The police were a branch of the Shuri military/justice administration. Most of them were lower-ranking Okinawan keimochi reporting to the military commander of the Okinawan government.

- **Satsuma samurai:** For 250 years the Satsuma samurai walked among the helpless Okinawans like wolves among sheep. If later Japanese behavior in Korea and China is any guide, the early occupation of Okinawa must have been very brutal. The samurai regarded the Okinawans as *gaijin* (barbarians) and conquered gaijin had the same social status as animals.[24]

- **Foreigners:** Naha was a deep-water seaport with many visiting sailors from all over the world. These visitors were armed with knives, clubs, swords, harpoons, pistols, and sometimes rifles. They made life exciting for the keimochi ministers and the unarmed Okinawan police.

- **Peasants:** Impoverished and downtrodden, these farmers and fishermen were little more than semi-naked agricultural slaves. They did not have the leisure or the freedom to study martial arts during the 1800s.

Until you understand the relationships among these five groups, karate history will make no sense at all.

Kobudo

Kobudo is the indigenous Okinawan art of weaponry. Okinawans have a unique tradition of sophisticated fighting techniques associated with common household and agricultural objects such as millstone handles, sickles, threshing flails, bridles, oars, turtle shells, machetes,

---

[24] Kim, 1974, p. 13, tells a story about a Japanese samurai trying to rape an Okinawan girl. A stalwart hero kills the samurai with an oar.

and staffs. Kobodu also includes some uncommon items such as the *sai*. Okinawan peasants used to receive the credit for developing kobudo, but this romantic idea is simply not supported by the facts.[25]

Okinawan sensei claim that kobudo has a 1000 year history, but the evidence of this seems very thin.[26] People have hit each other with sticks since the dawn of time. There was no pressing need for sophisticated kobudo until the 1609 Japanese invasion turned Okinawa into an enslaved nation. From that point on, makeshift weapons were a priority, and not just for peasants. Kobudo dates from this period.

McCarthy relates an obscure story that may explain the true origins of kobudo.[27] After sending all his troops to occupy Okinawa, Satsuma's Lord Shimasu began to feel a bit naked on the landward side. He decided to conscript a peasant self-defense force. His idea was to teach the peasants to use common objects as weapons against a samurai soldier. Shimasu knew that such techniques would be worthless without the input of skilled swordsmen. He ordered the masters of the *jigen-ryu* sword fighting school of Satsuma to determine how to use the long and short staff, sickles, oar and flute as makeshift weapons against the sword.

The sword masters collected peasant tools and began to experiment with them. They eventually produced a series of sophisticated folk dances which were taught to the peasant militia. Each dance demonstrated how to use a specific implement as a weapon. Such dances persist in Okinawa to the present day.[28] From Satsuma, these early kata quickly crossed the sea to beleagured Okinawa, where unarmed self-defense against the sword was a major social issue.

The ancient Okinawan kobudo experts were not peasants. They were keimochi nobles at Shuri, who had a unique need for non-weapon weapons. Most of the Shuri nobles whose names are prominent in

---

[25] McCarthy, Patrick, *Ancient Okinawan Martial Arts: Korryu Uchinadi*, Volume 2, Tuttle, 1999b, p. 92-93. The peasant origin of kobudo "can no longer support the weight of serious consideration."

[26] McCarthy, 1999a, p. 9, where Shinken Taira cites fragments of stick-fighting evidence running back to the 10th century.

[27] McCarthy, 1995, p. 51.

[28] McCarthy, 1999a, p. 9. Taira writes of a rural Okinawan *bo* dance.

this book as karate masters were also well-known kobudo masters.[29] Kobudo mastery is particularly evident among the keimochi who served as royal bodyguards and police, because they encountered Satsuma overlords and armed foreigners on a daily basis. They used "peasant weapons," but they were not peasants.

The theory of kobudo as the creation of agricultural slaves has all kinds of practical problems, too, chief among which is the sai. The sai is not a peasant farming implement. Peasants could not afford steel tools, which had to be imported from Japan or China.[30] The sai is a steel truncheon with a cross guard, almost identical to the *jutte* police nightstick used in Japan in the same period.[31] When we understand, however, that the chief proponents of kobudo in the kingdom of Okinawa were upper-class keimochi policemen, suddenly the sai makes perfect sense. It was a weapon issued to police. [32]

This is not to say that peasants never hit each other with sticks, or that the many branches of Okinawan kobudo were all invented by jigen-ryu masters. The seed may have come from Satsuma, but the tree grew in Okinawa. Kobudo is a robust and uniquely Okinawan martial art.

Shuri Castle

Shuri Castle is the palace of the Sho kings, built by Sho Shin on a limestone hill about three miles inland from Naha, where you can see a panorama of the East China Sea on the western horizon and the open Pacific Ocean to the east. The view is magnificent, and the castle lives up to the grandure of the site upon which it was constructed.

Shuri Castle was originally built by Sho Shin in the 1500s, imitating on a small scale the beautiful royal lodgings of China and Thailand. The castle was surrounded by graceful, curving walls that put blocky Welsh castles to shame. There were beautiful ramps and garden pools, all created with an eye for beauty that made Shuri Castle an incredible work of art. The central courtyard was laid out in stripes of white and

---

[29] McCarthy, 1999a, p. 10-11.

[30] This point was made by kobudo expert Fumio Demura at a seminar in Foster City, Calif., in 2001. The seminar was hosted by Bernard Edwards.

[31] Cunningham, Don, *Secret Weapons of Jujutsu*, Tuttle, 2002, Ch. 6.

[32] McCarthy, 1999b, p. 125, says the sai and bo were standard issue for Okinawan police from the time of Sho Shin onward.

Figure 1-6: The Seiden, or throne room, of Shuri Castle. These are students of the Shuri Dai Ichi Elementary School apparently practicing *pinan nidan*, led by Shimpan Gusukuma.[33] Pinan nidan later became *heian shodan*. Note the long front stances, a characteristic of Shuri-te. The teacher's white karate uniform indicates that the picture was taken after 1936.[34]

red pavement, with red-tile-roof buildings on all four sides. The castle contained multiple Okinawan national treasures dating back centuries.

In World War II, the Japanese Imperial Forces callously used Shuri Castle as their command post, and U.S. forces utterly destroyed it. The Okinawans have been rebuilding it ever since, and today it shines with more than its former glory.

One approaches Shuri Castle through a series of gates and ramps up the northwest side of the hill. The central courtyard, with its red and white pavement, dominates the hilltop. On the east side of the

---

[33] Shimpan Gusukuma and Shimpan Shiroma are the same person. Apparently "Gusukuma" is the Okinawan reading, while "Shiroma" is the Japanese reading of the same name.

[34] This famous picture is from page 61 of *Karate Do Dai Kan*, an anthology by Gichin Funakoshi, Genwa Nakasone, Hiroki Otsuka, Hanashiro Nagashige, Shimpan Gusukuma, Choshin Chibana, Kenwa Mabuni, and Shinken Taira, published in Tokyo by Tosho, Inc., in 1938.

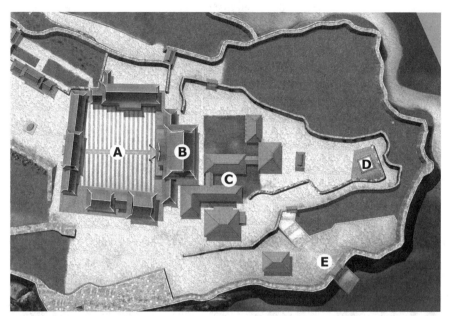

Figure 1-7: East half of Shuri Castle. You can see the striped courtyard at the left (A), dominated by the Seiden or throne room (B). The king's living quarters are the small buildings in the center of the image (C). The isolated square building on the right is the king's private mausoleum (D), and the private gate is at the bottom edge of the picture (E). This 3-D computer model of the castle was created by Rafael Malabanan.

courtyard is the palatial reception hall, the Seiden, where one has audiences with the king. It is the king's office building, devoted to the business and ceremony of running the government.

The two adjacent halls, forming the north and south sides of the square, were devoted to additional offices and facilities for foreign envoys. Part of the north building was used by emissaries of the Ming Emperor of China, who maintained the illusion that Okinawa was a Chinese province. Part of the south hall was allocated to representatives of the Shimasu clan from Satsuma, who secretly represented the shogun of Japan.

The fourth side (the west side) of the courtyard was occupied by another hall, with a reception area in one wing and offices in the other. The bureaucrats who ran the government at Shuri were members of the Okinawan keimochi nobility. They were proud of their warrior heritage, even if they had been disarmed for 200 years.

The west half of the castle area and the surrounding grounds were devoted to various gardens, temples and isolated buildings in scenes of great beauty. We are more interested in the eastern half, behind the Seiden, called the Ouchibara. This was the hidden half of the castle.

The king worked in the Seiden, but he did not live there. The royal family actually lived in a series of smaller apartments hidden from view in a parklike area behind the two-story pavilion. Here the king lived with family members and a large staff of female servants. Male servants and casual visitors were banned from this area. At the extreme east end of the hill, about 100 feet from the residential buildings, was a small mausoleum surrounded by a 10-foot high stone wall with a stout gate. The gate was locked and guarded. Only the king could enter.

On the southeast corner of the hill is a small gate and path down to the surrounding forest. This gate lies on the opposite side of the hill from the main entrance, and opens in the royals-only zone behind the Seiden. It looks like a convenient back door for times when someone undesirable was pounding on the front gate.

Inside the Seiden

The Seiden, the king's hall, is a two-story office building in the center of Shuri Castle. It contains two throne rooms, one on each floor, surrounded by offices and rooms with special purposes. The king spent most of his time on the second floor. These were the executive offices of the kingdom. From the second floor of the Seiden, elevated corridors lead to adjacent buildings in the private area of the castle.

There is a central stairway from the second floor down to the public throne room on the ground floor. This stairway, called the *ochokui*, opens directly behind the *urasuka*, which was the raised platform where the king sat during audiences. This staircase was the king's normal route to and from public appearances.

If the king were ever attacked during an audience on the ground floor, his bodyguards would have whisked him up the stairs to the secure second floor, and then to a prepared escape route away from danger. The ochokui is the tactical bottleneck in the escape route. It would be natural for the bodyguards to make a stand at the stairway to block pursuit.

This is another of the obscure clues to the Shuri-te *bunkai*. We will return to it at the appropriate time.

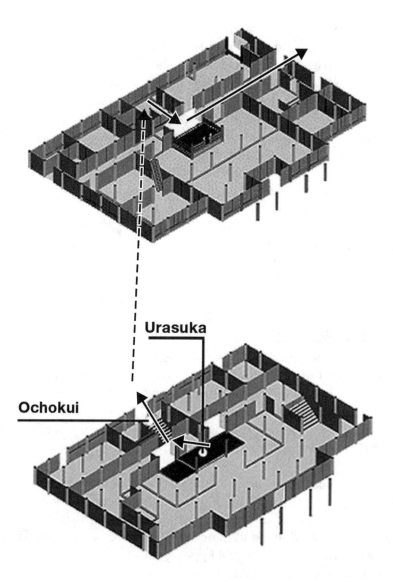

Figure 1-8: Interior of the Seiden, the royal administration building. The ochokui is the hidden staircase to the second floor, only a few feet behind the urasuka, the raised dais for the throne. The arrows show the escape route from the public throne room, up the stairs, through the upper offices, to the royal residence. The stairs were the defensible bottleneck in the route. [35]

---

[35] 3-D models of the interior of the Seiden adapted from the Shurijo Park web site. http://www.shurijo-park.go.jp/syuri_e/c/c409000.html.

Western Barbarians

One of the critical elements of the Shuri Crucible was a revolution in European seafaring skills at the end of the 18th century. In 1762 the English inventor John Harrison perfected a navigational chronometer accurate enough to let British naval officers calculate their exact longitude within 18 feet, even after a year at sea. This chronometer was the 18th-century technical equivalent of warp drive. Within 10 years Captain James Cook had circumnavigated the world using this new technology, going boldly where no Englishman had gone before. Within 50 years the technology had spread to other seafaring powers, including the upstart United States of America.

Naturally the Western seafaring nations wanted to open trade relations with the Orient, but it was really the whaling trade that lured Americans to the shores of Japan. By the 1840s there were over 1000 American whaling vessels hunting humpback whales in Japanese waters. They often needed to put into port to make repairs or to resupply, but were always refused. Landing on the Japanese mainland was a deadly mistake. Just a few days' sail to the south, however, was the legendary weaponless paradise of Okinawa.

Figure 1-9: Tomari from the sea showing western ships at anchor. This is the opposite point of view to Figure 1-1.[36]

---

[36] Perry, 2000, p. 316.

Figure 1-10: "Whaddaya mean, *not welcome?*" This whaling crew has dropped anchor and is looking forward to shore leave. Imagine being the unarmed keimochi official who has to send them back to their ship. (Courtesy of The New Bedford Whaling Museum.)[37]

Whalers thought they would get a better reception there, and if not, they could always *insist*.

It takes a daring man to stick a spear in the back of a whale from a tiny rowboat, and whalers were not the least bit squeamish about blood and gore. Each crew was answerable only to their captain. When these men came ashore, they were like a mob of gangbangers who had just spent five months in jail. They were ready to *party*. After months at sea, they wanted fresh food, liquor and women. These commodities were available in Naha.

In the 1820s, 1830s and 1840s, Okinawa received a steady stream of whalers putting in to Naha and Tomari to resupply, recreate or trade. They were met at the shore by regretful Shuri ministers who

---

[37] This photo comes from the collection of The New Bedford Whaling Museum, and was probably taken after 1900. The actual crew, ship and location are unknown.

explained that there was nothing Okinawa wanted to buy and nothing for sale on the entire island. The visitors were not welcome and should go back to their ships.

Whaling ships from Europe and America were very common in Okinawan waters, and hairy Western barbarians dropped anchor at Naha with distressing regularity. The captains expected to barter for supplies and trade items in Naha, and were not happy when the Okinawans inexplicably *refused* to trade.

> On their part, the Okinawans were shaken by fear and uncertainty when the Western ships began to call at Naha. Shuri had no firm precedents with which to govern its behavior. As we shall see, Satsuma's official attitudes veered with changing policies ... sometimes encouraging foreign intercourse for the sake of trade, sometimes frowning on it, and always meting out heavy punishments to those who violated orders. The Europeans who came were unacquainted with the rituals and procedures traditionally associated with the reception and dispatch of embassies and trading missions, and this led to many crises within Shuri Castle walls.[38]

This policy naturally led to many angry confrontations with visitors, where the Westerners became increasingly frustrated with the helpless Okinawan ministers. The visitors didn't understand the deadly three-way game involving the Sho kings, Satsuma and Beijing. They thought Okinawa was an autonomous island kingdom and didn't realize that it was really a part of Japan. As such it was a capital crime for Okinawans to engage in any commerce with foreigners. If the king's staff had dared to make any agreement with the visitors, even a secret agreement, they would have been risking the life of the king. The Shuri ministers simply wouldn't take that chance.

For example, in 1853 the people of Naha were plagued by an obnoxious Christian missionary named Dr. Bettelheim. The history books agree that Bettelheim was the kind of missionary who is hated by everyone he meets. Bettelheim could not get the Shuri officials to sell him any provisions, even to feed his starving wife and children.

---

[38] Kerr, 2000, p. 248.

He had plenty of money donated by charity organizations in England, but he could not spend it. Therefore, he simply *stole* anything he needed and dropped a coin on the ground in payment. When Bettelheim at last departed from Okinawa, the Shuri government presented him with a small chest containing *every coin* the missionary had distributed in six years. The Okinawans absolutely would *not* accept payment![39]

Sometimes the Westerners sailed away in frustration. Sometimes they shoved the Shuri officials aside and just took what they needed. Sometimes they rioted and caused so much trouble along the waterfront that the ministers purchased supplies out of their own funds and gave them to the visitors, just to get them to go away.

In every visit, there was a moment of truth when the unarmed Shuri ministers had to meet the barbarians face-to-face and say, "You are not welcome here. Go back to your ship." It was never pleasant or safe to do so. The same crisis played out, like a recurring nightmare, every time a Western ship dropped anchor in Naha harbor from about 1820 to 1868.

Meiji Restoration

The downfall of the shogunate in 1868 put the imperial family back in control of Japan for the first time in three centuries. This revolution is known as the Meiji restoration. (The first restored emperor was named "Meiji.")

The Meiji restoration was good news and also very bad news for Okinawa. On the one hand, it rescinded the shogun's laws about avoiding contact with foreigners, so a new era of trade began. The laws against carrying swords were not repealed, but instead were broadened to apply to everyone in Japan. Emperor Meiji disarmed the samurai. This must have been a great relief to nearly everyone. Sudden death was no longer a part of daily life.

The new emperor was not amused that Okinawa paid tribute to China, so the tradition of dual subordination ended abruptly. Japan was no longer afraid of war with China. In fact, the new Japan looked forward to a war with China.

These changes might all be considered improvements, but the changes didn't stop there. Emperor Meiji naturally felt that there was

---

[39] Kerr, 2000, p. 340.

room for only *one* king in Japan, so King Sho Tai was demoted to Mr. Sho, a common citizen of the empire. He was ordered to move to Tokyo as a ward of the government. Many of Okinawa's highest nobility were required to go with him as hostages. They resisted the move for several years, but were forced to comply in 1879.

The remaining keimochi families in Okinawa were dismissed from their government jobs and declared to be commoners. For three centuries these keimochi families had performed government functions in return for hereditary salaries. Suddenly they were thrown on their own resources with no social position, no jobs, no lands and no income. Virtually everyone in Shuri was suddenly unemployed with no market for their bureaucratic skills. This is why so many stories about karate masters describe their severe poverty in the late 1800s. The keimochi families were starving.

Early 20th Century

There was a 60 year period from 1880 to 1940, during which linear karate matured and went out to meet the world. During the first two decades (up to 1900), karate was still practiced in secret, at night, and in enclosed places like graveyards. During the second two decades (up to 1920), karate became well known in Okinawa, and attracted the attention of visiting Japanese dignitaries. During this period, karate was adopted by the Shuri public schools as a physical education program. In the final 20 years, karate invaded Japan and began its expansion into the world.

We will examine all of these developments in more detail as we meet the people involved. The new art had found acceptance in the public eye, and the future of karate looked bright indeed.

The Shuri Crucible

In this chapter we have established some of the historical background of Okinawa in the 1800s. These circumstances created a deadly trap for the Shuri nobles and resulted in the birth of linear karate. In summary:

- This island paradise was conquered by the Japanese shogunate, a government with open contempt for human life. In a brazen twist of foreign policy, this brutal regime wanted the conquest kept secret.

- The puppet government of the island was composed of keimochi bureaucrats, who carried out the business of the government in four large wooden buildings in Shuri Castle.

- The keimochi nobles were constantly watched by their Satsuma masters. If they made a misstep, Okinawa's king answered for it.

- The shogun's edicts prohibited Okinawa from having any commerce with Western visitors. When visitors showed up anyway, keimochi nobles were ordered to meet them at the beach and turn them away. The Japanese overlords stayed discreetly out of sight during these angry confrontations.

- This situation was workable for the first 200 years of the Japanese occupation, but in the 1800s Western whaling ships and naval vessels began to drop anchor at Naha quite frequently. Their crews didn't understand why the king of Okinawa was so rude to visiting sailors.

- As time went on, the confrontations became more frequent and more dangerous. The visitors carried every type of weapon known to man. The Okinawan officials were always unarmed.

The Shuri ministers had no choice but to confront the visiting sailors. They had no choice but to frustrate, disappoint and anger these dangerous barbarians. They had no choice but to enter these meetings outnumbered and unarmed.

After each such encounter, the Satsuma overlords must have demanded an accounting. The Shuri ministers were in mortal danger during these interviews, too. Again, they had no choice and no weapons. The Satsumas fingered their swords as they decided the fate of each Okinawan official.

This explains why the lords of Okinawa stayed up late every night hitting their makiwara posts until their knuckles burst through their skin. Trapped between the Satsuma overlords and the Western sailors, the Shuri lords were literally between the devil and the deep blue sea.

The situation just kept getting worse until 1853, when the Shuri ministers found themselves caught in a brink-of-war confrontation between the despotic shogunate and the United States of America. The Shuri ministers were ordered down to the beach yet again to put the barbarians back on their ships. This time the barbarians were United States Marines.

Sokon Matsumura was the chief bodyguard to the kings of Okinawa during this entire period. It was his duty to bring the elderly Shuri ministers safely out of any confrontation, whether against drunken sailors, Satsuma overlords, or U.S. Marines bristling with weapons. When violence erupted, Matsumura was in the front, first to fight and last to retreat. When he went into action, the odds were one against many, and the weapons were skin against steel. This was his destiny for 50 years of active service.

What was the Shuri Crucible? In a chemistry laboratory, a crucible is a ceramic cup used to heat crystals or metals to extremely high temperatures. Inside a crucible, conditions are so extreme that the original materials become changed into something new and different. Raw ore is smelted into metal. Sand turns into glass. With enough heat and pressure, carbon can be transformed into diamond. A crucible is a place where heat and pressure produce dramatic changes.

Shuri Castle in the 1800s was a martial-arts crucible. Matsumura faced the same threats repeatedly throughout his 50 year tenure as Shuri's chief military officer. During this period the Shuri Crucible forged a new martial art in Matsumura's mind, burning away unsuitable techniques and compounding new ones in their place. Decades later, Matsumura's protégé, Yasutsune Itosu, opened this scorched vessel and poured out the hard-style karate kata and techniques we practice in shotokan today.

In the next chapter we will meet the people who spent their lives in the Shuri Crucible. Matsumura faced Shuri's enemies bare-handed, but he did not face them alone.

Chapter 2

The Lords of Karate

Now that we have laid out the broad strokes of Okinawan history, we need to meet the people who lived and worked in Shuri in the 1800s. Most karate history books introduce the Shuri masters as isolated, elderly curmudgeons who practiced in secret to guard their special knowledge from each other. This picture is very superficial and incomplete.

The impression of hostile isolation was created in the early 1900s, and pertains mostly to the students of the original Shuri masters. Some of these young masters were bitter rivals with churlish attitudes toward one another. It is easy to see how we got the impression that karate masters were jealous and secretive.

Fifty years earlier, however, the original Shuri-te masters had been young officials of the Shuri government. They trained together and shared karate knowledge quite freely because it was their only means of mutual defense. On June 6, 1853, when the population of Shuri fled before an advancing column of U.S. Marines, four elderly ministers awaited the Westerners at the north gate of Shuri Castle. Behind them stood a dozen grim young men. Who were these courageous men if not Matsumura and his students? These men became the first masters of hard-style karate.

This chapter repeats some of karate's famous stories, but it does more than that. I have chosen specific anecdotes because they contain subtle clues about the personalities and circumstances of these men who invented linear karate. Who were they? What were they like? What lives did they lead? Who were their enemies? Who were their friends? This information is critically important to interpreting bunkai, the applications of our modern kata. To understand the creators of karate, we have to understand the context in which they lived. The context created the karate.

Japanese Language

Before we get into the details, I need to explain a few things about the Japanese language and culture. If this seems like a pointless detour, have faith. The Shuri masters played word games when they named kata and styles. We need to be aware of these games.

Written language did not exist in Japan before the third or fourth century A.D., when the Japanese began to imitate the very advanced kanji ideographs they observed in ancient China. There are thousands of these kanji characters, each representing a word or idea in the Chinese language.

The Chinese people use inflections (sing-song sounds) to distinguish similar words from one another in conversation. Unfortunately, the Japanese do not use these intonations, so when they adopted the Chinese written language they accidentally created thousands of homophones. These are words that sounded different when spoken in Chinese, but all sound exactly the same when spoken in Japanese. This created no end of confusion, resulting in the present-day situation where written Japanese uses kanji and two different phonic alphabets to sort it all out.

Each of the original kanji characters came with a Chinese *on* reading, meaning the sound of that word in ancient Chinese. To this the Japanese added a *kun* reading, which was a Japanese spoken word that had approximately the same meaning. Over the centuries this situation became more complex, until today each of the thousands of kanji characters may have multiple *on* and *kun* readings, and as many multiple meanings.

Therefore, just about anything written in Japanese kanji can have several possible meanings, and can be read aloud in multiple ways. Just about anything spoken in Japanese can have dozens or even hundreds of competing interpretations if encountered out of context.

When someone tells you "the meaning" of a Japanese word, the correct response is skepticism. They have told you only *one* of the meanings. There are always other meanings, and they may have chosen the wrong one. As we go forward, you may be surprised to discover what some of the familiar Japanese karate terms actually mean.

What is Truth?

As if karate history were not confusing enough, one eventually realizes that Japanese writers and karate masters enjoy a very special relationship with the truth. It confounds the naïve Western reader to discover that respected Japanese sensei casually conceal, distort or fabricate stories about karate's historical origins for their own purposes. In Japanese culture this is the normal thing to do, and it would not occur to them to do otherwise. In Japan, the official story is more important than the actual truth. In fact, they consider the official story to be another kind of truth, even if the story is completely inaccurate and deliberately misleading. For a person to question the official story is shockingly rude. People who insist on digging for verifiable facts are derided as *rikutsuppoi*, or "reason freaks."[40]

We can lay this philosophy at the feet of Ieyasu Tokugawa, the master of mind control. The Tokugawa edicts forced the Japanese people to adopt a double standard of truth. Every person had their private opinion, their secret *honne*, which was not safe to share even within the family. Instead, they all staunchly supported the official government story, the *tatemae*. It was the only safe thing to do in an era when a careless word could doom an entire family, or even a village.

This distinction between honne and tatemae appears again and again in karate history, right down to the present day. Honne refers to a person's true feelings, underlying motives, or the true facts of the case, and is written using the kanji for "true or real" plus the kanji that means "sound." Tatemae means the cover story, and is written with kanji that mean "to build" and "in front." In other words, tatemae is the screen we erect to hide the truth.

For example, in 19th century Okinawa, the tatemae (official story) was that the Sho kings were in charge of the kingdom, and they reported only to the Emperor of China. The hidden honne (the real situation) was that the Satsuma overlords were secretly in control. The Sho kings didn't make a move without Satsuma approval. That's the difference between honne and tatemae.

This curious relationship to the truth has an important corrolary: Japanese citizens are quite comfortable with information that is inconsistent, contradictory, ambiguous and incomplete. They're used to it. Ambiguity is a major feature of the language itself. It's normal. Contradictions cannot be investigated, because that would question the tatemae. Incomplete explanations cannot be researched and explained. Japanese citizens simply assume that they are being kept in the dark for a good reason that will be revealed to them, or not, in due course.

For instance, Japanese authors seem quite comfortable with the jumble of disjointed, self-contradictory information they have assembled on the history of karate. They often repeat tatemae directly

---

[40] Van Wolferen, Karel, *The Enigma of Japanese Power*, MacMillan, 1989, especially Chapter 9, "The Management of Reality."

to their readers as if it were real history. Japanese karate students see nothing contradictory about learning and endlessly repeating kata whose purpose and meaning are unknown. The fact that their masters can't explain the kata either doesn't seem to bother anyone. Their world is not supposed to make sense, so contradictions and inconsistencies are irrelevant.

As a Western scientist, I have a very different attitude toward the truth. As we go forward with this analysis, I'll point out the pretense (tatemae) and the truth (honne) in many situations, beginning with the myth of karate's ancient origins.

Is Karate Ancient?

Every karate book has some legend about the ancient origins of karate. Due to the lingering effects of the Tokugawa tyranny, the Japanese people still regard anything ancient as safe and respectable, but anything new is regarded as suspicious and dangerous. Therefore, Japanese sensei promote an official position (tatemae) that karate is "ancient." They make a ritual of pointing out that Bodhidharma, a sixth century monk, was both the founder of Zen Buddhism and the creator of Shaolin Temple boxing. Zen Buddhism is widely practiced and respected in Japan, so karate must be respectable, too!

It is sad to reveal, but there is also a strong element of racism involved in this issue. The Japanese, Chinese, Okinawan and Korean peoples share a deep respect for ancient Chinese culture. They also have a mutual contempt for one another that is quite dismaying. There is no love lost between Japan and her neighbors, including Okinawa. The fact that linear karate arose in Shuri was simply unbelievable to many Japanese in Funakoshi's time. Okinawans were regarded as too ignorant and backward to produce anything so sophisticated or as subtle as karate.

For this reason Funakoshi and his friend, Shito-ryu master Kenwa Mabuni, developed the story that hard-style karate was an ancient Chinese art, not a recent Okinawan invention.[41] This was their tatemae, their official story, intended to make karate more acceptable to the average Japanese citizen. Western readers might be willing to give up

[41] Sells, 2000, p. 17.

some of this purloined respectability in search of a better historical perspective (honne). Bodhidharma did not invent hard-style karate any more than King Arthur invented professional wrestling.

Make no mistake, most of the Chinese fighting arts, including the "soft" karate styles, possibly do reach back 15 centuries to Bodhidharma. That's not the issue. Linear karate from Shuri is only 150 years old. The *heian* (*pinan*) kata are less than 100 years old. Shotokan itself, and the white cotton uniforms we wear, are no more than 80 years old. The high kicks that adorn our logos and patches are about 60 years old. Most of the named karate systems in the world today are less than 50 years old. Most of the practitioners are under 15 years old. Compared to the ancient origins of chuan fa, "traditional" karate is as new as a shiny penny.

Chi-Niang Fang

If you are interested in the history of linear karate, the first person you should meet is not Bodhidharma but a young woman named Chi-Niang Fang of Yongchun village in Fukien Provence, China. (Fukien Provence is the seacoast area of China closest to Okinawa.) Sometime in the late 1600s, Chi-Niang Fang lost a fight with a stork.

According to one legend, the stork was eating Fang's grain, so she

Figure 2-1: Chi-Niang Fang fights a stork. Courtesy of The Martial Source (http://www.martialsource.com).

34

tried to drive it off with a stick. Using its strong wings and sharp beak, the stork fought back and gave Fang a beating. Fang, whose father was a murdered Shaolin monk, decided to base a fighting style on the antics of this stork and avenge her father.[42,43] This was the beginning of the Shaolin white crane branch of chuan fa. The new style quickly spread across southern China and became very popular.

White crane became known as a style of quick hand movements using fingers or knuckles to "peck" sharply at the vital points of the enemy. (Shotokan's *ippon ken* and *nukite* techniques come from white crane.) It is not an overly powerful style, but relies on a flurry of vital-point strikes to debilitate each opponent. The white crane fighter typically sidesteps a charging opponent and counters while the attacker is still lunging forward.

White crane kata emphasize punches, blocks and joint locks, and are frequently designed as two-person forms. The second half of the kata contains the countermoves to the first half, so you can practice solo or with a partner. This is important because one-on-one fighting encourages the study of joint locks and grappling. (You can't grapple against multiple opponents.)

The white crane style includes many weapons, such as the seven-star staff, the spear, three-sectional staff, halberd, cane, horse-cutter broadsword, the tiger fork, the double iron rods, the double broadswords, and the southern short swords. Additional weapons include the single broadsword, straight sword and the fighting fan.

Okinawan unarmed fighting in the 1700s consisted mainly of white crane chuan fa imported and re-imported countless times from mainland China. The only clear difference between mainland and island fighting arts was that Okinawans could not openly study the white crane weapons. (They substituted kobudo weapons instead.) Some of Naha's Chinese families, particularly in the Kumemura district of Naha, must have studied the weapons anyway, but only in private.

The important things to remember about the white crane style are the use of *tai sabaki* to evade attack, the forms where you grapple

---

[42] De Tourreil, Paul, *Fukien Shaolin White Crane Kung fu: A Portrait of Grand Master Lee Kiang Ke*, http://www.aei.ca/~straycat/kungfu/w-crane.html.

[43] McCarthy, 1995, p. 62 for another stork legend with the same general theme.

with a single opponent to subdue him, the vital-point "pecking" designed to wear an opponent down, and the plethora of weapons. These ideas are important because modern linear karate has discarded most of white crane. Shuri-te is a shocking departure from the Chinese arts on several levels.

In shotokan, you can still see the crane peeking out of kata like *kanku dai, gankaku* and *unsu*, but for the most part hard-style karate has renounced the white crane heritage. As we will see, there were good reasons for this development.

Satunushi "Tode" Sakugawa

Peichin Satunushi Sakugawa is the first teacher in the shotokan lineage who made specific contributions to the karate we study every day. His martial technique was very different from ours, based on white crane chuan fa, but his ideas about teaching were very modern. He represents the third generation before Funakoshi.

Sakugawa's Training

Sakugawa was born March 5, 1733, about 40 years before the American Revolution.[44] His father died from internal bleeding after a beating by drunken bullies when Sakugawa was a teenager, sometime around 1750. The father took several hours to die, and spent the time in agonized conversation with his family. He exacted a promise from his grieving teenage son, that he would never allow himself to be a helpless victim of violence.

After burying his father, Sakugawa sought expert instruction in the martial arts. He found a Buddhist monk, Peichin Takahara, who was an expert in *tode*, the Okinawan version of chuan fa.[45] Takahara was an Okinawan noble who worked as a surveyor and mapmaker at

---

[44] Birth dates and death dates of Okinawan karate masters are cited authoritatively, and *inconsistently*, by every author in the field. McCarthy, 1999b, p. 124, lists Sakugawa's birth year as 1733, 1744, or 1762, depending on who you believe. Death dates are equally random and unreliable.

[45] Okinawan sensei claim that *tode* ("Chinese hand") was a uniquely Okinawan form of fistfighting with a long, independent history. This is their tatemae. On the evidence, it is difficult to demonstrate that *tode* was more than the local name for a haphazard mix of imported Chinese skills.

Shuri Castle.[46] He accepted Sakugawa as an apprentice. The teenager studied with Takahara for six years and was a very dedicated and proficient student.

In view of subsequent events, I'd like to suggest at this point that Peichin Takahara was one of Shuri's bodyguards to the royal family. It turns out that the Shuri government made a policy of employing very skilful martial artists to fill routine staff positions in the immediate vicinity of the king. These bodyguards were also bureaucrats, secretaries, translators, diplomats, inspectors, military officers, tax collectors, accountants and administrators, but they performed their daily duties within a few yards of the unarmed king. Takahara was a prominent martial artist with a position at Shuri, and may well have been one of these bodyguards. If so, then Sakugawa's apprenticeship eventually qualified him as a Shuri employee and royal bodyguard, too.

We would like to think that our karate ancestors were all noble and dignified men of wisdom, but even wise men begin as passionate and foolish youths. Sakugawa was daring and mischievous at 23, and one night contrived to push a visiting Chinese dignitary into a stream for the fun of it.[47] The Chinese, Kong Su Kung, used his own martial arts knowledge to turn the tables on Sakugawa. The young prankster was shamed and humiliated, and thus was forced to humble himself and apologize.[48]

Showing astonishing mercy and wisdom, Kong Su Kung invited the shamed Sakugawa to become his student and study white crane chuan fa with him. With the enthusiastic support of Takahara, Sakugawa accepted. The white crane style was a new and exciting development at that time, and Takahara probably expected to learn about it through his student. Sakagawa studied with Kong Su Kung for another six years.

---

[46] Sells, 2000, p. 23.

[47] There is documentary evidence that Kong Su Kung was a Chinese chuan fa expert who arrived in Okinawa in 1756 (or just a few years prior to 1762). This is one of the very few actual facts in early Okinawan history. It also validates Sakugawa's birthdate as 1733. See McCarthy, 1999b, p. 47.

[48] Kim, Richard, *The Weaponless Warriors*, Ohara, 1974, p. 21.

"Tode"

Somewhere in this period, Takahara sickened and died. On his deathbed, he asked Satunushi Sakugawa to take the name "Tode" in honor of his teacher's art. Sakugawa wore the name with honor for the rest of his life.

Kanji symbols can be "read" in multiple languages. "Tode" is written using two kanji symbols that mean "Chinese hand." Tode is a mix of *on* and *kun* readings. The Japanese *kun* reading of the same two symbols is "kara te," which still means "Chinese hand." The same characters, when read in Korean, are pronounced "tang soo" (as in *tang soo do*) and still mean "Chinese hand."[49] A Western reader would think that tode, kara te, and tang soo do were three different arts, but the Asian reader sees at a glance that all three terms mean the same thing. They mean "Chinese fist-fighting."

"Tode" Sakugawa and "Karate" Sakugawa are the same man. In Korea they might call him "Tang Su" Sakugawa, depending on who reads the kanji.

Figure 2-2: *Kanji* symbols for Tode, with *on*, *kun* and Korean readings. [50]

Pirates In the Dark

According to multiple sources, Kong Su Kung taught "night fighting" and grappling techniques to Sakugawa. During this period of history, military combat usually occurred in the daytime, but self-defense fighting usually occurred at night. It was not unusual to be set upon in the darkness, beaten unconscious and robbed—even in peaceful Okinawa. Grappling is the natural approach to night-fighting,

---

[49] Haines, Bruce, *Karate's History and Traditions*, Tuttle, 1995, p. 110.

[50] *Kanji* images with *on* and *kun* readings are based on Mark Spahn and Wolfgang Hadamitzky, *The Kanji Dictionary*, Tuttle, 1996.

because it is difficult to punch or kick someone you cannot see.[51]

Sakugawa became one of the rising stars of the Okinawan royal government, probably in a dual role as junior diplomat and bodyguard. He was sent to China to learn Chinese and perhaps to study Chinese martial techniques. He got a ride on the annual tribute ship, laden with taxes, from Okinawa to China. As his ship approached Fuzhou harbor late at night, another ship loomed beside them in the darkness. It was a pirate vessel, and Sakugawa's ship was attacked.

There were no cannons as we might expect of Caribbean pirates. It was hand-to-hand combat in the dark, in which the pirates simply grabbed everyone on Sakugawa's ship and threw them into the sea to drown. Their plan was to kill the crew and sail away with the entire ship, Okinawan treasure included. (The "treasure" probably consisted of a cargo of rice, which explains why they had to steal the whole ship.)

Sakugawa was a bitter surprise to the pirates. Try as they might, they could not get a grip on him. With his extensive knowledge of night-fighting, he single-handedly defeated the pirate crew and drove them over the rail into the sea. Outnumbered severely, he grabbed the last few pirates and heroically hurled himself overboard, saving the ship.

Fortunately, the Chinese harbor patrol rescued all the swimmers. Unfortunately, they then threw them all in jail. Sakugawa was almost executed for piracy before he learned enough Chinese words to protest his innocence. We can only imagine how many fights he had in prison with the pirates before winning his freedom and returning to Okinawa.[52]

Kusanku Kata

In later years, Sakugawa created a new kata to honor his Chinese teacher, Kong Su Kung. The teacher's name is also rendered as Kusanku, depending on whether you pronounce it in Chinese or Okinawan.

The *kusanku* kata of night-fighting techniques[53] was the basis of shotokan's *kanku sho* and *kanku dai* kata, and people often point out that it looks like an ancestor of the pinan (heian) kata as well. Kanku is the living heart of shotokan, and it comes from Sakugawa.

---

[51] Sells, 2000, p. 25. In the era before automobiles and electric lights, walking home at night was a dark and dangerous adventure.

[52] Nagamine, Shoshin, *Tales of Okinawa's Great Masters*, Tuttle, 2000, p. 13-14.

[53] McCarthy, Pat, *Classical Kata of Okinawan Karate*, Ohara, 1987, p. 139.

Sakugawa's Legacy

Sakugawa is credited with creating the dojo system of teaching, and with writing the first set of *dojo kun*, the rules of behavior for a karate student. Kong Su Kung also introduced Sakugawa to the principle of *hikite*, the pullback hand. In kobudo circles Sakugawa is honored as the inventor of the famous bo kata, the *Sakugawa no kon*.[54]

In 1811, when Sakugawa was 78 years old, he was introduced to a troubled 14-year-old named Sokon Matsumura who had an ambition to become the greatest fist fighter in Okinawa. He wanted to study under Sakugawa, possibly to apprentice as a royal bodyguard. For some reason Sakugawa hesitated to accept the new pupil. "Master," insisted Matsumura, "I will not disappoint you."[55] Sakugawa was impressed by the boy's spirit and decided to give him a chance. This meeting was one of the seminal moments in the prehistory of linear karate.

The important things to remember about Sakugawa are that he invented the dojo training system and the original Kusanku kata, and was the first teacher of Matsumura. It seems clear that he did not make the leap to the raw power of linear karate. He relied heavily on circular (soft) technique and grappling, to judge from the branches of karate that still practice primitive versions of the Kusanku kata.

Tode Sakugawa died on August 17, 1815, at the age of 82, after training Matsumura for only four years. This was quite an advanced age. He lived more than twice as long as an average person in that time and place. After his death, Western ships began to call at Naha more and more frequently. The death of Sakugawa marked the beginning of the Shuri Crucible.

Sokon "Bushi" Matsumura

Sokon "Bushi" Matsumura is one of the two central characters in our story. Linear karate apparently did not exist before Matsumura, but it was recognizably modern in the next generation to follow him. Matsumura represents the second generation before Funakoshi. He was the commander of the Shuri Castle garrison for 50 years.

---

[54] McCarthy, 1987, p. 28.

[55] Kim, 1974, p. 32.

Figure 2-3: Sokon "Bushi" Matsumura in old age, as pictured by Okinawan artist Akira Miyagi.[56] According to Funakoshi, Matsumura was known for his piercing, hawklike eyes. Every story about Matsumura mentions his unusual eyes.

It seems clear that Matsumura was a prime mover in the development of linear power technique, and yet it is hard to prove the case. The reason is that Matsumura was intelligent, creative, ambitious, ruthless, manipulative and deceptive. He was a driven man who embraced the martial arts with fanatical devotion. At age 14 he was determined to become the greatest fighter in the kingdom. At 25, he was widely acknowledged as having achieved this goal. How does something like that come about?

"Matsumura"

Let's take a quick look at Matsumura's name. It is composed of two kanji symbols. "Matsu" means "pine tree." "Mura" is a common suffix that means "village."

---

[56] Nagamine, 2000, p. xix for the artist's credit, and p. 17 for the portrait. Unfortunately the provenance of this portrait is not explained.

Figure 2-4: **"Matsumura"** means "pine village."

"Matsumura" is the *kun* pronunciation of the name. It could equally well be translated or spoken using the *on* reading, which is "Shoson." Take note of the "pine tree" image in Matsumura's name. Pine trees and forests are very common symbols in the karate styles that trace their roots to Matsumura. We'll encounter them again and again in later sections.

Matsumura's Skills

We first see Matsumura as a disciple of Tode Sakugawa, when the ancient teacher was approaching 80 years of age. Born in 1796,[57] Sokon Matsumura had a passion for martial arts that consumed his entire life.

Karate historians usually pass over Matsumura's early years without special comment. They say he studied with Sakugawa and "became" the chief bodyguard to the king of Okinawa a few years later. I find this incredible. How did an untrained teenager become the most feared martial artist in the kingdom in just a few years?

George Alexander says that Matsumura originated a "scientific" theory of martial arts that gave his blows astonishing power compared to the competition. The theory was stated as, "torque plus speed equals true power."[58] From John Sells, "Matsumura evidently believed that speed was the key to power."[59]

---

[57] Nagamine, 2000, p. 17 insists Matsumura was born in 1809, based on an interview with an elderly woman who thought her mother once said she was born in the same year as Matsumura's 88th birthday. This tenuous chronology contradicts every previous account of Matsumura's life and should not be taken seriously.

[58] Alexander, George, *Okinawa, Island of Karate*, Yamazato Publications, 1991, p. 44. The quote is not attributed.

[59] Sells, 2000, p. 30.

To a person schooled in the basic principles of shotokan power, these statements leap off the page. In them one can see the core of linear impact technique. In a technique like *oi-zuki*, one generates knock-down momentum (power) through rapid forward motion of the *hara*. The more speed, the more power.

There is an obscure scientific principle that may explain Matsumura's technical breakthrough. Matsumura may have been the first to appreciate that kinetic energy increases exponentially with the square of the speed. Kinetic energy is the ability to do work, which in this case means the ability to damage or move the other person's body. This means if you can double your forward speed at the moment of impact, you can quadruple the damage. Move three times faster, hit nine times harder.

If you are feeling skeptical, think of a pistol bullet. A bullet is just a small lead pebble. Take a pistol bullet in your hand and toss it at your *senpai*,[60] at a speed of about 10 feet/second. The bullet bounces off his chest and rattles harmlessly to the floor. If you fire the same bullet from a pistol, however, it will strike senpai's chest traveling about 1,000 feet/per second. This is 100 times faster than before, so the bullet hits senpai with 100 x 100 = 10,000 times more kinetic energy, and well-known lethal consequences. The lead pebble is identical in both situations. The only difference is speed.

Even a modestly-capable person can knock an opponent completely off his feet by hurling the hara forward at high speed behind the punch.

Legend has it that Matsumura was in many fights and never lost because of this discovery. He became famous by publicly challenging and defeating one fighter after another until no one would agree to fight him. If Matsumura was the first to fully realize the exponential nature of power, he might well have cut a swath through the local chuan fa and tode fighters.

Linear impact technique lets small people knock down large, muscular opponents. This was not the case with chuan fa, where the best fighters were the ones with the biggest muscles. That fact explains why hard-style karate swept across the world in a few decades, while the traditional Chinese arts have mainly lingered in China for the last

---

[60] I am addressing my remarks to the *sensei*. The *senpai* is then the senior student of the dojo; the sensei's assistant.

15 centuries. Shuri-te was different. Shuri-te let smaller, weaker people fight larger, stronger people and win.

The discovery of exponential power could explain how Matsumura defeated the proud fighters of Okinawa, but it does not explain why. From an early age he desperately wanted to fight and defeat the toughest, most dangerous men he could find. This is not the portrait of a normal teenager. We recall that Sakugawa was driven to greatness by the tragic death of his father. Something powerful drove Matsumura, too, but the legends are silent. We have only one clue. Every story says there was something unusual about Matsumura's eyes. One witness after another mentions these eyes. That might be the key to the whole mystery. The final chapter of this book will further explore this idea.

Matsumura's Career

Having established a superhuman reputation, Matsumura rose quickly through the ranks to become chief of security to the royal family. (Funakoshi says he was the "minister of military affairs," which would be a very high position indeed, reporting directly to the king.)[61] This was during the reign of King Sho Ko, who was deposed by Satsuma in 1828, so Matsumura probably received this appointment when he was in his 20s.

Matsumura continued as the chief of security to King Sho Iku from 1828 until he was deposed in 1847, and for Sho Tai from 1847 to the date he was deposed in 1879. Matsumura died in 1893 at the age of 97.

Matsumura's Fights

There are many stories about Matsumura that provide insight into his character, five of which shall be sumarized here. The first has to do with fighting a street robber; the second with fighting a bull; the third with fighting his wife; and the fourth with using psychology on a superstitious opponent. The last story has to do with punching out the king.

In the first story, Matsumura as a young man was walking home

---

[61] Funakoshi, Gichin, *Karate-Do Nyumon*, Kodansha, 1988, p. 102.

late at night after having had a little too much to drink.[62] A masked or hooded figure suddenly attacked him using a pair of sai. The attacker threw a sai at Matsumura, who dived to the ground to avoid it. Then Matsumura drew a *tessen* (iron fan) from his belt and returned the attack. The attacker ran away with a broken wrist.

There are two important features to this story. The first is that Matsumura avoided a thrown sai by diving to the ground, as one does in kanku dai. (Remember that the original Kusanku kata was created by Matsumura's teacher and passed down to us through Matsumura himself.)

The second interesting point is that Matsumura defeated the mugger by using a tessen he carried in his belt. The tessen is an iron truncheon disguised to look like a folding fan. (See Figure 9-39.) In skilled hands it is lethal, and can even give a man a fighting chance against a sword.

The next story concerns King Sho Ko, the first of the three kings Matsumura served as bodyguard. Sho Ko was a well-known lunatic. This is often a problem with hereditary kings, and it led to his early retirement when the Satsuma overlords decided he wasn't a reliable figurehead for Okinawa's government.

One day, shortly after his "retirement," Sho Ko announced a spectacle for his own entertainment. On a certain day his bodyguard, the great Matsumura, would fight a raging bull bare-handed. Sho Ko invited the whole island to come watch the fun. This was exciting news for the islanders because Okinawan bull fights usually pitted a bull against another bull.[63] For a man to fight a bull was very unusual. But barehanded?

One can only imagine the look on Matsumura's face when he learned of this. There was no way that he could decline without losing his position. He had to fight the bull.

The stories agree that Matsumura faced the bull on the legendary day, but there was no fight. Matsumura met the bull in the middle of the arena, and fixed his hawk-like gaze on the animal. The bull

---

[62] People who have had too much to drink are prominent in the karate stories from Okinawa. They lived stressful lives, and had no TV or other modern distractions in the evening. Over-indulgence in "adult analgesics" was common.

[63] Sells, 2000, p. 32.

suddenly lost its nerve and ran away, bellowing in terror. King Sho Ko was delighted. His bodyguard was so fierce that his very *gaze* would terrify a bull! He issued a royal degree, granting the title "bushi" (warrior) to Matsumura. This was the highest honor awarded to any karate artist in history, until very recently.[64]

Some versions of this story explain that Matsumura achieved this feat by visiting the bull in its stall every day for a week before the fight. There he would gaze fiercely into the eyes of the bull while jabbing its nose with a needle.[65] He trained the bull to run away. One story says he enlisted the aid of the bull's keeper after swearing him to secrecy.[66] You have to admire Matsumura. He planned for success and didn't leave things to chance.

Matsumura married a legendary woman named Tsuru Yonamine, who was a formidable fighter in her own right. Some writers romanticize Yonamine as a demure Japanese maiden who happened to know some martial arts. Others openly state that the incredible stories about her just can't be true.[67] They underestimate the lady. The stories about her are completely consistent and entirely plausible.

Yonamine enjoyed sumo wrestling with men, and often won. She enjoyed tode fighting, too, bare-knuckle and full contact. The girl's father despaired of arranging a marriage for her, and offered a large dowry to anyone who would dare to court her.[68] Courting Yonamine was asking for a beating. She was a lady with attitude.

One story, repeated as folklore in Okinawa, says that Matsumura first encountered Yonamine as an anonymous opponent in a full-contact street match. He didn't realize he was fighting a woman, and was puzzled that repeated kicks to the groin had no effect. "Later on, Matsumura found out that this person was a woman and they got

---

[64] On November 3, 2000, shotokan master Hidetaka Nishiyama was designated a Japanese living national treasure by the Emperor of Japan in a special ceremony conducted at the Imperial Palace in Tokyo.

[65] Nagamine, 2000, p. 25, says Matsumura used a club instead of a needle. Silvan relates that Matsumura beat the bull with either a *bo* staff or with his bare fist. Silvan, Jim, "Oral Traditions of Okinawan Karate," *Journal of Asian Martial Arts*, Vol. 7, No. 3, 1998, p. 73.

[66] Kim, 1974, p. 39.

[67] Cook, p. 20, says he can't believe that Yonamine could have developed a version of *seisan* kata that would let her fight with a baby strapped to her back. Sells (personal communication) cautioned me that stories of Yonamine's feats were probably "apocryphal."

[68] Nagamine, 2000, p. 27.

married."[69] It must have seemed like the only decent thing to do under the circumstances.

Matsumura's student Chotoku Kyan once saw Yonamine lift a 132-pound sack of rice with one hand while sweeping up the kitchen.[70] Whatever Yonamine was, she was not demure.

After the wedding, the stories say, Matsumura harbored secret doubts about his wife's ability in actual combat. The stories vary in detail, but the central idea is that Matsumura contrived to send Yonamine on a journey by herself at night. He then disguised himself and waylaid her on the road as if he were a robber. The legends agree that Yonamine knocked him out with an *uraken* to the temple, then tied him to a tree with his own belt. Matsumura spent an uncomfortable night by the roadside and had some explaining to do the next day.[71]

The fourth Matsumura story has to do with his duel with Uehara, a skilled metal craftsman who was also a well-known if undisciplined martial artist in the Shuri area. The story says that Matsumura sought out Uehara to have some slight repair made to his pipe. Uehara recognized Matsumura, and asked the great bushi to accept him as a student. Matsumura declined, claiming that his only student was the king himself. Uehara, hoping to learn something (or to prove something), challenged Matsumura to a fight.

There are many versions of this story, some in substantial conflict with others. Matsumura apparently knew that Uehara was superstitious, so he suggested that the fight take place before dawn in a nearby graveyard. At the time of the fight, Matsumura used careful staging and his legendary hawk-like gaze to unnerve Uehara, who lost his composure and begged forgiveness.[72]

Matsumura served at the pleasure of the king, and was once suspended for several weeks when he lost patience with his royal student.[73] The king launched a flashy but impractical attack, and the bushi knocked him out to teach him a lesson. It was his duty to protect

[69] Silvan, 1998, p. 79.

[70] Bishop, Mark, *Okinawan Karate, Teachers, Styles and Secret Techniques*, Tuttle, 1999, p. 55.

[71] Kim, 1974, p. 36, tells a more elaborate version of this story in which Matsumura goes to Sakugawa for advice, and then defeats his wife in a rematch by punching her in the breasts.

[72] Funakoshi, 1974, p. 101-108. Also Kim, 1974, p. 42.

[73] Funakoshi, 1975, p. 23.

the king, but he had no control over the king. This has always been a problem for bodyguards.

What do these stories tell us about Matsumura? First of all, a man who marries a woman after repeatedly kicking her in the groin has very unusual priorities, and the same might be said of the woman. Second, Matsumura was very well-prepared for his encounters. He studied his enemies ahead of time and made plans for their defeat. Third, he had a secretive and deceptive side. He wasn't above disguising himself or disguising a weapon if it suited his purpose. He would sometimes enlist assistants under an oath of silence. Fourth, he was a master of psychology. He not only outwitted Uehara, he outwitted King Sho Ko and the bull. Fifth, he was impatient with his students, even royal students. After all, punching out a king takes nerves of steel.

Patsai (Bassai) Kata

Matsumura is rumored to be the author of the *patsai* (*bassai*) kata, but his love of secrecy makes this hard to prove. Several of his students practiced and taught the kata, however, and some called it "Matsumura Patsai."[74] If bushi Matsumura is the original or primary source of shotokan's bassai dai, then the kata tells us a little more about him.

Bassai dai is the black-belt test kata of shotokan, a place of central honor that seems significant to me. Our linear technique comes from Matsumura, and we honor him by using his kata to rank our black belts. The kata is asymmetrical, powerful, brutal, and there is a sense of impatience in it. The legend is that patsai means "to break into a fortress," and that it "turns disadvantage into advantage." It is interesting that Matsumura defended the Shuri fortress, and he did so from a position of extreme disadvantage. He must have had nightmares about people breaking into his castle. Reversing this disadvantage was his life-long mission. It is entirely appropriate that patsai would be his kata.

By the way, the widespread legend that "bassai" means "to penetrate a fortress" is not true, even if it does come directly from Funakoshi.[75] The kanji characters for "bassai" don't mention a fortress. They don't

---

[74] McCarthy, 1987, p. 120. Kim, 1974, p. 44.

[75] Funakoshi, Gichin, *Karate-Do Kyohan*, Kodansha, 1973, p. 36.

mention "penetrating" or "breaking into" anything, either. In fact, "breaking into a fortress" appears to be a karate urban legend.

"Batsu" means extract or escape. "Sai" means block as in blocking a passage or corridor.

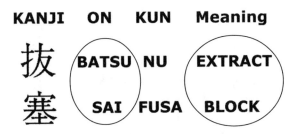

KANJI   ON   KUN   Meaning

BATSU NU   EXTRACT

SAI FUSA   BLOCK

Figure 2-5: "Bassai" means to "extract" and to "block." It has nothing to do with storming a fortress.

Bassai is supposed to be Matsumura's own kata. As you progress through this book, the possibility that bassai originally meant to "extract" and to "block" will suddenly assume a special significance.

King vs. Karma

From your own experience in tournaments you know that the rules of kumite have a profound impact on the strategies and techniques used by the contestants. For instance, karate didn't use any high kicks until contest rules outlawed strikes to the testicles in the 1930s. Suddenly it was safe to expose the groin during a match, because the rules protected the testicles. High kicks became very popular.

The profound difference between Shuri-te and the previous Chinese styles is that Matsumura changed the rules. Shuri stylists fight in a different moral context than Chinese stylists, and all of the subsequent differences in technique, kata selection and bunkai flow from this difference.

The Chinese styles owe a large debt to the Buddhist monks of the Shaolin Temple. These monks learned the martial arts for self-discipline and self-defense. Wandering monks penetrated the worst sorts of neighborhoods and were often attacked by bullies, thieves and thugs. A Buddhist monk under attack had a serious moral dilemma to resolve. He wanted to defend himself, as we all do, but he also had to protect his *karma*, the future of his spirit. He believed that the pain he inflicted on others would return to him in the next life. Nathan Johnson, a martial artist and Zen Buddhist, makes it clear that inflicting unnecessary pain and destruction is antithetical to the Zen Buddhist point of view.[76]

The monk must minimize the damage he does to his opponent because of this karmic backlash. If you are trying to minimize damage to your opponent, you naturally favor submission fighting because it gives the opponent every opportunity to admit defeat without serious injury. Combat becomes a series of escalations that eventually force the opponent to surrender or flee.[77]

A natural corollary is that the monk is going to get hit a few times in every encounter. It is a very monk-like attitude to strengthen and harden the body to withstand this kind of punishment. We see these fighting strategies at the core of the Chinese arts, including such neo-Chinese arts as goju-ryu and uechi ryu. Goju/uechi stylists may not think of themselves as Buddhist monks, but they diligently practice *Sanchin* kata. Sanchin builds up your muscles for grappling while training your body to withstand pain and impact. People who practice Sanchin are on the Shaolin Temple path.

When you are under attack, you are at liberty to behave like a monk. When someone else is under attack, however, you do not have the same degree of moral freedom. You may sacrifice yourself to protect your karma, but it would be karmic suicide to sacrifice someone else. The moral landscape shifts abruptly when a third party is in danger.

Matsumura was not a monk. The Shuri bodyguards were keimochi, born to live and die in the service of their lord. As military bodyguards, their opponents were not lone drunks and robbers. Their opponents were mobs of sailors, armed samurai and sometimes organized military units. In order to protect the king, the Shuri bodyguards had to be absolutely ruthless. They couldn't afford to worry about karmic consequences.

Which is more important to you, king or karma? The monk defends his soul. The bodyguard wages war. Their different goals force them to play by different rules.

---

[76] Johnson, 2000, p. 124. "Dreadful karmic penalties."

[77] McCarthy, 1999b, p. 13-14.

This is what makes hard-style karate so different from the soft Chinese styles. Matsumura optimized Shuri-te to inflict maximum injury in minimum time. He was unconcerned about the damage he might cause. Between the block and the lethal counterstrike there is no time to surrender or withdraw. The instant passes in the blink of an eye, followed by the sickening sound of bones breaking.

It could be extremely intimidating for a monk-like chuan fa stylist to confront the bodyguard mindset in a one-on-one match. The old stories make it clear that matches between Okinawan masters were brutal but not lethal. Suppose the young Matsumura didn't see it that way and fought his opponents ruthlessly? Just a few matches that left people dead or maimed would have created the reputation he certainly had. The chuan fa masters would have backed away and refused to fight him.

Maybe Matsumura was not the most skillful fighter on the island. Maybe he was just the most ruthless one.

Matsumura's Legacy

Matsumura was the focal point of a revolution in combat technique in the middle 1800s. Due to the Shuri Crucible, he had a different set of combat priorities than his predecessors. His discovery of exponential impact gave him a new tool to exploit. He seems to have developed or invented most of the high-impact techniques we use in shotokan today.

Matsumura made trips to China and Japan to study their martial arts, including a pilgrimage to the Shaolin Temple, and allegedly brought back several kata including early forms of *naihanchi (tekki)*, *seisan (hangetsu)*, and *gojushiho*, among others. Most accounts agree that Matsumura created the kata called *chinto (gankaku)* using techniques he learned from a shipwrecked Chinese martial artist in Tomari. Some accounts say he is the original author of the kata we know as *heian nidan*. The kata passed down to us by Matsumura eventually formed the very core of shotokan.

Matsumura is also well-known in kobudo circles for his mastery of the bo staff, the sai, and the *ekubo* (oar). He created kata for all three weapons.

Matsumura spent over 50 years as the chief military officer of Shuri Castle, from the mid-1820s until 1879. It is no wonder that his style became known as Shuri-te. All branches of modern linear karate descend from Matsumura, most of them through his remarkable protégé, Yasutsune Itosu.

Yasutsune Itosu

Matsumura is one of the two central characters in the birth of Shuri-te. The other is Yasutsune Itosu. Matsumura was the inventor; Itosu was the teacher.

Figure 2-6: Yasutsune "Anko" Itosu, as depicted by Akira Miyagi.[78] Compared to Matsumura, Itosu has a friendlier expression and a more relaxed attitude. He had remarkably Caucasian-looking eyes. His body was as hard as rock.

When we turn our attention to Itosu, we have at last reached a teacher who taught the same karate that we practice in shotokan today. In Itosu's classes the principles of hard-style karate became a reality. If Funakoshi was the father of shotokan karate, then Itosu is definitely

---

[78] Nagamine, 2000, p. xix for the artist's credit, and p. 45 for the portrait.

the grandfather. In fact, most of our daily karate activities come directly from Itosu, with the exception of *jiyu kumite* (free-fighting), which he would not have liked.[79]

"Itosu"

Itosu's name has confused a lot of people. As a practical matter, the interpretation of Okinawan names from written kanji is very uncertain. You can see the man's name written in kanji, but the translator has to guess at pronunciation. Translators render the famous names consistently, but the names of obscure persons can become garbled.[80]

Figure 2-7: Kanji characters of Itosu's name, with on and kun readings.

"Itosu," for instance, is the *kun* (Japanese) reading of Itosu's family name. The *on* (ancient Chinese) reading of the same name is "Shishu." Itosu's personal name is read "Yasutsune" (*kun*) or "Anko" (*on*). Both readings are correct and are used interchangeably.

---

[79] See McCarthy, 1999b, p. 24, for Kenwa Mabuni's opinion that sport karate brings out "the worst in human behavior." Most traditional sensei agree with that opinion.

[80] Eri Takase, www.takase.com, calligrapher and translator, in personal communication with the author. Ms. Takase is San Ten's Japanese translator and calligrapher, and has helped us create many beautiful and authentic karate grading certificates, including the *judan* certificate we presented to Master Hidetaka Nishiyama on November 1, 2003.

Yasutsune Itosu and Anko Shishu are the same man, and in fact it is the same name. There is no rule against mixing *on* and *kun* readings, so Anko Itosu is often seen.

I have adopted the Western habit of placing the personal name first and the family name last as a courtesy to the reader.[81] Experienced Nipponophiles can recognize the names in either order, but newcomers need some help. I have chosen to accommodate the beginners by presenting the names in a familiar English fashion: title, personal name, family name.

Many karate writers, however, make a virtue of showing their respect for Japan by reversing the name order. This means that Yasutsune Itosu is often presented as Itosu Yasutsune, or Itosu Anko, or Shishu Yasutsune. This can be very confusing, especially when they throw the "peichin" title into the mix. I have seen Itosu's name in print in half a dozen different forms.

The real trouble begins when a Japanese translator forgets himself and shifts back and forth between two readings of a name in the same book.[82] In Funakoshi's early book, *To-Te Jutsu*, translator Shingo Ichida used "Itosu" on page 18, but shifted abruptly to "Shishu" on page 22. This creates the illusion that he is talking about two people when there is really only one.

The opposite problem occurs, too. Sometimes several masters actually do share the same name. Seisho Arakaki and Kamadeunchu Arakaki are two names for "Arakaki the Cat," but *Ankichi* Arakaki is a different person. There are many subsequent Arakaki's in Goju-ryu and Shorin-ryu lineages. You may also encounter quite a few masters named Shimabuku or Shimabukuro, not all of whom are related. When you read a story about Master Arakaki or Master Shimabuku, you have to stop and ask, "Which one?"[83]

---

[81] Except for the names of the Sho kings.

[82] Funakoshi, Gichin, *To-Te Jutsu*, Masters Publication, 1994. See also Nagamine, 2000, p. 86, where "Kyan Chotoku" suddenly turns into "Chan Mi-Gwa." This last is a nickname, which makes things even more arbitrary and confusing.

[83] See Hassell, 1995, p. 174, where Ankichi Arakaki gets the credit for creating Seisho Arakaki's kata. Also McCarthy, 1999b, p. 11, where Shinken Taira tells us that "Arakaki Sensei" was a great kobudo expert. He means Seisho Arakaki, but he doesn't actually say so.

Itosu's Skills

Itosu was born in 1830 and as a child was regularly beaten by his father, who wanted the boy to develop an aggressive martial spirit. He studied directly under Bushi Matsumura as an apprentice bodyguard from age 16 to 24, which would be the years 1846 to 1854, roughly during the period when King Sho Tai was a small child.[84] During his apprenticeship Itosu joined the peichin class, became the king's personal secretary, and continued to work side-by-side with Matsumura for the next 30 years. This seems to have been a typical arrangement for the Shuri bodyguards, as we will see.

Funakoshi described Itosu as barrel-chested and of average height. He had a kindly face and, in old age, a long beard. Itosu's punch and grip were legendary. Funakoshi says Itosu could crush a green bamboo stalk in his fist.[85] After eight years with Matsumura, Itosu's body was so hard he could absorb heavy blows without any sign of discomfort. He liked to arm-wrestle with his friends, and was so strong that he always won. There is a story about someone who tried to punch Itosu on the back and found himself caught by the wrist, unable to break away. Itosu then dragged the miscreant through a crowded restaurant and forced him to kneel and wait (sobbing for mercy) while Itosu ordered drinks. He released the man's arm only after the drinks arrived.[86] In another story, Itosu found himself in the path of a charging bull. He literally took the bull by the horns and wrestled it to the ground. (These stories are significant because some of Itosu's kata applications might have required his immense strength.)

Itosu's punch was simply awe-inspiring. There are many stories about his fists. A makiwara punching post was not sufficient for his workouts, so one day he found a solid stone wall to hit instead. He hung a leather sandal on the wall as a pad for his knuckles. After a few punches, however, the stone behind the sandal pushed through the wall and fell out the other side. He moved over and tried a different stone, but the same thing happened. Nagamine says that Itosu's workout ultimately destroyed the wall.[87]

---

[84] Kim, 1974, p. 51.

[85] Funakoshi, 1988, p. 16.

[86] Funakoshi, 1988, p. 33-34.

[87] Nagamine, 2000, p. 49, for the stories of the bull and the wall.

Itosu's Fights

In *The Weaponless Warriors*, Richard Kim tells several stories about fights Itosu won as a young man in Naha. In one adventure, Itosu challenged a loud bully named Tomoyose at Naha who was openly disdainful of the Shuri style of fighting, calling it "parlor karate." Expecting a fair fight, Itosu was instead attacked by members of Tomoyose's gang, some of them armed with clubs.[88]

- The first opponent threw a powerful but looping right-hand punch. Itosu pounded his face with a triple *renzuki* (multiple rapid punches), knocking out the attacker before his punch landed.

- Two more opponents rushed in with clubs. Itosu caught one man's arm and held it in his bamboo-cracking grip while landing a side-kick on the jaw of the second man. This produced another knockout. Itosu finished off the first man with a snap kick to the groin. The man went down moaning in agony.

- This was too much for Tomoyose, who waded in to finish off the upstart from Shuri. Tomoyose threw a killer punch aimed at Itosu's head. The Shuri-te expert sidestepped it and broke the bully's arm (maybe the collarbone?) with a single *shuto* strike.

Once his opponents were disabled, Itosu stepped back and the fight was over.

When Itosu was 75 years old he was challenged to a *shiai* (arranged fight) by a Japanese judo player half his age. The challenge was blown out of all proportion by antagonism between Okinawa and home-island Japanese citizens. The Okinawans hoped karate would win the match, while the Japanese hoped judo would prevail.

Itosu showed up for the match and introduced himself to the judo champion. The judoka was very condescending, promising to defeat the elderly Okinawan as gently as possible without doing any serious damage.

As the match began, the judo champion took hold of Itosu's jacket, preparing to throw the old man to the ground. Itosu punched the younger man *once* in the solar plexus, using his left hand. The judoka collapsed in a heap, unable to move or breathe. Itosu gave him first

---

[88] Kim, 1974, p. 51-52.

aid until he could breathe again, and then left the arena.[89]

It is important to notice how *suddenly* Itosu defeated each of his opponents, generally by using a single blow delivered while the opponent was making his opening attack. The ability to consistently end a fight with a single blow is a very significant development in karate, and is quite different from chuan fa.[90] Itosu didn't "peck" his opponents with vital-point strikes, or subdue them with joint locks. He simply destroyed them in a fraction of a second. This ruthless strategy was a new and somewhat disturbing characteristic of Shuri-te.

"Saint" Itosu

Itosu lived to be 85 years old and died in 1915. After his death, local martial artists gave him the title *kensai*, (fist saint)—Saint Itosu.[91] Unfortunately, some people have taken this honor too seriously.

Grandmaster Shoshin Nagamine is the author of *Tales of Okinawa's Great Masters*, a book that describes Itosu as a saintly man who never had a fight in his life. "In his 85 years," states Nagamine, "there was not a single episode describing such an encounter."[92] Nagamine did not say that the Itosu fight stories are untrue. He said that no such stories exist. That is nonsense. There are many such stories, but you won't learn about them from Nagamine. Why not? Nagamine thought his students needed a saint to admire, so he created one. This was Nagamine's official story (tatemae) that none of his students dared to challenge.

Mark Bishop commented on this issue, too, describing other writings of Shoshin Nagamine:

> "One should read works on 'eminent masters' with a pinch
> of salt, taking into consideration the generational time
> frame of the writer. For people of Shoshin Nagamine's age

---

[89] Kim, 1974, p. 57.

[90] In contrast, Kanryo Higaonna's first real fight (using White Crane and Praying Mantis chuan fa) lasted 15 minutes and ended when both fighters were too winded to continue. Kim, 1974, p. 98.

[91] "Ken" is the reading for a kanji symbol meaning "fist" and also for a different kanji symbol meaning "sword." "Kensai" is usually translated "sword saint" when applied to Musashi Miyamoto, but "fist saint" for various Okinawan masters.

[92] Nagamine, 2000, p. 46.

group, exaltation and veneration of the deceased is far more important ... than is the recording of objective facts; yet many younger writers have been highly influenced by mythical works, mistaking descriptive, poetic fantasy for unbiased information."[93]

It isn't just Nagamine. Official lies, tatemae, are everywhere in the karate history books. Credulous Western readers need to understand that this, too, is a part of karate history. If a Japanese master thinks the truth isn't appropriate, he'll often make up a new truth that sounds better. Nagamine's attempt to whitewash Itosu's life is just one example.

The unspoken truth is that the great Okinawan masters were just people like ourselves. They had strengths and weaknesses. With the insights of modern psychology we can see that they became masters *because* of their weaknesses. Funakoshi, Kyan and Higaonna were all very small men, for instance. Karate helped them compensate for their size. Sakugawa was haunted by the horrible death of his father. Tsuru Yonamine was a most unfeminine woman. There was something strange about Matsumura's face. These people all had psychological issues that karate helped to alleviate.

Itosu, beaten and abused by his father as a child, was no saint. By every account he was a powerful fighter, a gifted teacher, a noted scholar, and in every sense a pillar of the community. Now and then he was attacked on the streets of Naha and forced to defend himself. The stories of these fights emphasize how easily he dealt with his attackers.

Itosu's Career

Itosu, like many Shuri inhabitants of the keimochi class, was trained in Chinese language, philosophy and calligraphy so he could serve as a clerk or bureaucrat in the government. In fact, he served as the personal secretary to King Sho Tai for three decades until Japan ended the Sho dynasty in 1879. Itosu did not follow the king into exile in Tokyo, but remained in Shuri and started a family printing business. He taught karate to a small circle of students that included, at long last, Gichin Funakoshi. These classes were conducted secretly

---

[93] Bishop, 1999, p. 79.

in Itosu's house in the middle of the night, over a span of 20 years, roughly from 1880 to 1900.

During this period, Itosu was approached by a youth named Choki Motobu (Motobu the Monkey), who would become a famous karate master in his old age. In his youth, however, Motobu was the worst sort of brawler. Each time Itosu taught him a new technique, Motobu would rush down to Naha's red-light district and try it out on someone. Since Shuri-te is much more lethal than chuan fa, this was not a good policy. When Itosu found out about these experiments, he publicly humiliated Motobu by expelling him from the class.[94] (Motobu became a life-long enemy of Gichin Funakoshi, who was a student in the same class. One wonders if Funakoshi was involved in this incident. It seems almost inevitable that he was.)

In 1902, Itosu broke entirely new ground by reversing his stand on secrecy and taking karate public. Up to this time karate had been taught and practiced in the strictest privacy, but in his 71st year Itosu obtained permission to teach karate in the public schools at Shuri. By 1905, Itosu was teaching karate classes at the Prefectural Dai Ichi College and the Prefectural Teachers Training College. Karate was finally out in the open.

Itosu's Kata

During this period, Itosu produced his matchless masterpiece: the five pinan (heian) kata.[95] These kata were designed to bring a raw beginner up to a level where he could be introduced to naihanchi (tekki), and then to patsai (bassai). They were first taught to junior high school students in 1905.

Itosu is generally credited with the expansion of the naihanchi (tekki) kata into three kata, although there is some argument about that as well. Most people give him credit for introducing the *chinte* kata after learning the techniques from a Chinese fighter. He standardized kusanku (kanku) into sho and dai versions, and did the same for patsai (bassai) and gojushiho. He created the *rohai* kata,

---

[94] Bishop, 1999, p. 68

[95] Bishop, 1999, p. 89. Itosu's authorship of the pinan kata in 1905 is common knowledge among karate historians. These kata are not "ancient."

from which Funakoshi extracted *meikyo*. Shotokan's *empi*, a very old kata dating from 1683, is usually traced through Itosu.

Itosu laid his hands on the ancient kata and changed them. He seems to have revised nearly all the Shuri kata to standardize their portrayal of linear, hard-style technique. When we practice our shotokan kata, we are repeating the lessons designed and laid down by Itosu himself. Films of shotokan kata in the 1920s, a few years after Itosu's death, show only minor differences from the kata we practice today.[96]

Itosu's Legacy

Every biography of Itosu mentions that the students he secretly trained in his home during the 1880s and 1890s include some of the greatest names in karate, men who established famous schools and styles in later years.[97] One of the things Itosu taught his students was absolutely revolutionary: *You can do karate in public.* If Itosu had maintained the extreme secrecy of previous karate teachers, karate would still be a secret in Okinawa.

The important things to remember about Itosu are that he felt the need to revise the kata, he demonstrated well-developed single-blow victories, and he took karate public in 1902. The other interesting thing about Itosu is that his famous students uniformly established karate styles where the form of the kata was well documented but the meaning of the bunkai was not.

Itosu invented the pinan (heian) kata. They distilled his lifetime experience as a bodyguard and martial artist. Is there any doubt that he had applications in mind for them? He must have known the applications of his own kata! Even so, no branch of karate seems to know the revealed truth of the pinan bunkai. Itosu taught the moves but not the explanations. Why would he do that? We'll explore that question later in this book.

---

[96] People talk about how much the shotokan kata have changed over the years. Compared to the sweeping changes Itosu made, subsequent alterations have been trivial, bordering on invisible.

[97] A chart showing how Matsumura's teachings found their way into our modern karate styles has been included as an appendix.

The karate legends make it clear that Itosu studied kobudo kata,[98] but he doesn't seem to have created any. He put his energies elsewhere.

"Shorin-ryu"

Legend has it that the Shuri-te type of karate was called "shorin-ryu" by Itosu.[99] He must have had a great deal of fun applying this name to the art. "Shorin" is the Okinawan pronunciation of "Shaolin," as in the Shaolin Temple of China. Western readers naturally assume that Itosu named shorin-ryu after the temple, acknowledging his debt to the ancient Shaolin monks. Maybe he did, but Itosu had more pressing debts to pay and the language gave him a lot of room to be clever.

Itosu wrote a famous letter that mentions both the shorin and shorei styles of karate. He spelled "shorin" using kanji characters that mean "bright/clear forest" instead of the traditional "young forest" characters of the Shaolin Temple.[100] Itosu was a linguist and scholar, secretary to the king, so this was a deliberate decision, not an error. I will take a momentary liberty and translate Itosu's bright/clear forest ryu as "shining forest style" for the sake of this discussion.

Spoken out loud, the "shorin" label is open to multiple interpretations in the mind of the listener. In the martial arts context it is natural to assume that "shorin" really refers to the Shaolin Temple, but that is not the only direction we can go. The "sho" syllable of "shorin" could be interpreted as honoring the royal family of King Sho Tai, the first family of Shuri. Flattery is always a good idea when you work with a king every day as Itosu did. "Rin" is "forest." Listeners might interpret "shorin" as simply meaning "sho's forest" instead of "shining forest."

There is a more compelling possibility, however. As you know, it is very common to name a new style after the master who founded it. (What else is "shotokan?") Shuri-te was founded by Itosu's teacher, Matsumura, whose name means "pine village." The first kanji character in Matsumura's name has the *kun* reading "matsu," meaning "pine tree."

---

[98] Kim, 1974, p. 30.

[99] Alexander, 1991, p. 27.

[100] Sells, 2000. p. 72.

The *on* reading of this same character is "sho," as in "shorin."

When Itosu and his students called the Shuri-te style "Sho's forest," they might have been referring to their own Master Sho. Matsumura was the big pine tree; his students were the young forest of saplings springing up around the big tree; and shorin-ryu was the style they practiced in the shining forest.

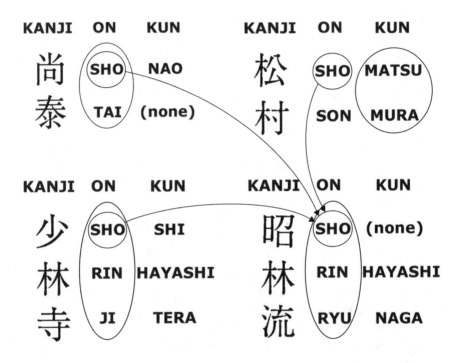

Figure 2-8: Itosu's "shorin-ryu" subtly compliments Matsumura, King Sho Tai, and the Shaolin Temple (Shorinji) by working their shared name (sho) into the name of the style.

Over the years "shorin-ryu" broke up into multiple styles founded by various masters. By using different selections of kanji characters with the same readings, these "shorin-ryu" styles have meanings such as "young forest style," "small forest style" and "pine forest style." The alternate spellings also have alternate readings, such as *"kobayashi-ryu,"* *"shobayashi-ryu"* and *"matsubayashi-ryu,"* but the Japanese reader can tell at a glance that they are all variants of Itosu's "shorin-ryu."

Matsubayashi-ryu, (pine forest style), is a shorin style named by Shoshin Nagamine using the first character of Matsumura's name as "sho." Nagamine may have seen through Itosu's games to the deeper meanings of shorin-ryu.

Yasutsune Azato

Born in 1828, peichin Yasutsune Azato is a very intriguing character in our story because very little is actually known about him. Funakoshi called Azato the greatest karate master he ever met, which is high praise considering the 20 years Funakoshi spent with Itosu.[101] Like Itosu, his best friend, Azato is one of the grandfathers of modern karate.

Peichin Azato himself was another direct student of the redoubtable Bushi Matsumura. His role in the Shuri government was "military attaché" and foreign affairs advisor to the Sho kings.[102] He was the hereditary lord of the village of Asato, located halfway between Shuri and Tomari, a little north of Naha. The Asato neighborhood is still on the maps today. (See Figure 1-3.)

Azato was Funakoshi's first teacher, and Funakoshi was Azato's only student, at least at that time. Funakoshi paints an amusing picture of his training under Azato, which was conducted secretly after midnight in the courtyard of Azato's house. Azato drilled Funakoshi in the naihanchi (*tekki shodan*) kata over and over again for three years. Most sessions consisted of Funakoshi performing the kata by lamplight, and Azato sipping tea and muttering, "Do it again." Rarely did Azato unbend and grunt, "Good."

Funakoshi was amused, maybe even proud, that his secretive midnight journeys to Azato's house led his neighbors to conclude that he was sneaking out to visit the red-light district in Naha.[103] He was about 12 years old at the time, and undoubtedly found this flattering.

Azato and Itosu were close friends, often found in each other's company. They were almost the same age, shared similar names, similar heritage, similar employment, and they both loved the martial arts. They were best friends throughout their lives.

---

[101] Funakoshi, 1988, p. 30.
[102] Funakoshi, 1988, p. 31.
[103] Funakoshi, 1975, p. 6.

In Azato we have yet another legendary martial artist and shotokan forefather in daily attendance with King Sho Tai at Shuri Castle. He was part of the inner circle, like Matsumura and Itosu, and often advised the king on questions of international politics. Funakoshi says Azato used his influence to get Itosu the position of secretary to the king. It's likely that Matsumura had something to do with that, too.

We know that Azato was a highly-trained swordsman, horseman and archer. He was expert at *jukendo*, which is a form of bayonet fighting in which you jab your opponent with the padded end of a carved wooden rifle.[104] He regarded hands and feet as deadly weapons: "Think of the hands and feet of anyone who has trained in karate as swords. They can kill with a touch."[105] He was not impressed with Itosu's ability to withstand heavy blows because that strategy is a disaster in a sword fight. Azato felt that a true martial artist should step out of the way (of the sword or bayonet) and avoid being hit. He was an expert at lightning-fast tai sabaki.

Azato once tested his ability in an extreme way by challenging a sword master to a match. Azato fought Yorin Kanna, a master from the jigen-ryu school of the sword in Satsuma prefecture. Kanna had a sword; Azato used his bare hands. The legends say that Azato deflected Kanna's incoming strike "with his arm" and immobilized the master, not once but several times.[106]

Azato drops out of the history of karate at about the same time King Sho Tai was forced to abdicate and move to Tokyo. He may have been one of the keimochi hostages who went into exile with the king, as several other nobles and court officials did. Funakoshi says cryptically that Azato "served as an ambassador to Tokyo for many years" (which sounds better than "hostage"). Azato died in 1906 at the age of 78.

Azato has been neglected by history. He had few students and left little heritage. Most of what we know about him comes directly from Funakoshi. It turns out that Azato was a pro-Japanese patriot, which would have made him very unpopular with his peers in the Okinawan gentry. This may be another reason why Azato moved to Tokyo and

---

[104] Sells, 2000, p. 58.

[105] Funakoshi, 1988, p. 31.

[106] Funakoshi, 1975, p. 14. Not everyone believes this story, however. See Sells, 2000, p. 59.

became the "invisible man" of karate.

In terms of kobudo, Master Azato clearly preferred real weapons. He doesn't seem to have left any kobudo heritage. In terms of karate kata, there are rare references to Azato versions of kusanku and patsai, but there are no details.

It is certainly a shame that "the greatest karate master" Funakoshi ever met didn't leave us any more heritage than he did. To date, no one has located a photo or drawing of Azato. It leaves us sadly wondering what he was really like. Whatever it was, Funakoshi admired him very much.[107]

Chofu Kyan

Chofu Kyan (*not* Chotoku Kyan) was a respected martial arts expert who held the hereditary office of Royal Steward to the Sho kings, and had the additional honor of being the Keeper of the Royal Seal. The position of "steward" sounds like Kyan was a valet or butler, but I suspect that the Keeper of the Royal Seal was someone who could disburse funds and sign orders on behalf of the king. The seal is the *hanko*, which is literally the king's signature. In other words, we are close to the truth if we think of Kyan as the king's "chief of staff." He was certainly a powerful and trusted member of the inner circle.

Born in 1835, Chofu was just a few years older than Itosu. During his career, Kyan was in constant attendance of the king. When Sho Tai was deposed in 1879, Kyan moved to Tokyo for four years "on assignment." The king still needed his chief of staff, even in exile.[108] Kyan died in 1889.

There isn't much known about Kyan except that he was the father of Chotoku Kyan, the sickly little boy who later became one of the most notorious figures in karate history. Stories about the father and son training together during their exile in Tokyo show that the senior Kyan was the kind of sensei who believed that training barefoot in the snow builds character.[109] He held his son to a brutally high

---

[107] Azato's grandson, Yoriyuki Azato, moved to Tokyo in 1933 and established the *Shobukan* dojo. It is possible that Azato's teachings persist there. He used the "Sho" royal family name kanji in "Sho bu kan."

[108] Bishop, 1999, p. 72.

[109] Nagamine, 2000, p. 82.

standard. Kyan trained the sickly little boy relentlessly in an attempt to improve his health. Behind the ruthless sensei was a loving father trying to strengthen his weak and ailing son.

Kyan is the fourth legendary martial artist who was employed in the immediate vicinity of the throne. He was there every day with Matsumura, Itosu and Azato.

Seisho Arakaki

Unless you are a student of kobudo, you have probably never heard of Seisho Arakaki. Born in 1840, he was 10 years younger than Itosu and Azato. He was employed as a Japanese and Chinese language interpreter at the Shuri court in the 1860s, and served as an envoy to China as late as 1870.[110] He was one of Chotoku Kyan's teachers.

Arakaki was a master of monk fist and white crane chuan fa, and is said to have been the first teacher of Kanryo Higaonna.[111] He was the source of the *niseishi (nijushiho)*, *sochin*, and unsu kata that we practice in shotokan. His nickname was "Maya," (the Cat), because he could leap high into the air and land without making a sound.

Arakaki is also known as *Kamadeunchu*, the sickle master. He is famous in kobudo circles for his mastery of the sickles, sai and bo. He is said to have practiced over two hundred bo techniques for use against a swordsman.[112]

As a court interpreter, Arakaki was yet another shotokan ancestor who worked every day within a few yards of the throne. When you stop to think about it, that's an astonishing concentration of martial arts talent in one room.

The Seeds of Shotokan

Matsumura was Shuri's chief military officer, in charge of all military and law-enforcement personnel. Azato was the king's foreign affairs advisor, like a modern secretary of state. Itosu was the king's secretary, translating his letters and legal documents. Kyan supervised the staff and paid the king's bills. Arakaki translated documents and

---

[110] Sells, 2000, p. 41. Also McCarthy, 1995, p. 36.

[111] McCarthy, 1999b, p. 6.

[112] Sells, 2000, p. 296.

represented Shuri to foreign governments. All five of these men could deal out instant death with either hand. All of the modern Shorin styles point straight back to this exact group of men as the source of hard-style karate—as well they should. These are the chief players, noting their contributions to modern karate, especially shotokan:

- Matsumura: bassai, gankaku, heian nidan, tekki shodan, kanku, gojushiho, hangetsu. Inventor of linear technique.

- Itosu: heians, tekki 2 and 3, *jion, jitte, jiin*, chinte, rohai (meikyo), empi. Source of sho/dai versions of bassai, kanku and gojushiho. Funakoshi's mentor.

- Azato: First teacher of Gichin Funakoshi. Master of tai sabaki and disarming techniques.

- Chofu Kyan: Father (and first teacher) of Chotoku Kyan. Emphasized health and character development issues.

- Seisho Arakaki: Source of unsu, nijushiho, sochin.

In this list we can see the shotokan style coming together a decade or more before the birth of Funakoshi. This list accounts for all 26 of the shotokan kata except for *wankan*, which seems to have been created by Funakoshi's son, Gigo, at a much later date.[113]

It looks as if Matsumura quietly surrounded the king with a team of world-class bodyguards, all performing routine duties as members of the Shuri staff. Think of them as the Shuri Secret Service. They had legitimate government positions and stipends, but they arranged their routine duties to keep them near the king so that they could protect him. Other than these few men, Sho Tai was completely defenseless. As we have seen, the unarmed king was often in danger and needed protection.

Five men cannot provide around-the-clock protection without help. There must have been others. Who else might have been part of this special team?

---

[113] Sells, 2000, p. 266, 277. Wankan seems to have been invented by Gigo Funakoshi, and possibly also the JKA version of Sochin.

Shuri Spear Carriers

The cast of a play is divided into the lead actors, the supporting actors and the people who stand around in the background and don't say anything. In Shakespearean theater, these background actors are called "spear carriers" because they literally stand around holding spears.

When you picture the Shuri throne room, Matsumura and Itosu stand out as lead actors on the right and left sides of the throne. Azato plays a supporting role as a military advisor. Chofu Kyan and Arakaki pass through frequently as their duties require. As you read about karate history, you gradually become aware of additional figures standing silently behind the throne. They didn't carry spears, of course, but they were there, just on the edge of vision.

There were quite a few famous martial artists employed in the immediate vicinity of the king in the middle 1800s. To recognize these men in your reading, look for individuals with the title "peichin," who were born about the same time as Itosu in 1830. You will find these men casually mentioned in the karate history books as the teachers of Chotoku Kyan.

This is a critical point. The Shuri martial artists firmly believed that karate improved health and promotes longevity. Chotoku Kyan was the sickly son of the Shuri chief of staff. Picture him as "the boss's son." Little Chotoku was a pathetic figure—emaciated, stunted, wheezing with asthma and nearly blind with myopia. When the chief of staff asked the Shuri bodyguards to train his son, he was really asking them to save the boy's life. The Shuri bodyguards understood the reason for the request, and undertook the challenge with grim determination. As a result, Chotoku Kyan grew up to be the most relentlessly over-trained martial artist in history.

Here is a short list of "spear carriers" who may have been part of Sho Tai's bodyguard team. They all became very well-known masters in later years, as if the Shuri throne room had served as a martial arts graduate school. They all knew each other, worked together, and spent years training little Chotoku.

Kokan Oyadomari

There is little doubt that Kokan Oyadomari was part of the team of martial artists surrounding Sho Tai. Oyadomari was born around 1830, which makes him the same age as Itosu. He is often listed as a student of Bushi Matsumura. He is regarded as one of the patriarchs of Tomari-te karate. Tomari-te has not survived to the present day, mainly because it looked so much like Shuri-te. Oyadomari was trained at Shuri, and his karate had that Shuri flavor.[114]

Oyadomari's title of "peichin" means he held some kind of position at Shuri. When Chotoku Kyan was eight years old, his father asked Matsumura, Itosu and Oyadomari to be the boy's first instructors.[115] This argues that Chofu Kyan knew Oyadomari as well as he knew Matsumura and Itosu. In other words, Oyadomari must have been a familiar face to the king's steward.

In terms of kobudo, there are rare references to Oyadomari kata for the sai, *tonfa* and bo.

Oyadomari is a respected and legendary master. If he was there in the throne room, he was part of the bodyguard team. He would not have shirked this duty, even if he had a choice. Let's pencil him in as another bodyguard to Sho Tai.

Kosaku Matsumora

If Oyadomari was one of the Shuri bodyguards, then Kosaku Matsumora must have been one, too. Matsumora (not the same as *Matsumura*) was born around 1830 like Itosu and Oyadomari. Matsumora was yet another government figure, had a legendary reputation as a fighter, taught Shuri-like technique in Tomari when he retired, and was an early instructor to Chotoku Kyan, son of the chief of staff.

In addition, karate historians emphasize that Oyadomari and Matsumora were "on very good terms," that they were inseparable friends, that they traded kata and shared students—to the extent that some people speculate that they might have been brothers. If Oyadomari was one of Bushi Matsumura's special agents, Matsumora would not have been far behind. They did everything together. One possible explanation is that they both lived in Tomari, but both worked two miles away in Shuri. If they walked to and from work together

---

[114] Empi kata, which Okinawans knew as wansu or wang shu, has been practiced in Okinawa since 1683, and is vaguely associated with Tomari. Our version came from Matsumura and Itosu.

[115] Nagamine, 1976, p. 40.

every day, it would explain much of their reputation for "togetherness."

Kosaku Matsumora became famous at the age of 20 (around 1850) when he stole a sword out of the hands of an angry Satsuma overlord using only a "wet towel" as a weapon.[116] The Japanese overlord was disorderly, probably drunk, and was threatening a crowd of unarmed Okinawans with his sword when young Matsumora confronted him. Nagamine says, "Matsumora quickly removed the moist Japanese towel which he had recently been in the habit of carrying concealed inside his garment." Matsumora hit the astonished samurai with the wet towel and grabbed the sword. In the process, Matsumora lost a thumb. He threw the thumb and the sword in the nearby Asato River.

In budo there was no greater contempt than to humiliate your opponent and then turn your back and walk away. There is an implication that the opponent is so cowardly that you do not fear his revenge. This episode was so insulting to the hated Japanese overlords that Matsumora became an Okinawan folk hero overnight. He had to hide out in the woods for a couple of years until the Satsumas stopped hunting for him.

Let's stop and read between the lines here. The official story (tatemae) comes from Nagamine and doesn't sound quite right. Nobody in his right mind would habitually carry a wet towel wrapped around his body under his garments. What was the unspoken honne?

Responding to the emergency, Matsumora probably created an expedient weapon by urinating in the towel-like loincloth he wore "concealed under his garments." It was easy for him to hike up his kimono to "unwind" it. He flung the dripping underwear in the opponent's face as a distraction, and stole the sword in the moment of gagging shock that followed.

Kosaku Matsumora's admirers must have *loved* telling this story. Nagamine may have cleaned it up a little for publication.

There is no question that Matsumora would have been welcome at Shuri. He was a daring fighter, a hero and a natural team member or advisor. He was also a student of Bushi Matsumura, and both learned the famous chinto kata from a Tomari pirate at the same time. More about that later.

---

[116] Nagamine, 2000, p. 32.

Peichin Yara

Peichin Yomitan Yara belonged to the generation between Bushi Matsumura and Itosu. His reputation as a martial artist rests mainly on various kobudo kata. (The kobudo masters were not peasants!) He also passed down a second kusanku kata, inherited from Chatan Yara, a relative, who was a contemporary of Sakugawa and another student of the legendary Kong Su Kung.

Peichin Yara was a noted martial artist, a Shuri government employee, and another teacher of little Chotoku Kyan.[117] It is very likely that he was one of the bodyguards. There isn't very much known about him, but he fits the bodyguard profile.

Sanda Kinjo

About 10 years younger than Itosu, Sanda Kinjo was a famous kobudo expert. According to George Alexander, Kinjo was the chief of the civil police at Shuri for 40 years and did double duty as a bodyguard to the king.[118] It is likely, almost inevitable, that he reported to Matsumura, the minister of military affairs. Because of his duties as a policeman, Kinjo had to be proficient with all weapons used by the lower classes of criminals. Matsumura recognized and rewarded this kind of talent.

There isn't much evidence that Kinjo was part of the daily retinue of the king in the throne room. He clearly had duties that took him elsewhere. In an emergency, however, he and his constables would have quickly filled in the second rank behind the bodyguards. They were there to back up Matsumura's play.

Peichin Kiyuna

Little is known about Peichin Kiyuna, except that he was a contemporary of Itosu, had a government position as a security guard (night watchman) at Shuri Castle, was trained by Bushi Matsumura, and had a very powerful punch. He once used a tree on the castle grounds as a makiwara, but after ten days of pounding the tree wilted and died.[119]

---

[117] Sells, 2000, p. 26.
[118] Alexander, 1991, p. 49.
[119] Nagamine, 2000, p. 48.

In later years, Kiyuna contributed training to both Taro Shimabuku and Gichin Funakoshi.[120] Shimabuku was a student of Chotoku Kyan, and of course Funakoshi was a protégé of Itosu. These connections demonstrate that Kiyuna was connected to the inner circle of martial artists at Shuri and was a good candidate to be another shadowy bodyguard lurking near the throne.

Additional Bodyguards

There appear to have been other "spear carriers," but they are only names with no details. In 50 years of service, Matsumura must have trained dozens of young men for service in Shuri Castle.

Their stories are lost, but I think it is evident that the inner circle of Shuri Castle was a college for martial-arts masters. In later years these masters all went their separate ways in Shuri and Tomari, but in the 1850s and 1860s they were a highly-trained team, and protecting Sho Tai was their collective mission.

In retrospect, the Shuri bodyguards must have done rather well. They kept the king and the elderly ministers safe from both the Satsuma overlords and from the crews of visiting ships who periodically overran the waterfront of Naha. They kept the peace, protected their lord, and did their duty. We have to respect them for succeeding in this very difficult situation.

Their nemesis turned out to be a ruthless gaijin barbarian from the United States of America. He marched up the road to Shuri, leaving utter ruin in his wake.

---

[120] Alexander, 1991, p. 51.

Chapter 3

The Japan Expedition

By this point, veteran readers of karate history may be getting restless while revisiting these well-worn stories about Okinawan masters. It was necessary to include these stories because the clues to the mystery of hard-style karate, as well as the bunkai, lie in the details and personalities revealed by these specific tales. The story of Commodore Matthew Perry, however, will take many karateka by surprise. As far as I can tell, karate history books haven't acknowledged Perry.[121] He played a crucial role in the creation of shotokan.

Perry's visit to Naha is not a story that Okinawans like to repeat. Perry destroyed Japan's Tokugawa dynasty and Shuri's entire way of life. Documentation of his visit comes from English-language sources almost 150 years old. Japanese masters don't seem to be aware of these rare publications.

Commodore Matthew Perry

By the 1840s, Ieyasu Tokugawa's long-standing policy of isolation from Western contact was rubbing a lot of people the wrong way. There were many U.S. ships in Japanese waters—mostly whalers—and shipwrecked Americans who washed up on the shores of Japan were treated very badly indeed. They were often killed.[122] Friendly attempts to open diplomatic relations with Japan were very rudely rebuffed, to the considerable embarrassment of the U.S. government.[123]

There was a strong feeling in the U.S. Congress that "the Japan question" needed to be resolved, by force if necessary. In 1853, President Millard Fillmore dispatched Commodore Matthew Perry with a fleet of 15 sail-and-steam-powered warships to force Japan to open its doors and establish diplomatic and financial relations with the rest of the world.

Perry knew that the Japanese respected only strength and brutality, so he decided to give them something to think about. Instead of sailing directly for Tokyo, he took his fleet to defenseless Okinawa instead. His idea was to act like a bully in Okinawa in order to create a reputation that would serve him later in Tokyo.

---

[121] Nagamine, 2000, p. 37, mentioned Perry but didn't expand on his history. Sells, 2000, p. 34-35 gives Perry two short paragraphs.

[122] Sells, 2000, p. 34.

[123] In 1845 a U.S. emissary was shoved back into his boat by a Japanese soldier when he tried to come ashore at Edo (Tokyo). He never got ashore.

Figure 3-1: Commodore Matthew Perry, shortly after the conclusion of his mission to Japan.

Perry Arrives in Naha

Most historians portray Perry as a pompous egotist, based on the testimony of his officers, but consider that. Perry was a shrewd negotiator who had read every available book and report on Japan before embarking on this expedition.[124] It stands to reason that he deliberately imitated the behavior of a Japanese *daimyo* in order to generate respect for his authority and power. Perry's personal journal shows a deep awareness of honne and tatemae to which his assistants were simply blind.[125]

---

[124] Kerr, George, Okinawa: *The History of an Island People*, Tuttle, 2000, p. 301.

[125] Perry, M.C., *The Japan Expedition 1852-1854: The Personal Journal of Commodore Matthew C. Perry,* edited by Roger Pineau, with an introduction by Samuel Elliot Morrison, The Smithsonian Press, Washington D.C., 1968.

When Perry arrived in Naha he began by throwing the port authorities off his ship and rejecting their gifts, claiming they did not have sufficient rank to speak to him. This was an official lie intended to bring the real authorities into the open.

Shortly thereafter he was visited by Sho Taimu, who introduced himself as the regent (acting king) of Okinawa. Sho Taimu was a member of the royal family and the hereditary lord of Mabuni village.[126] At that time king Sho Tai was still a boy, too young to take command.[127] The regent came aboard Perry's flagship with a small number of grim-faced keimochi assistants. Matsumura and Itosu were almost certainly in this group. They took a tour of the ship and had dinner with the Commodore.

Perry then made a series of demands. He wanted to speak to the Okinawan king about signing a contract to cover such items as the price of provisions sold to U.S. ships visiting Naha. He wanted a building to use as his base onshore. He wanted to establish a coal depot for visiting steamships. He was politely but firmly refused on every front.

Perry then demanded to speak with the real king. Sho Taimu made official excuses, saying the king was just a little boy and not yet in power. His mother, the dowager queen, was terribly ill and was not seeing anyone. It was so regrettable, but Okinawa could not sell any supplies of any kind to visiting ships. Sho Taimu would not compromise on any point.

The regent was simply enforcing Japan's iron policy of zero contact with Western nations (the unspoken honne), but the Satsuma overlords didn't allow him to say so (the official tatemae). For his part, Perry was deliberately picking a fight over false issues (tatemae) in order to create a confrontation that he would certainly win (honne). He needed a hard reputation and he meant to obtain it. Sho Taimu played right into Perry's hands.

---

[126] Historians have come to the conclusion that Sho Taimu was only pretending to be the regent (tatemae) while the real regent was in hiding with the young king and the king's mother (honne). From Perry's point of view, however, Sho Taimu was the acting king. Perry, 1968, p. 61.

[127] In the history books, Sho Taimu appears as Shang Ta-mu. "Shang" is the Chinese reading of the kanji character for the royal "Sho" family name. Perry's translators were Chinese.

Perry Invades Shuri Castle

On Monday, June 6, 1853, Commodore Perry forced the issue by landing two cannons and two companies of U.S. Marines bearing Springfield rifle-muskets and flashing bayonets. Along with 50 naval officers and two brass bands, Perry set out for Shuri Castle.

It was an impressive parade. The vanguard was a party of 30 sailors dragging two cannons. Behind them was a brass band in red coats. Next came a company of Marines proudly displaying Old Glory. Perry himself was carried forward in a sedan chair made just for the occasion. The chair was carried by eight Chinese coolies exactly as if he were the Shogun himself. Behind the commodore came his 50 naval officers in blue jackets and white trousers. Each officer carried a saber. The second brass band in red coats followed the officers. Bringing up the rear was another American flag and the second company of Marines. It was literally a red-white-and-blue procession.[128]

Figure 3-2: Commodore Perry brings two companies of U.S. Marines to force the gate of Shuri Castle.[129]

---

[128] Perry, 1968, facing page 93. Perry's personal journal contains a watercolor painting of the procession. Unfortunately, it could not be reproduced here with any clarity.

[129] Perry, 2000, p. 188.

It was an invasion disguised as a parade. In modern terms, it was "deniable." Perry was very good at this sort of thing. The column looked like a parade (tatemae), but the cannons and the bristling bayonets sent a clear message (honne). It takes enormous effort to offload two cannons, transport them to shore in rowboats, and drag them three miles uphill by hand. This was not an innocent or casual act.

The column arrived at Shuri and found the castle gate closed and locked. Perry made it clear that the ancient and beautiful "Gate of Courtesy" was not going to stop him. The Okinawan officials conferred with one another and stared fearfully at the cannons. After a few minutes they reluctantly opened the gates. Perry and his officers marched into the heart of Shuri Castle, leaving most of the Marines behind to secure the gate.[130]

Shuri Castle was the seat of the Okinawan government, and must have employed at least a couple of hundred bureaucrats and clerks. We know there were a hundred female servants attending the royal family. When Perry entered, however, the castle was deserted except for Sho Taimu, three senior ministers, and a dozen shadowy assistants. Perry and his officers were escorted into the large reception hall on the north side of the central courtyard (apparently not the Seiden). The Americans filled the hall, except for one corner occupied by the Okinawan officials. The two parties stood and glared at each other, sipping weak tea and chewing twists of stale gingerbread supplied by the grim Okinawan hosts.

Figure 3-3: Commodore Perry at the gate (close-up of Figure 3-2). Okinawan officials greet the Commodore (foreground). Ranks of U.S. Marines carrying rifles and fixed bayonets are visible against the white wall in the background.

---

[130] Perry, 1968, p. 65.

The Okinawans were very tense, because in their experience there was only one reason a military force would invade Shuri. They expected Perry to declare himself the military governor of Okinawa, and declare the island to be a United States possession. (Okinawa did in fact become a U.S. possession about 90 years later.) They could not understand why he would invade the castle at gunpoint and then stand there silently chewing that disgusting gingerbread.

This tension naturally resulted in some awkward silences. Francis Dawks, the principal author of Perry's *Narrative*, noted that "the interview was becoming rather uninteresting, and it was quite plain that the magnates of Lew Chew, for some cause or other, were not quite at their ease."[131] Small wonder, considering they expected to be arrested or killed at any moment.

For his part, Perry had no intention of seizing the castle because

Figure 3-4: Commodore Perry received with stale gingerbread at Shuri Castle. The Okinawan officials are huddled in the far left corner of the room.[132] Except for this room, the castle was deserted.

---

[131] Perry, 2000, p. 191. "Lew Chew" is Dawks's rendering of "Ryukyu," a synonym of Okinawa.

[132] Perry, 2000, p. 190.

he had accomplished his real goal by forcing his way in. He knew he would be taken seriously when he reached Tokyo. He didn't care about conquering Okinawa. Who would want to conquer Okinawa?

Perry at the Regent's House

After a while, the regent invited Perry's officers to his home for dinner (tatemae, again), which was really a weak attempt to lure the barbarians out of the castle (honne, the hidden motivation). To the astonishment of Sho Taimu, Perry accepted this invitation. The invasion force turned around, marched out of the castle again, and settled down for a 12-course meal at the regent's home. (The courses were almost all soup.) We can be certain that the castle gate was firmly bolted behind them as they left.

While dining at the regent's house, Perry apparently demanded a photograph of their royal host for his report. The picture of Sho Taimu (Figure 3-5) speaks eloquently of his attitude toward his guests. He looks absolutely furious. He was appalled by the barbaric behavior of the Americans, and was still quite uncertain about Perry's intentions. Who can read the mind of a barbarian from a wilderness like America?

The repeated courses of dishwater soup, like the stale gingerbread, were probably a calculated insult on the part of Sho Taimu. Eventually Perry got the message. He led his entourage back down the hill to Tomari, and spent the afternoon getting the cannons back on board ship. Shuri residents breathed a large sigh of relief to see him go.

After Perry was out of sight, Sho Taimu turned grimly back toward the castle. The Satsuma overlords had ordered him to keep Perry aboard his ship. Sho Taimu had failed spectacularly. The barbarian had not only left his ship, he had marched soldiers within a few feet of the Japanese overlords themselves! Sho Taimu collected his dignity as he walked back to the Seiden. There he made his report and submitted himself to the terrible wrath of Satsuma.

Just after this incident, Perry made a brief excursion to the nearby Bonin Islands. When he returned to Okinawa, he was surprised to discover that Sho Taimu had disappeared and was rumored to have committed suicide because of Perry's visit to Shuri. No one knows what actually happened to Sho Taimu. The Satsumas would certainly have punished him for his spectacular failure, and *hara kiri* was a possibility. All we really know is that there was a new regent when Perry returned from the Bonin Islands, and Sho Taimu was not seen again.[133]

Perry could not officially admit that he had caused the old man's death, so he "determined" in his report that the former regent had simply resigned. The lesson of Sho Taimu's disappearance was not lost on the Commodore, however. A few weeks later he wrote a brief passage in his personal journal, sympathizing with the lethal plight of the Shuri ministers:

> "Those in power can never know how soon any of their acts, however harmless in their own estimation, may be construed into some offence against the state, and finding their lives consequently in jeopardy are compelled to purchase safety by humility, or a good share of their substance. These failing, they commit suicide to save their families from ruin, and their fortunes from confiscation."[134]

Who was he speaking of, if not Sho Taimu?

Perry had many other adventures in Okinawa, almost all of a threatening and invasive nature, but never quite resorting to actual violence. Eventually he sailed for Japan to complete his diplomatic mission. Japan was forced to open her doors to the rest of the world, and the shogunate lost so much face that it soon lost control of the country. Perry's mission was a great success. It toppled one of history's great dynasties and ushered in the Meiji restoration. (The Meiji restoration, as you recall, absolutely ruined Shuri.)

Perry made a final call at Naha after humiliating the shogunate, and by association, the Satsuma samurai. This time the Okinawans were much more cooperative, and even agreed to open the marketplace to Perry's officers. Once a degree of free trade had been established, the Okinawan ministers turned out to be very shrewd businessmen. They wanted payment in silver for everything, and they drove very hard bargains.

---

[133] Perry, 1968, p. 83.
[134] Perry, 1968, p. 115.

Figure 3-5: The regent of Okinawa, Sho Taimu, during his last public appearance on June 6, 1853. Sho Taimu was a very angry man that night. (Note the *hachimaki* hats and haori topcoats, signifying the wearer's high rank.)[135]

---

[135] Perry, 2000, p. 218.

Perry's Report

Commodore Perry edited the official report of the expedition and his personal journal so that they reflected very well on him (tatemae), but some of his men kept private diaries and journals of which Perry was not aware (honne). The writers of these journals criticized the commodore severely for his pompous and irrational mistreatment of the peaceful Okinawans. These accounts are very entertaining to read and provide a wealth of information on daily life in Okinawa in the 1850s.[136]

In all the months that the Americans spent exploring the island, they didn't see *anything* they recognized as a weapon. They also never saw the child king or his mother, whom they called the "dowager queen." They met two different men playing the role of "regent," always flanked by the same grim attendants. The American visitors never had the faintest idea that martial arts like karate, tode, or kubudo even existed. They never saw a sai. Their reports do not mention any names we would recognize except for the king himself.

But they kept journals, wrote letters, drew sketches and took photographs all over the island. Those few months are the best documented period of Okinawan history.

The Perry expedition published their two-volume narrative report of their visit to Okinawa in 1856.[137] The photographic plates were destroyed in a fire, but the original lithographs from the expedition's report show near-photographic detail of scenes in and around Shuri Castle in 1853. This brings the birthplace of karate to life in a way that vague oral histories just can't do.

---

[136] Kerr, 2000, Chapter 7. Kerr contrasts the official narrative with the private accounts.
[137] Perry, 2000.

Chapter 4

Dispossessed and Abandoned

The Meiji restoration ruined the *keimochi* nobles of Shuri. Prior to 1868 the lords of Shuri were in constant danger but their hereditary stipends made them financially secure. After 1868 the danger evaporated, but so did the stipends. Karate continued to develop, but karate's "next generation" suffered from poverty and indignity. They became known as *shizoku*, the Japanese Meiji-era term for the former keimochi families.[138]

The men described in this chapter did not share the common bond of the Shuri bodyguards. They had no common interests and no common dream. They inherited a remarkable martial art that no one needed anymore. Many of them didn't like or trust one another. They became "lost souls" who went into the world to establish their own independent karate "styles." Linear karate fragmented down new paths toward new destinies.

For the purposes of this study, the two giants of this generation were Gichin Funakoshi and Chotoku Kyan.

Chotoku Kyan

Chotoku Kyan is not one of our Shotokan forebears. If Funakoshi is the father of Shotokan karate, then Kyan is the black-sheep uncle the family never talks about. Funakoshi's silence about Kyan is eloquent.

In Kyan's biography we see tatemae at war with honne. When you read Richard Kim's or Shoshin Nagamine's accounts of the life of Chotoku Kyan, you can see the authors struggling to portray Kyan as a heroic and noble master. His life doesn't lend itself to that interpretation. After reading every available story about Kyan, I found myself describing him as "Funakoshi's evil twin." It is very disturbing when every story about a famous sensei has some ugly twist to it.

However, it turns out that Kyan was an incredible fighter who had deep emotional and moral problems.

Half of the Okinawan "Shorin" karate styles are based on the teachings of Kyan. His faithful students believe the official story that they are preserving Itosu's Shorin tradition (the tatemae), but that is doubtful. For instance, Kyan learned the same pinan kata as

---

[138] McCarthy, 1999b, p. 123. Karate history is a wild mix of languages. Keimochi is the traditional Okinawan term for the upper-class families. Shizoku is the later Japanese term for the dispossessed upper class families.

Figure 4-1: Chotoku Kyan, or Chan Migwa, the most overtrained martial artist in history. Note the enlarged knuckles from pounding the makiwara.

Funakoshi and Mabuni, but the pinan kata he *taught* are almost unrecognizable. Most of Matsumura's revolutionary linear techniques are *missing* from these kata. Kyan was no fan of Shuri-te.

On the other hand, Kyan made some unique contributions of his own, and his story is worth telling. At one point in this analysis, Kyan's iconoclasm becomes very important.

Kyan's Health

Kyan was born in 1870, which makes him almost the same age as Funakoshi and about 40 years younger than Itosu. He was not part of the inner circle at Shuri Castle, but his father was. As you recall, Chofu Kyan was chief of staff to the king, a position that Chotoku would have inherited except for the abolishment of the keimochi class while he was a child.[139]

---

[139] Nagamine, 2000, p. 81.

Chotoku Kyan was a sickly baby, with some of the problems one associates with a premature birth. As a child, he was small, weak and thin. He wheezed with asthma and squinted with myopia. Other boys made fun of him, and nicknamed him "squinty-eyed Chan," or Chan Migwa. The small body contained a brooding and angry spirit. Kyan trained from the age of eight under the iron supervision of the Shuri bodyguards, who were all friends of his father. Kyan was small, but Nagamine says that trying to fight him was like trying to swallow a needle. The size of the needle just isn't relevant.

Kyan was a ferocious fighter and an inspiring teacher, judging from his remarkable students, but he had serious character problems. Photos of Kyan show a sour little man with a grim mouth. He glares bitterly at the world. He might have become the second most-powerful man in Okinawa, the royal chief of staff, except for Perry's destruction of the shogunate. Instead, he struggled with poverty all his life.

Kyan's Attitude

Chotoku Kyan's father loved his sickly son and wanted to make him healthy. He arranged for the boy to undergo the most vigorous martial training available, thinking that hard training would strengthen the youngster's failing health. Given the circumstances, little Chotoku probably had nothing to say about this decision. In fact, Chotoku Kyan might not have wanted to become a martial artist. It was a destiny forced upon him by his domineering father.

According to Richard Kim, Matsumura put the sickly little boy through "the type of training that would have done justice to a Zen temple."[140] From the age of eight onward, little Kyan suffered through private lessons with all of the most accomplished martial artists of Shuri and Tomari. He learned every kata and every weapon from at least a dozen sensei, who must often have contradicted and undermined each other. Kyan had been training for 11 or 12 years by the time his father died in 1889. By the time Kyan was about 19 years old, he had become the most grimly over-trained (but healthy) youth in karate history. He also seems to have developed a teenager's rebellious anger toward his tormentors.

The Kyan stories convey a sense of backlash against his father and

---

[140] Kim, 1974, p. 63.

the Shuri masters. Most martial artists show a life-long loyalty to their principal teachers (*giri*), but this doesn't seem to be the case with Kyan. He spent his life changing the Shuri kata in various ways, although not always constructively. It may be that Kyan saw no advantage to linear technique, so he discarded it and reverted to vital-point technique instead. Kyan's unique contribution was that he combined China's vital-point strikes with Shuri's ruthless philosophy of *ikken hisatsu*. One strike, sudden death. He went for the eyes and throat *first*, which a Shaolin monk would never have done.

Late in his life, Kyan apparently abandoned Shuri-te completely and taught only pre-Matsumura kata and techniques. That tells us quite a lot about his attitude toward Shuri-te and the Shuri masters. In the end, he completely turned his back on them.

Kyan's Fights

Because of his small size, Kyan specialized in rapid sidestepping and vital-point strikes. The stories of his fights show Shuri-te's amoral commitment to single-blow victories, but no sign of linear impact technique. He turned vital-point technique into a lethal art. Let's look at some of these stories.

Kyan had two young followers who walked around with him like bodyguards, often just causing trouble. These friends were Ankichi Arakaki[141] and Taro Shimabuku.[142] There is a famous story in which the trio went to a cockfight, and Kyan entered his favorite fighting cock in the contest. As they were about to leave, Arakaki and Shimabuku circulated in the crowd, telling several men that Kyan had said insulting things about the men. Then they hid nearby to watch the fun.

When Kyan came out, every fist was against him. He had to fight his way through the crowd.

This is where the story gets interesting. Kyan cut though the mob so effortlessly that he never had to let go of his pet rooster![143] The stories

---

[141] First teacher of Shoshin Nagamine. Not the same as Seisho Arakaki who gave us nijushiho, sochin and unsu.

[142] Brother of Tatsuo Shimabuku. Taro used to beat up his little brother. Tatsuo decided to take karate lessons, too, and later founded isshin-ryu.

[143] Alexander, 1991, p. 60, and Bishop, 1999, p. 74.

of this incident say that Arakaki and Shimabuku were astonished, as if Kyan drew on secret techniques the two troublemakers had not seen before. It turns out that the ability to cut through a hostile mob was an essential skill for a Shuri bodyguard, and it appears that Kyan was adept at it. (See Figure 9-26.)

There is another story involving Kyan and chickens. Kyan once set a trap for a gang of four strong-arm robbers. He bought two live chickens and carried them back and forth along the Naha-Shuri road each evening for several days, waiting to be mugged. When the gangsters finally appeared, Kyan threw the squawking chickens in their faces as a distraction, and then leveled the criminals with a series of vital-point strikes to the eyes, throat and testicles. According to Richard Kim, Kyan gave the moaning gang members a sermon about their moral obligation to society, followed by a stern warning to mend their ways or face the consequences! According to George Alexander, Kyan simply killed all four and went home.[144] This may be another example of face-saving tatemae contrasted with more brutal honne.

Kyan once provoked a bully, Matsuda, to a match by the riverside. Matsuda charged in to crush the frail-looking youth with the thick glasses. Kyan sidestepped and kicked Matsuda in the thigh, hitting the sciatic nerve. Matsuda lost control of his leg and hurtled into the water.[145]

Alexander relates a story in which Kyan fought Tairaguwa, a famous strongman and, one hopes, some kind of outlaw. Kyan killed Tairaguwa by jumping out of a tree and breaking his neck.[146] (Try to picture Funakoshi leaping out of a tree to break someone's neck!)

Challenged to a friendly match by a 6th dan in judo, Kyan stuck his thumb inside the opponent's mouth, dug his nails into the man's cheek, and yanked him down to the ground "in an attempt to separate the skin from the bone."[147] He then finished off his opponent with a hammerfist blow to the face. To give him credit, he held back the final blow after nearly ripping the terrified man's face off. It was a friendly match, after all.

---

[144] Kim, 1974, p. 61. Alexander, 1991, p. 59.

[145] Nagamine, 2000, p. 85.

[146] Alexander, 1991, p. 59.

[147] Nagamine, 2000, p. 87.

Bishop also tells an unsavory story about Kyan selling piglets in the marketplace for his wife, then stealing part of her money so he could accompany his friends to brothels at night. The traits of morality, humility and honor one expects of a karate master were not always evident in this bitter little man.

Apparently Kyan, Arakaki and Shimabuku were in the habit of issuing open challenges. One of these challenges resulted in the early death of Arakaki at the age of 28 (or maybe it was 31). Karate teaches you humility because there is always someone who is bigger and faster than you are. The handsome and dashing Arakaki met this man and died, apparently of internal bleeding.[148]

According to Bishop, Kyan admonished his students that hard drinking and fornication with prostitutes were an essential part of their martial arts training.[149] This seems very amusing until you think about it. To me, it sounds as if Kyan was mocking his fanatical father, who had forced him to suffer every type of physical abuse as "an essential part of your martial arts training."

Kyan survived the terrible Battle of Okinawa in 1945 but starved to death in the aftermath. There is a legend that he gave up his ration of rice so that destitute children might eat. This noble legend (the tatemae) is repeated much more widely than the stories about the disrespect, the fights, the drinking, the stealing, the whoring and the apparent murders (the honne).

In spite of the noble gesture toward the children, Kyan's death was a suicide. Food was available and Kyan could have eaten it, but he chose not to. In Japan, starving oneself to death is a noble gesture.

Kyan's Kata

Our modern idea that kata are immutable would have taken the Shuri masters by surprise. The "ancient" masters of Okinawa, including Kyan, did not hesitate to change the kata that they learned from their teachers. Kyan studied many different versions of common kata, and made no attempt to teach a consistent system of his own.

---

[148] Bishop, 1999, p. 74. Shoshin Nagamine loyally insists that his beloved teacher really died of stomach ulcers. Nagamine, 2000, p. 113. This tatemae diverts attention from the fact that Arakaki lost the fight.

[149] Bishop, 1999, p. 73.

Attempts to preserve kata "exactly as taught by Kyan" are noble but pointless, because he seems to have taught every student something different. Anyone who preserves a Kyan kata is preserving something that Kyan himself eventually abandoned.

Kyan's iconoclastic attitude must be a problem for the karate styles that are based on his teachings, but it is actually a blessing in disguise for our present purposes. His lack of respect for Shuri led him to teach pre-Shuri kata to some of his students. As a result, some of Kyan's students established styles based on kata that were not modified by Itosu. In particular, Tatsuo Shimabuku studied under Kyan during the 1930s when the master was in his 60s. At that time, Kyan had gone back to basics by teaching older versions of Okinawan kata instead of the forms modified at Shuri.[150] These kata are preserved in Shimabuku's style, isshin-ryu. This forms a basis for comparative kata studies later in this book.

Kyan's Legacy

Some say that there are only three philosophies in the world. The first is the lighthearted philosophy of people who have never been shot at. The second is the more sober view of people who have been shot at. The third is the deadly philosophy of people who have been shot at and hit. Think of couples who have never had children; couples who have raised children; and couples who have seen their children die. They have three different views of the world.

The Shuri Crucible makes one thing very clear: Chotoku Kyan was an incredible fighter, perhaps the most formidable ever trained at Shuri. Even so, he never stood with his back to the wall, facing 200 American Marines like Itosu did. Itosu was a grim and sober veteran of the Shuri Crucible. In comparison, Kyan was a bitter amateur who didn't understand the problem. It made a significant difference in their behavior toward the art.

Kanryo Higaonna

Kanryo Higaonna really has little or nothing to do with the history of Shuri-te and shotokan, yet it is very important to know who he was.

---

[150] Sells, 2000, p. 189. Also see "The Complete Tatsuo Shimabuku" by Victor Smith at http://www.fightingarts.com/content01/shimabuku.shtml.

Higaonna is regarded as the founder of Naha-te, the principal rival of Shuri-te in Okinawa. We'll explore the rivalry between Naha and Shuri in the next section.

Higaonna (sometimes the kanji are read "Higashionna") was born in 1853, the year Commodore Perry marched on Shuri Castle.[151] That made him about 20 years younger than Itosu and 15 years older than Funakoshi. He was never a royal insider. He came from a high-ranking keimochi family that opened a firewood business when the gentry were dispossessed in 1868. From this point on, Higaonna's family was too poor to have him educated, so he grew up illiterate.

Higaonna may have studied tode or even Shuri-te with Seisho "The Cat" Arakaki as a teenager.[152] When he was 16 his family lost their royal stipend and had to rely entirely on their firewood business. Higaonna ran away to China where he spent 14 years weaving baskets while studying white crane and praying mantis chuan fa.[153] He practiced sanchin kata to the point that he developed a physique of a bodybuilder.

Higaonna suffered profoundly from depression during the long, dark years of his self-imposed exile. He taught himself Chinese and painfully struggled through the Confucian classics to educate himself. He dreamed of a triumphant return to Okinawa, where he would become a famous teacher loved by all as a master of Chinese fighting technique and philosophy.

Higaonna returned to Okinawa in 1881 (roughly), but his hopes were cruelly dashed. The Japanese Meiji government had forbidden Okinawa to have any further contact with China. In fact, the Japanese were busy stamping out the Okinawan language itself, forcing everyone to speak Japanese. Old schools that taught Okinawan and Chinese languages were forced to close. New Japanese schools opened in their place. A teacher of Chinese arts and philosophy was not only useless but officially unwelcome.

---

[151] Nagamine, 2000, p. 60, says Higaonna was born in 1853. Or maybe it was 1845 (Kim, 1974, p. 95). Or 1851 (Alexander, 1991, p. 51). Higaonna's history contains very few verifiable facts prior to 1902.

[152] Nagamine, 2000, p. 60.

[153] The published stories of why Higaonna went to China, how he made the journey, when he arrived, where he went, how long he stayed, what he studied, and who he studied with are wildly contradictory. We really have no idea what he did in China, except that he studied martial arts.

Instead of opening a school, Higaonna resumed his family's firewood business and, according to Nagamine, did not teach martial arts for 20 years. Driven by depression, he regularly abandoned himself in Naha's red-light district. One story from this period emphasizes how well he could fight even when too drunk to stand up.[154] He was immensely strong and extremely fast in combat, and was a master of unexpected attacks to the legs and knees. People called him the "secret bushi," a warrior pretending to be a mere woodcutter.

Itosu and Higaonna naturally found each other and became friends. When Itosu started teaching karate in public schools in 1902, Higaonna dusted off his chuan fa and opened a class, too. He accepted a few students and quickly established a reputation as a demanding but rather boring teacher. He followed the mainland chuan fa philosophy that a student should practice sanchin kata for three years before being taught anything else.

Sanchin kata is grueling. It consists of about a minute and a half of exhausting isometric muscle contractions during which your teacher strikes your chest, back and legs with a stick to inure you to pain. It leaves bruises on your body. Imagine what it would be like to do sanchin 50 times a night for three years. I suspect this is the tradition that prompted Bruce Lee's famous remark that "kata is organized despair." Sanchin comes close. On the other hand, it builds huge muscles and eventually makes you tough as a tree root.[155]

Higaonna's most famous student was the remarkable Chojun Miyagi, the founder of Okinawan goju-ryu.[156] Higaonna was also one of the teachers of Kenwa Mabuni and Shimpan Gusukuma (Shimpan Shiroma), the founders of the two Shito-Ryu styles.

The most important thing to remember about Kanryu Higaonna is that he taught traditional chuan fa newly imported from China.[157] He didn't teach at all before 1902, and yet there is a widespread tatemae

---

[154] Nagamine, 2000, p. 63-64.

[155] Chojun Miyagi, a champion of sanchin, suffered from high blood pressure and died suddenly of a heart attack at age 65. John Porta and Jack McCabe, "Karate of Chojun Miyagi," *Journal of Asian Martial Arts*, Vol. 3, 1994, p. 69.

[156] Nagamine, 2000, Chapter 6.

[157] Sells, 2000, p. 37. "Southern Chinese Fujian kung fu."

that Naha-te is an ancient Okinawan branch of karate.[158] It would be very hard to justify that idea. Certainly there had always been a few martial artists in Naha, particularly among the secretive Chinese families, but there was no developing martial tradition there before Higaonna began to teach at the turn of the century.

Naha-te vs. Shuri-te

Now that we have met Higaonna, we can sort out the differences between "hard" and "soft" karate.

It is not clear to the casual reader that there are two very different kinds of "Okinawan karate," with different masters, different origins, different histories, different kata, and different means of generating power. This causes a lot of confusion about "karate" history. There are, in essence, two different histories.

When karate became popular in Japan in the 1920s (largely due to Funakoshi), Okinawan masters felt a bit left out. In 1926 they made an effort to organize their local arts and get some national recognition. As part of this reorganization, they coined the terms "Shuri-te," "Naha-te," and "Tomari-te," to describe the types of karate they were teaching in these three towns.[159]

To clarify, this book is mainly concerned with the development of Shuri-te under the influence of Bushi Matsumura and Yasutsune Itosu. Shuri-te is also known as linear karate, hard-style karate, and Shorin karate. The tatemae of "Shorin" is that it refers to the original Shaolin Temple. This type of karate arose in Shuri among upper-class royal bodyguards in the 1800s. It is said to be best for people who are light and quick on their feet because it uses body momentum to generate impact. It has many long-range weapons such as *oi-zuki* (front punch), which require enough light to be able to *see* your opponent. This hard-hitting karate first appeared in the 1820s when Matsumura was young, and developed steadily through Itosu's death in 1915. In traditional shotokan karate, we continue to research and refine the Shuri-te principles to the present day.

---

[158] Sells says Higaonna taught a few private students beginning in 1889. That makes the same point. Sells, 2000, p. 47.

[159] McCarthy, 1999b, p. 3-4.

The second school of Okinawan karate is called Naha-te. It is also known as soft-style karate, circular karate, or the Shorei style. "Shorei" refers to the Shorei-ji, the *Southern* Shaolin Temple![160] Naha-te is sometimes listed as a branch or example of White Crane chuan fa. It was founded by Kanryu Higaonna in 1902, and according to Nagamine was almost pure chuan fa, newly re-imported from China at that time. Higaonna emphasized body building and stationary, rooted stances. There was an emphasis on muscle power, and on keeping your hands in contact with the opponent while you fight. This lets you grapple with an opponent in the dark. For this reason, Funakoshi says that Shorei technique is best for muscular body-builders like Higaonna.[161]

Naha-te quickly evolved into Okinawan goju-ryu. The other branch of modern Naha-te is uechi-ryu, which didn't arrive in Okinawa (from China, via Japan) until 1945. Chuan fa may be ancient, but the unspoken truth of Naha-te is that it arose and was named in the 20th century.

For the record, we also see other kinds of "karate" in Japan and Okinawa, usually labeled *"kenpo."* These are soft-style arts based on chuan fa from China, and are only distantly related to Shuri-te. Kenpo is the Japanese pronunciation of the Chinese "chuan fa" kanji. It is a Chinese art performed in a Japanese uniform.

Comparing Shuri technique with Naha is like comparing the irresistible cannonball with the immovable post, yet both are known as "karate" simply because both towns are in weaponless Okinawa. When people write about "karate," it is important to know which kind

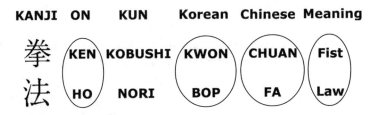

KANJI	ON	KUN	Korean	Chinese	Meaning
拳	KEN	KOBUSHI	KWON	CHUAN	Fist
法	HO	NORI	BOP	FA	Law

Figure 4-2: Kenpo (Japanese) is chuan fa (Chinese), *the law of the fist.* It is read as *kwon bop* in Korean.

---

[160] Sells, 2000, p. 47.

[161] Funakoshi, 1973, p. 8. Note that Shorei technique is not for heavy people, but for *muscular* people.

of karate they mean. They have very little in common except for the uniform, and even that was a modern innovation.

Quite a lot of rivalry arose between Shuri-te and Naha-te between 1902 and 1930 due to the extreme differences in their philosophy, origins and technique.

- Naha-te arose on the grimy waterfront; Shuri-te came from a sparkling palace. That alone would cause friction.

- Naha-te was rooted in muscular strength and grappling, while Shuri-te was rooted in speed and impact.

- Naha-te was used to subdue an opponent; Shuri-te sought to destroy the opponent. This created quite a bit of moral tension between the two styles.

- Naha-te teaches you to fight in the dark; Shuri-te assumes that you can see the enemy. This is literally a "night and day" difference.

- Above all, Naha-te and the southern Chinese styles place an enormous emphasis on sanchin kata, both for body-building and for testing black belts. Shuri-te abandoned sanchin completely, a dramatic difference that set Shuri-te completely apart from the Chinese styles. If you are not doing sanchin, you simply are not a white crane or Naha stylist.[162]

It is clear that neither Shuri nor Naha can claim that their art is based on "hundreds of years of secret development" in weaponless Okinawa. That romantic tatemae might apply to kobudo, but is not valid for any form of karate. The period of "secret development" for Shuri-te lasted about 50 years, during Matsumura's tenure at Shuri Castle. There was never a period of secret development for Naha-te. Higaonna's techniques were imported straight from Fuzhou, and were not developed in Okinawa at all. Any subsequent development that took place happened under the direction of Chojun Miyagi after the veil of secrecy was lifted.

What about Tomari-te? After careful consideration I see little reason to mention Tomari-te, although I greatly admire Kosaku Matsumora

---

[162] Shotokan technique is mainly Shuri-te, but Funakoshi wanted his students to sample a wider experience. Therefore several of Shotokan's "advanced" kata are borrowed from the older Chinese tradition. Even so, he did not include sanchin.

for that trick with the wet towel. The men who taught karate in Tomari were retired Shuri bodyguards. The idea that Tomari-te is significantly different from Shuri-te strikes me as tatemae by someone who had a dojo in Tomari in 1926.

Tatsuo Shimabuku

It is hard to imagine a martial-arts master whose contributions are less relevant to shotokan than Tatsuo Shimabuku, who founded the isshin-ryu style in 1956. He's in the wrong karate lineage, with the wrong kata and the wrong techniques, and he arrived a hundred years too late. This is his charm, however. In isshin-ryu we find several Okinawan kata taught to Shimabuku by the elderly Chotoku Kyan during one of Kyan's rebellious periods in the 1930s. It's like finding a time capsule of soft kata from the pre-Shuri-te period.

We will examine these kata in a later chapter to get a feel for the changes Itosu introduced when he took the original kata and revised them.

Gichin "Shoto" Funakoshi

As a shotokan sensei, I always have Master Gichin Funakoshi in my thoughts. A brief sketch of Master Funakoshi is necessary to connect the events of karate's prehistory to our own experience in the modern era. (Most shotokan students know nothing about karate before it arrived in Japan, as if Funakoshi invented it. He didn't.)

Funakoshi was a schoolteacher. He had faults, like other masters, but his were the faults of fanaticism. This man was unflinchingly honorable and rather severe. He avoided fights, respected his wife, and apparently never lied, cheated or stole. He never challenged a gang of bullies. He never climbed a tree to jump on the neck of an enemy. He never fought a bull with his bare hands. He defended himself only two times in his life, and was deeply ashamed afterward. He believed that a *real* master can win without fighting. Being forced to use his fists humiliated him.

Funakoshi led a blameless and somewhat boring life, setting an austere standard very few of us would want to equal. At the age when most men retire, he left his family behind in Shuri and became a karate missionary in Tokyo. He was very successful in popularizing karate in the nation's capital. For this he is widely acknowledged as "the father of modern karate."

Funakoshi's life is amply described elsewhere, including his own autobiography,[163] so I will confine myself to a few significant events of his life that are pertinent to this study. The first is that Funakoshi was born around 1868, the year of the Meiji restoration. This means he was 10 or 11 years old when the Sho dynasty ended. He was never a part of the inner circle at Shuri Castle.

Figure 4-3: Gichin Funakoshi in maturity.

If you search the web for information on Funakoshi's boyhood, you may discover allegations that his father ruined the family by spending all their money on alcohol and dissipation. As we now know, *every* Shuri family was impoverished and destitute while Funakoshi was growing up. There is no need to blame Funakoshi's father for the ruinous edicts of the Meiji government. It was Emperor Meiji who destroyed the Funakoshi family fortune and left them starving. If Funakoshi's father became a drunk as a result, who can blame him? His entire world had collapsed.

The son, however, was made of sterner stuff.

---

[163] Funakoshi, Gichin, *Karate-Do, My Way of Life,* Kodansha, 1975.

Funakoshi's Career

Funakoshi's autobiography describes growing up in Shuri under the instruction of Azato and his friend Itosu. Funakoshi hoped to become a physician, but was excluded from medical school because he would not shave off his keimochi topknot. This was a hot political issue following the Meiji restoration. He eventually cut his hair to get a position as an elementary school teacher, which stunned and shamed his family, and he followed this career for 30 years. He turned down promotions so that he wouldn't have to leave Shuri and interrupt his karate training.

When Funakoshi married and had a family, his teachers Azato and Itosu behaved as *de facto* grandparents to the Funakoshi children. The masters spoiled the children with candy at a time when Funakoshi himself was so impoverished that he could barely put food on the table.[164] He mentions occasional training with a very elderly Bushi Matsumura, but has little to say about him except that the bushi had remarkable eyes.

One suspects that Funakoshi had some influence on Itosu's appearance in the public elementary schools, junior college, and teaching college in the years 1902 to 1905. In some instances Itosu presided while Funakoshi and others did the actual teaching, but he did some of the teaching himself. Itosu was vigorous in 1905, in spite of his advanced age.

Karate Missionary

When Itosu passed away in 1915, Funakoshi was 47 and one of Itosu's senior students. At this point, something very remarkable happened.

Itosu's senior students felt an enormous debt to their teacher, and apparently formed a pact to dedicate the remainder of their lives to spreading karate. They made a conscious commitment to take Shuri-te karate out of Okinawa and introduce it to the world. A moment's reflection reminds us that middle-aged men generally do not uproot their comfortable lives in this fashion. They must have felt that they had learned something extraordinary that could not be allowed to languish quietly along the road from Naha to Shuri. Note that chuan

---

[164] My own master, Hanshi Vincent Cruz of Roswell, NM, spoils my children by sending them cartons of bakery items. It may be a karate tradition.

fa, or kung fu, was already well-known throughout the Orient. There was something special about Shuri-te karate that made missionaries of these men. Shuri-te offered something that chuan fa did not.

So why choose karate as a life path? Why did Funakoshi and his classmates believe that karate was a special way to a better life? The answer, I am convinced, is *longevity*.

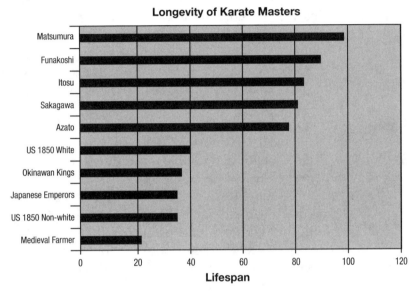

Figure 4-4: Longevity of Okinawan karate masters compared to other groups. Shuri masters lived remarkably long lives.

In a medieval, agricultural society the average life expectancy of a peasant farmer was as low as 22 years. Conditions were somewhat better in Okinawa in the 1800s, but the islanders suffered from repeated famines and epidemics of rubella, cholera and other diseases.[165] At least they bathed regularly and practiced reasonable sanitation, which put them way ahead of medieval Europeans. (Perry's personal journal says that Shuri was the cleanest town he had ever seen in his worldwide travels.)

You might assume that the kings would have the highest standard of living and the longest life expectancy of anyone on the island.

---

[165] For Okinawan famines and epidemics in early 1800s, refer to http://www.niraikanai.wwma.net/pages/base/chap1-4.html.

Including Sho Tai, the average lifespan of the last five Sho kings was only 36 years.[166] Sho Tai was a standout at 60 years.

That average seemed very low to me, so I also looked up the lifespan of the five Japanese emperors whose reigns covered roughly the same historical period. Their average life span was only 35 years! I kept digging for comparable data. The expected lifespan of a white American in 1850 was only 40 years.[167] European data is very similar.

Compared to this dismal record, what was the life span of the karate masters in our direct Shotokan lineage? At a time when emperors lived to be 35, Peichin Azato lived to be 78. Tode Sakugawa lived 82 years. Itosu was 85 on his last day. Funakoshi himself was 89. Matsumura lived to be 97. Shosei Kina, the last surviving direct student of Itosu, died in 1981 at the age of 100.[168] All of them lived to be twice the age of their contemporaries. Compared to the Sho kings, Matsumura and Kina lived 2-1/2 normal lifetimes.[169]

Wouldn't you follow a path that doubles your life expectancy? No wonder they thought karate was special!

Fired with commitment, Itosu's students nevertheless waited several years before putting their plan into action. As the senior man, Funakoshi had both the right and obligation to go first. In 1922 he traveled to Tokyo to perform karate demonstrations for various groups, and was so well-received that he eventually opened the first public karate school, the Shoto-kan, in Tokyo.

He never returned to his wife in Okinawa. It was 25 years before they were reunited in Tokyo.

Karate in Tokyo

Funakoshi received a special welcome from respected judo master Jigoro Kano at the Kodokan. Kano asked Funakoshi to teach some karate moves to the senior judo instructors, and judo's advanced *atemi waza* is the result. Funakoshi, in turn, adopted Kano's colored-belt

---

[166] I drew their birth and death dates from the table at http://www.worldstatesmen.org/Japan.htm.

[167] http://www.infoplease.com/ipa/A0005140.html

[168] Sells, 2000, p. 310.

[169] Apparently one did not see this effect among the chuan fa masters, possibly because of the side-effects of practicing sanchin.

ranking system, and had lightweight judo uniforms sewn for his karate students. This was the origin of the white cotton *gi* and colorful belts we wear today.

The 1930s were the golden years of the Shoto-kan. It was during this time that the shotokan style matured and spread through the universities of Japan. Funakoshi became very well known and widely respected. Then World War II came. The war did not go well for the Japanese, and in 1945 the fire bombings began.

At the close of World War II, Japanese civilians suffered horribly from the B-29 aerial fire bombings and atomic bombings. It is hard for modern Americans to imagine in this age of precision warfare, but in the summer of 1945 our nation set fire to Japan's largest cities and burned them to the ground. There were 70 cities that were more than half destroyed, and scores more that suffered partial damage. Millions of Japanese civilians died in the flames, and millions more still carry scars from the burns. The appalling atomic bombings of Hiroshima and Nagasaki in August, 1945, amounted to only 3 percent of the total destruction.[170] Funakoshi describes trying to survive as a homeless refugee in Japan by foraging for scraps of seaweed on the beach, because he could find nothing else to feed his starving wife. He was 78 years old at the time.

One of the buildings that burned to the ground in the Tokyo fires was the Shoto-kan. Fortunately, Master Funakoshi survived these events, but many of his friends and students did not. He lost his favorite son, Gigo Funakoshi, during this black year and his wife shortly afterward.[171]

Unlike Chotoku Kyan, Master Funakoshi did not despair and turn to suicide. He somehow found the courage to start again. Before his death at the age of 89, Funakoshi saw his surviving students rebuild the Shoto-kan and set it on the path that spread his teachings all over the world.[172] Today it is estimated that over five million people practice shotokan karate in 68 countries around the world.

---

[170] Caiden, Martin. *A Torch to the Enemy*, Ballantine, 1960, p. 158. Again, this was only 60 years ago. We have forgotten, but they have not.

[171] Gigo (Yoshitaka) Funakoshi was his father's protégé, the creator of the *taikyoku* and tenno kata, and wankan. He was the first to use high kicks in contests. He died of tuberculosis. Streptomycin could have cured him, but was not available in wartime Japan.

[172] Funakoshi states that he is 90 years old in his biography (Funakoshi, 1975, p. 96,) and also that he changed the date of his birth certificate when applying for medical school (p.1). This may account for varying estimates of his lifespan.

"Karate"

After he moved to Japan, Funakoshi changed the first kanji character of "kara te do" to mean "empty-hand way" instead of "Chinese-hand way."[173] This was part of his campaign to make karate seem more Japanese and less foreign. Pronounced in Korean, this new label came out "kong soo do," another early name for taekwondo.

"Karate" was not the only label Funakoshi changed. When karate invaded Japan, the old Okinawan/Chinese kata names were replaced by politically-correct Japanese names. Pinan became heian; naihanchi became tekki; patsai became bassai, kusanku became kanku; seisan became hangetsu; chinto became gankaku; and wansu became empi. Karate's Okinawan labels were painted over to make the art more respectable in the eyes of mainstream Japanese bureaucrats.

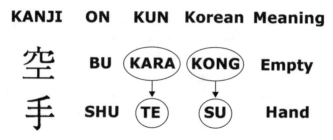

Figure 4-5: *Kanji* for "karate," with *on*, *kun* and Korean readings.

Why bureaucrats? Funakoshi wanted karate to be accepted as an official martial art like kendo and judo. To accomplish this feat, he had to persuade the all-powerful *Dai Nippon Butoku-ka*, the bureaucracy that licensed and supported the legitimate martial arts.[174] By this time, Funakoshi's tatemae had evolved. This time he convinced the ministers that Okinawan karate had been completely reorganized into a new *Japanese* martial art, and was no longer

---

[173] Funakoshi, 1975, p. 33.
[174] McCarthy, 1999b, p. 78-79.

Okinawan or Chinese at all. This pleased the bureaucrats, but caused problems back home in Okinawa.

Funakoshi succeeded in making karate very popular in Tokyo. Within 10 years there was a definite sense of envy growing among the old guard in Naha. Tokyo had become the world center of karate activity, and Okinawa was suddenly an unimportant backwater. Worse than that, it was Shuri-te that was so popular, not Naha-te or kenpo.

On October 25, 1936, the Okinawan masters met in Naha to discuss this problem.[175] Masters in attendance included Chojun Miyagi, Chotoku Kyan, Choki Motobu, and Shimpan Gusukuma (Shiroma), among others. They were quite concerned that karate had become so popular on the mainland and they were getting so little credit for it.

After some discussion, the Okinawan masters decided to follow Funakoshi's lead and adopt "kara (empty) te" as the common name of all branches of Okinawan unarmed fighting (not just Shuri-te). They also resolved to adopt a standard uniform for all karate styles, which eventually turned out to be Funakoshi's uniform. They made a clear decision to capitalize on Funakoshi's success in every way they could. They did all of this without once mentioning Funakoshi's name … or so says the transcript.

The transcript is the tatemae, the official record of the meeting taken down and transcribed by the staff of the local newspaper. The honne is more interesting. The moderators of the meeting respectfully addressed each master in rotation, seeking their views. The replies in the transcript are measured and polite, but there are several places where the subject changes abruptly, as if parts of the transcript have been deleted.

One of these abrupt changes occurs just as Choki Motobu begins to speak. Motobu was a vicious critic of Funakoshi. He is famous for publically calling Funakoshi an "impostor" who taught false karate.[176] If he said anything of substance at this meeting, it has been diplomatically edited from the official record.

Another attendee was Chotoku Kyan, who was also quite outspoken. Kyan's comments about the "Tokyo problem" are completely missing from the transcript, as if he wasn't there at all.

[175] McCarthy, 1999b, p. 57-69, for the transcript of the meeting. The meeting was sponsored by the local newspaper, and careful notes were taken for later publication.
[176] McCarthy, 1999b, p. 126.

It is unlikely that the respectful moderators would have overlooked Kyan, and I don't believe Kyan would have been silent. This was a much more colorful meeting than we know.

"Shoto"

Funakoshi published poetry under the pen name "Shoto." He wrote "Shoto" using the kanji characters that mean "pine waves," which he explained as "waves of wind in pine trees." In English, we would say "whispering pines." At least, this is Shotokan's official tatemae version of the story.

This is a very vivid and poetic image. The image of waving pine trees subtly acknowledges Funakoshi's connection with the Shining Forest style of his teacher, Itosu. There may also be a mischievous hidden meaning in "Shoto." When spoken aloud, "Shoto" can refer to the smaller of the two samurai swords in a *daisho* display (the *wakizashi* or even the *tanto*). There is no question in my mind that this was deliberate. Funakoshi the scholar, who was only five feet tall, was as short and sharp as they come.

But even that isn't all. "Shoto" is the on reading of the kanji selected by Funakoshi for his penname. The *kun* reading is "matsuto." That's *matsu*, pine tree, exactly the same kanji character as in *Matsu*mura. *Matsu* is the first character of "*Sho*tokan." The name of the Shotokan style points straight back to the man who invented linear karate. That is the hidden truth (honne) of "Shotokan."

Every time we say "Shotokan" we mention Matsumura.

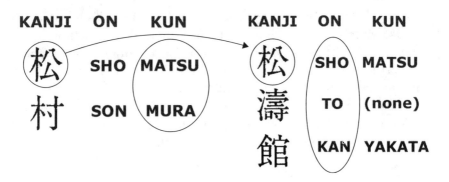

Figure 4-6: *Kanji* for Matsumura (left) and Shotokan (right). The "Sho" in "Shotokan" is drawn directly from Matsumura's name.

More Hidden Language

In my research, I noticed an interesting item from postwar Japan. The shotokan kata often exhibit a special kamae called *manji uke*. You see it at the very end of *heian godan*.[177] One stands in back stance, doing a down block to the front and a very high block to the rear (see Figure 9-29). The odd thing is that the famous shotokan writers such as Nakayama never seem to use the name of this technique in print. This is very puzzling until you see the kanji symbol for manji.

KANJI ON KUN

卍 **BAN MANJI**

Figure 4-7: **Manji** does not appear in print because it resembles the Nazi swastika.

The ancient Chinese kanji character for "manji" is a *swastika*. "Manji uke" means "swastika block," which makes sense considering the position of the arms. "Manji uke" is a term they didn't write down in the postwar period, when the authorities censored all publications for militaristic content.

Even today we might shy away from teaching students the "swastika block." Fortunately, this character is sometimes associated with the idea of swirling snowflakes.[178] Perhaps we could regard it as "swirling block" or "spiral block" instead of the swastika block.

Shotokan and Kobudo

If you have grown up with shotokan in the West, you are probably under the impression that shotokan is the art of the "empty hand" and does not involve weapons. Other Shorin styles study tonfa and bo sticks, but not shotokan. That's the tatemae. In fact, Shuri-te, Funakoshi and shotokan have strong connections to the modern art of kobudo.

---

[177] Sugiyama, Shojiro, *25 Shoto-kan Kata*, privately published by the author, 1989 edition, p. 54.

[178] Spahn and Hadamitzky, p. 347.

Kobudo is a product of Shuri, just like Shuri-te, and comes from the same masters who created hard-style karate. Chinese chuan-fa included both unarmed fighting and a wide selection of military weapons. These weapons were illegal in Okinawa, but the keimochi lords continued in the same tradition by substituting the kobudo weapons for the Chinese weapons. They did not view karate and kobudo as two separate arts, but parts of the same art. Most karate styles derived from Shuri still study the Okinawan weapons even today. Why not shotokan?

The prewar Shoto-kan dojo did contain kobudo weapons at one time, and certainly we have seen pictures of Gichin Funakoshi doing bo, sai, and tonfa kata during that period.[179] In postwar Japan, however, all martial arts were banned by the army of occupation. In order to re-open karate classes, Masatoshi Nakayama told the authorities that karate was a harmless form of Chinese boxing, like tai chi chuan on steriods.[180] The authorities demanded to know if karate students used swords or other banned weapons. Nakayama apparently assured them that shotokan students never play with weapons. From that moment on, shotokan students didn't touch weapons. This is a unique example of the official story becoming transformed into official policy. The tatemae became honne.

Shinken Taira was one of Funakoshi's early students at the Shoto-kan, long before the war. Taira studied for seven intense years (1922-1929) under Funakoshi's direct supervision. Apparently Funakoshi's kobudo kata intrigued Taira, because he subsequently devoted his life to collecting and codifying the disappearing knowledge of Okinawan kobudo. Taira became known as "the Father of Modern Kobudo."[181] Without his efforts, many rare forms might easily have died out.

Taira was one of the teachers of Fumio Demura, the well-known shito-ryu and kobudo master. This explains why my shotokan students seem so comfortable learning kobudo kata at Demura's seminars. The kata not only come from a long line of Shuri-te masters, just like the

---

[179] Hokama, 2000, p. 43. See also the back of the dust jacket of *Karate-Do, My Way of Life*, (Funakoshi, 1975.)

[180] Hassell, 1991, p. 83.

[181] McCarthy, 1999a, p. 101-113.

shotokan kata, but the "Father of Modern Kobudo" was a shotokan black belt who learned his first kobudo moves from Funakoshi himself. No wonder kobudo seems so natural to us!

It is only an accident of history that removed kobudo from shotokan. A strong case could be made that traditional shotokan is incomplete without it. Warriors need to understand weapons.

Much later in this book we will revisit kobudo, in the form of "kitchen kobudo." This is what kobudo would be if we had to invent it all over again in our own households.

Typhoon of Steel

Karate teachers repeat another misleading tatemae, the idea that the ancient masters were so secretive that they didn't leave any written records. They repeat this story to cover up their own ignorance. The truth is more stark and simple. The Shuri karate masters might have built entire libraries about karate, but their notes did not survive World

Figure 4-7: Naha city, after the Typhoon of Steel. The city of Naha was burned to the ground. Any written records of karate history that might have existed were lost in the fire. (U.S. Marine Corps photo)

Figure 4-8: Shuri Castle, after the Typhoon of Steel. Nothing was left but churned earth. Even the streets were gone. Shuri was destroyed more completely than Hiroshima or Nagasaki. (U.S. Marine Corps photo)

War II. Shuri-Naha was destroyed in 1945, swept away by a "Typhoon of Steel."

By 1945, the original Shuri masters were all deceased and the next generation after them had grown elderly. The third generation, young enough to fight in World War II, were already well-trained and deeply involved in the war. The war did not go well for them.

When U.S. forces closed in on Japan in 1945, they needed a secure base for the expected invasion. Once again, the unfortunate geography of the island made Okinawa a battle zone. The Americans thought that Okinawa was the perfect place to stage an invasion of Japan. The Japanese thought so, too, and defended the island at all costs.

The Battle of Okinawa in April 1945 was incredibly destructive. The Japanese forces used Shuri Castle to anchor one end of their defensive line, and fought so bravely that the Americans had to bring the battleship *U.S.S. Mississippi* close to shore to reduce the castle with her 16-inch guns.

The bombardment lasted for days, and in the end Sho Shin's ancient and beautiful castle was a pile of smouldering rubble. The Japanese commander had to evacuate his headquarters from the caves beneath the ruins.[182] He made his last stand in the highlands to the south, and finally killed himself when he reached the ocean cliffs and could retreat no farther.

The Japanese forces made no provision for the evacuation or safety of the Okinawan people, who were caught between two implacable war machines and received no mercy. Every building between Shuri Castle and the Naha coastline was destroyed by bombardment or fire.

Shuri, the second town of Okinawa, lay in utter ruin. There was no other city, town, or village in the Ryukyus that had been destroyed so completely ... It was estimated that about 200,000 rounds of artillery and naval gunfire had struck Shuri. Numerous air strikes had dropped 1,000-pound bombs on it. Mortar shells by the thousands had arched their way into the town area. Only two structures ... had enough of their walls standing to form silhouettes on the skyline. The rest was flattened rubble. The narrow paved and dirt streets, churned by high explosives and pitted with shell craters, were impassable to any vehicle. The stone walls of the numerous little terraces were battered down. The rubble and broken red tile of the houses lay in heaps. The frame portion of buildings had been reduced to kindling wood. Tattered bits of Japanese military clothing, gas masks, and tropical helmets-the most frequently seen items-and the dark-colored Okinawan civilian dress lay about in wild confusion. Over all this crater-of-the-moon landscape hung the unforgettable stench of rotting human flesh.[183]

The homes of the great masters burned, along with all of their possessions. Official and personal documents, letters, journals and diaries were forever lost. Nearly all of the local residents, including the relatives, friends and students of the great masters, were killed in

---

[182] Kerr, 2000, p. 470.

[183] Appleman, Roy, et al, *United States Army In World War II, The War in the Pacific,* "Okinawa: The Last Battle," Center Of Military History, United States Army, Washington, D. C., 2000, p. 401-402. http://www.army.mil/cmh-pg/books/wwii/okinawa/

the conflict. More than 90,000 Japanese soldiers died in the Battle of Okinawa, and more than 60,000 Okinawan civilians perished along with them.[184] This was less than 60 years ago! There are many people still living who remember the Typhoon of Steel.

This is the reason there is so little known about the history of karate. The Shuri masters were not paranoid and secretive. The witnesses, the records, the buildings—in fact the very streets where the karate masters walked—were obliterated in the spring of 1945. Nothing was left. The history of karate was erased.

Conclusion

The Shuri masters kept the new art, linear karate, out of sight of the Japanese overlords by practicing in secret. They had to keep it secret because martial arts were forbidden by the Satsuma edicts. They did not keep the art secret from one another, however. They were all on the same team, and the team was in danger.

Any actual documentation that might have existed about the beginnings of Shuri-te was shredded by the Typhoon of Steel. We are left with some broad historical realities, a few facts, some colorful stories, and the art itself.

Based on these fragments, we are going to recreate the birth of the Shuri-te bodyguard fighting system using our own expertise, common sense, and some well-informed imagination. This isn't precise scholarship, but it is an exercise that teaches us many things we didn't previously know about karate. We will predict the kinds of techniques and tactics Matsumura would have needed, and then we will test the prediction by looking for these techniques in the bunkai of the shotokan kata.

The Shuri bodyguards were not hobbyists, and they were not amateurs. They were deadly professionals who often faced superior numbers of angry, armed men. We can assume that any kata practiced at Shuri had some direct application to their problem. They didn't study karate for fun, and they didn't waste time on techniques that didn't work—and neither should we.

---

[184] Kerr, 2000, p. 472. McCarthy, 1999b, p. 92, says 200,000 civilian deaths.

Chapter 5

Defending Shuri Castle

In the previous chapters we have examined what is known about Okinawan history and the role of the Shuri masters in protecting their unarmed king. The Shuri Crucible was the political trap they were in, caught between implacable Satsuma overlords on the one hand, and armed Western visitors on the other.

In this chapter we will take a closer look at the situation that existed at Shuri Castle in the mid-1800s, and we will ask how a man like Bushi Matsumura would have organized the defense of the Sho family using, literally, his own bare hands.

The Shotokan kata teach hand-to-hand combat techniques, but they don't stop there. They also contain tactics, and a commander's tactics are shaped by the ground he defends. We need to get our feet on the ground at Shuri Castle, to see the battleground from Matsumura's point of view. Shuri must come to life in our imaginations.

Shuri Threat Analysis

Matsumura must have done what every bodyguard does. He would have assessed the various threats to his principals (the royal family and their aides). Then he would have provided defenses against each of these threats. He was a man who attacked problems, and this was the central problem of his life.

There are three classic threats to the life of a monarch. The first is assassination, often by a trusted member of the king's own family. The second is assassination by an outsider, such as a *ninja*, who must penetrate the fortress by stealth while the target is sleeping. The third threat is conquest by a warlike neighbor who attacks the castle and captures the king. Let's look at each threat closely to see how Matsumura might have planned his defense.

Assassination

The Sho kings were not in an enviable position. They had been figureheads in their own country for most of the history of the Second Sho Dynasty. They lived at the sufferance of their strict Satsuma masters, and were often deposed and carried off to Tokyo when their masters were displeased. It's hard to imagine an ambitious relative plotting to kill the king and seize the throne under these circumstances. Only a fool would envy a Sho king. The throne of Okinawa was the family curse.

Would anyone have tried to assassinate Sho Tai by stealth? Okinawa had been united under one government for almost 300 years. There were no neighboring warlords, and no local revolutionary movement. Sho Tai was not a despotic king, even though his subjects were poor and often hungry. He wasn't a key player in any strategic intrigues. He had no real power. The Chinese and Japanese governments both wanted him left in place. When he was eventually deposed by the Japanese, they simply sent him a letter telling him to pack a bag and report to his new home in Tokyo. When he didn't respond to the letter, Tokyo sent a boatload of soldiers to read it to him. There was never any need for stealthy assassins in black pajamas to creep into the palace.

Even so, there was one serious threat to the king's life. There must have been very difficult meetings with the Satsuma overlords, and the threat of sudden death was the backbone of samurai power. Matsumura must have prepared for a fight to the death against the Satsuma swordsmen.

As it happens, we know a little about Matsumura's strategy for this lethal confrontation. The bushi took a leave of absence early in his career and went to Kagoshima to study at the jigen-ryu fencing school. This was the same sword-fighting school the Satsuma overlords had attended as teenagers. Matsumura returned a few months later with a *menkyo kaiden* (a certificate of absolute mastery) from this famous sword school.[185]

From that moment on, the Satsuma overlords were on notice: Matsumura was a better swordsman than they were. He entered the meetings unarmed, but they knew how easily he could snatch one of their swords from its sheath. They also knew what would happen to them if he did. The threat of sudden death can cut both ways.

Conquest

Was Sho Tai in any danger of military conquest? You would not think so until you look at the context of the times. Matsumura served at Shuri Castle from the mid-1820s until 1879. Britain and China went to war in 1839-42 over China's refusal to open its ports to British trade. Matsumura watched from the ramparts of Shuri Castle as the unthinkable happened: China lost. Five ports were opened to British

[185] McCarthy, 1995, p. 51.

commerce, and China was forced to give Britain the island of Hong Kong. Matsumura received veiled threats from English and French naval captains that Shuri could easily be brought to heel in the same manner.[186] Military invasion was a real possibility. After all, how many troops does it take to subjugate a disarmed nation?

Then the United States sent Matthew Perry and his Marines to the very doors of Sho Tai's throne room in 1853. The Okinawans clearly expected Perry to seize the castle and declare himself military governor of Okinawa. At a later date, Perry grew weary of Okinawan diplomatic delays and bluntly threatened to seize Shuri Castle if he didn't get better cooperation. He got it.[187]

Matsumura was intelligent and thorough, and would have made a plan for protecting his principals in the event of a frontal assault on the castle. He had little hope of defending the battlements with his bare hands. If attacked, the castle would certainly fall, so the plan must have involved removing or concealing the principals instead of defending the walls. It is significant that Perry found the castle deserted on the day he came to visit. He also never saw the child king, nor the real regent, and didn't see but one woman the entire time he was on the island. Sometimes the things the visitor didn't see tell us more than the things he did see.

Battery and Abduction

Finally, we come to the key problem Matsumura repeatedly faced. The Shuri officials often confronted angry and dangerous barbarians (such as Chinese, Korean, British, French, German, Russian and American sea captains, some of whom were pirates). The danger was not assassination but battery or abduction during an angry meeting.

When negotiations fail for no good reason, one feels an irrational temptation to seize the uncooperative negotiators and beat some sense into them. If you throw the first negotiator in jail, the next negotiator is likely to be more respectful and cooperative. For instance, Commodore Perry might well have thrown regent Sho Taimu in the brig and tried his luck with the next regent. What could the Okinawans do about it, anyway? Fight back? Without any army

---

[186] Kerr, 2000, p. 249.

[187] Kerr, 2000, p. 325.

or navy? Without so much as a police constable that anyone could see? Without any weapons more formidable than a stick? Against US Marines and a flotilla of modern steam warships! Perry didn't have any doubts about who was actually in charge. He was.

Turn back to Figure 3-4, which shows Perry's naval officers confronting 20 unarmed ministers in the Shuri Castle reception hall. Had Perry given the word, 50 men would have pounced on the Okinawans, bound them hand and foot, and carried them away as prisoners. We can be confident that Perry would never have tortured or murdered these ministers as a Japanese daimyo would have done, but he might have put them in irons until they decided to cooperate. Perry had very broad discretionary powers, and there was no one within 8,000 miles who could countermand his orders.

Desperately outnumbered and unarmed, what would Matsumura have done if Perry had tried to arrest Sho Taimu? It's difficult to imagine him standing aside without a fight. He would have anticipated this situation, planned for it, and trained to meet it. Matsumura was a genius. He would have had a plan.

Our challenge is to reimagine this plan. Understanding the plan and the tactics helps us understand Matsumura's choice of weapons. We have inherited the weapons through Itosu and Funakoshi, but somehow the operator's manual got lost. It's time to recreate it.

Intelligence

The first layer of defense is pure intelligence. Both Matsumura and Azato were in the habit of repeating Sun Tzu's advice about intelligence: "The secret of victory is to know both yourself and your enemy." In pursuit of this goal, Azato kept a private diary of the skills and weaknesses of all martial artists in the Shuri/Naha area.[188] He knew exactly how he would fight each one of them if they challenged him in the street.

Knowing this principle, Matsumura would certainly have set up surveillance on Perry and his men. Perry's narrative makes frequent mention of the quiet Okinawan officials who followed the Americans everywhere they went on the island. Everything the Americans did was observed and reported in detail. The Americans at first found

---

[188] Funakoshi, 1975, p. 15.

this amusing, but were later astonished to discover that some of their quaint guardians could understand English![189] Matsumura enjoyed a great deal of intelligence on both the actions and conversations of these visiting barbarians.

Matsumura would also have taken pains to make himself invisible to his enemy. Several times Perry's men were face-to-face with palace

Figure 5-1: *Keimochi* **bodyguards serving food at the regent's lunch.** Perry is the figure making a toast on the right. Sho Taimu and the ministers are seated in the center of the picture. Note that one of the keimochi "stewards" stands almost unnoticed in the shadow five feet to Perry's left.[190] Incidentally, there are no women in this picture. The women were hiding.

security agents but didn't realize that they were in the presence of trained warriors. How did Matsumura accomplish that? How did he make his men so invisible to Perry that the admiral barely mentioned them in his reports?

The solution was laughably simple. He had the warriors serve tea. He turned the warriors into waiters.

---

[189] Perry, 2000, p. 159.

[190] Perry, 2000, p. 191.

Remember that Matsumura was a master of psychology and disguise. Keimochi men of that time and place observed certain taboos, one of which was that men don't belong in the kitchen. (Apparently Funakoshi himself never entered his family's kitchen.[191]) The Perry narrative contains a picture of keimochi knights in hachimaki hats humbly serving trays of food to American naval officers, just like the naval stewards Matsumura observed on Perry's flagship. American naval officers don't look twice at a steward unless he spills the coffee. Matsumura may have come within inches of Commodore Perry without alerting him to his danger. The bushi would have enjoyed that.

Intelligence is best when it is timely. In this regard, you can stand on the battlements of Shuri Castle and look directly into Naha harbor only three miles away. Matsumura would have created a forward observation post at the shoreline, equipped with a nautical telescope to monitor the American warships. When Perry hoisted the first cannon off the deck of the *U.S.S. Susquehana* for the march on Shuri Castle, we can be confident that Matsumura knew about it within minutes.

Concentric Architecture

Shuri Castle is a maze of concentric walls and gates. This is classic castle architecture designed to force an attacker to mount a series of battles in order to penetrate the central keep. In peacetime, these concentric walls not only channeled traffic through checkpoints on the castle grounds, but they created zones where the rules of access could be clearly defined. Tradesmen were allowed to enter the outer bailey to make deliveries. A person entering the central square would have been on official business. Someone trying to enter the throne room would need a royal invitation and probably an escort. A person trying to sneak into the royal living quarters was committing suicide.

It is clear that Shuri Castle had policies about access. You couldn't just wander around in there. If there were rules, then there was someone who was ready to enforce them. There were a few official guards, and quite a few unofficial ones.

---

[191] Funakoshi, 1975, p. x.

Bushi Bureaucrats

The clerks and ministers who ran the Okinawan government were all recruited from the families of the keimochi class. They had the warrior heritage and a liege obligation to defend the Sho family. Many of them were proud of their family ties to the dynasty. The warrior heritage was part of their manhood and identity. These men formed an extensive pool of ever-present keimochi soldiers if Matsumura needed help in a crisis. They were unarmed, but they were on-site and available during daylight hours. They weren't far away at night, either, since they all lived within walking distance of the castle.

These keimochi bureaucrats were scattered in offices all over the grounds of Shuri Castle, and certainly kept an eye on wandering visitors. To draw on this invisible fighting force, all Matsumura needed was an alarm of some kind, like a fire bell. Every castle in the world has a fire bell.[192]

Special Agents

I think it is reasonable to conclude that Matsumura recruited and trained a team of formidable martial artists to help him in a crisis. There is no question that Itosu was part of this team. Matsumura and Itosu worked on opposite sides of the throne for 30 years. Azato was also part of this inner circle, and was frequently in the throne room conversing with the king. Chofu Kyan worked in the same room as chief of staff. Seisho Arakaki was their Japanese interpreter. Peichin Kiyuna was one of Matsumura's guards inside the castle. Sanda Kinjo was Matsumura's man in charge of the Shuri police. Kokan Oyadomari and Kosaku Matsumora were part of this group. After the Shuri government was dissolved in 1879, all of these men became legendary karate teachers. They had the same alma mater: the Shuri Crucible.

We remember these men because they were teachers. There could have been many others who trained but did not teach. For example, at the official coronation of Sho Tai in 1866, there were 10 martial arts demonstrations given by peichin knights whose names are not

---

[192] In fact, a giant bronze bell was one of the only castle artifacts to survive the bombardment of World War II. http://www.army.mil/cmh-pg/books/wwii/okinawa/chapter15.htm#p5

immediately recognizable in the lore of karate.[193]

We can assume that many of the people in daily contact with the king were hand-picked by Matsumura for their fighting ability. The fact that they were highly educated in Confucian classics and had good penmanship helped to camouflage them to visitors. "There goes Itosu-san. He's a clerk who writes letters for the king." (And crushes bamboo stalks with his bare hands.)

In this context, let us revisit the confrontation between Matsumura and Uehara, the metal craftsman. A castle like Shuri, built in imitation of the grand Chinese tradition, needed constant repairs and enhancements. A fine metal craftsman might have been a good addition to the palace staff. For one thing, a metal craftsman under Matsumura's control could have created some very interesting disguised weapons. Matsumura's excuse for visiting Uehara, to repair his pipe, seems like a transparent pretext. Matsumura was too well prepared for that interview. It was not a casual visit.

Why did Matsumura visit Uehara's shop? I suggest that Matsumura saw a chance to recruit a notorious tode fighter to be a castle craftsman and to secretly double as the armorer to the bushi's security force. Did Uehara get the job? All we know is that Uehara lost his nerve in the graveyard, a humiliating experience that cost him his reputation as a bully and fighter. This surely must have made him bitter. Then, according to Funakoshi, Uehara suddenly became an ardent admirer of Matsumura![194] Something happened behind the scenes there, but we don't know the full story.

Note that modern police departments need a staff of at least twelve officers to provide 24-hour response in a small town, and Matsumura probably discovered the same geometry. I believe there must have been at least a dozen trained agents. When looking at Figure 3-4, we see 55 Americans confronting about 20 Okinawan men in an otherwise deserted castle. This is a portrait of Shuri's department heads backed up by Matsumura's unsmiling security force. Matsumura and Itosu *must* be two of the figures in this picture.

---

[193] Cook, p. 10-11. peichin Chiku Maeda, peichin Tsuji Aragaki, peichin Chikudan Tomura, among others.

[194] Funakoshi, 1988, p. 108.

Female Servants

The royal residence behind the Seiden was highly restricted space, rather similar to a harem in the Middle East. Free access was restricted to the family members and the all-female staff. This is an obvious security precaution. It creates an inner defense zone that no stranger can penetrate without detection. One result of this tradition was that it created an area that even the Satsuma overlords could not enter and inspect—a rather clever move on the part of the Okinawans.

It creates an interesting problem, too. Matsumura could not enter the king's residence except in a life-and-death emergency. As far as we know, Matsumura, Azato, Itosu, Kyan and the other Matsumura agents were all men.

How, then, could he send a bodyguard into the royal household in an emergency? There was only one solution. We can imagine Matsumura looking around for a truly formidable *female* warrior. Where would he find such an Amazon?

The story of Matsumura's marriage to Tsuru Yonamine suddenly makes a new kind of sense. The legend that Matsumura mugged his own wife because he was jealous of her reputation doesn't ring true. Matsumura was the quintessential karate master, and masters are not insecure. If he tested Yonamine in such a dangerous way then we can conclude he had a serious reason. There was something he had to know. Taken by surprise, alone on the road, could she fight effectively and win? Could she defeat a trained attacker in an unfair fight in the dark? Yonamine passed the test beyond all expectations, proving herself a capable bodyguard.

Did Yonamine actually serve as a palace guard? There is one tantalizing story. Sells reports that Matsumura once sent Yonamine to deal with a gang of "hooligans" who were causing a disturbance on the castle grounds.[195]

Matsumura could have handled the situation himself. He commanded the entire military and law-enforcement branch of the government, so he could have ordered the Shuri constables into action. He could have sent Itosu or Azato. Why did he send for Yonamine? It seems likely that this disturbance was in the females-only section of the castle. He sent Yonamine because she was the

---

[195] Sells, 2000, p. 33.

122

only one he could send.

Yonamine located the hooligans and killed them. Perhaps this is the real explanation of Matsumura's extraordinary taste in women.

Matsumura and Itosu

Matsumura was a fighter, not a manager. In any tense confrontation, Matsumura would have been in the front rank, standing in the signature position at the right shoulder of the person he was guarding. This gives the bodyguard complete freedom with his sword hand. (Matsumura carried a tessen [an iron truncheon disguised as a folding fan] instead of a sword, but the principle is the same.) This was almost the last layer of defense before reaching the skin of the king.

If the man to the right of the throne was the king's chief bodyguard, the man guarding the king's left shoulder would be an agent, too. Who more natural than Itosu, the king's secretary, there to take notes and write letters in the king's name? Matsumura left nothing to chance.

There are faint indications that Itosu might have been left-handed. I can't prove it, but if true it would make him the perfect agent for the left side of the throne. It might have been the one situation where left-handedness would not have been a social handicap.[196]

Sho Tai Himself

Logically, there was only one trained warrior who was *always* near the king, every minute of every day without fail. This was the king himself.

This is why the king's personal bodyguard also had to be the king's personal karate teacher. Part of protecting the king was teaching him to protect himself. Sho Tai was one of his own bodyguards.

Escaping the Room

One threat scenario is that violence erupts against the king, or the ministers, in a meeting inside the Seiden. The ground floor of the Seiden was largely devoted to an audience chamber where the king and the department heads would meet "the public." This would include the more important visiting Westerners.

---

[196] Even in modern Japan, a left-handed child is forced to learn calligraphy with his right hand, according to our translator, Eri Takase.

Suppose tempers were to flare and it became necessary to get the king out of the room? Exactly how to do that is the subject of the following chapter, but for now let's recall about the hidden staircase behind the throne, shown in Figure 1-8. If the bodyguards could get the king up the stairs, they could block pursuit on the stairway while he fled from the castle. This turns out to be an interesting source of bunkai later in the book.

Escaping the Castle

We say that "discretion is the better part of valor," meaning it is sometimes better to avoid a fight than to stubbornly insist on losing it. When the enemy has a hundred soldiers with swords, cannons, rifles and bayonets, and you have a handful of agents armed with fake fans, it is probably better to avoid the fight completely. I'm sure you agree.

Every rabbit warren has a back door. Most castles do, too. It is no surprise that there is a back door to Shuri Castle, called the Keiseimon gate. It opens on the opposite side of the ridge from the front entrance. This little gate is conspicuously near the king's bedroom, and was used only by the royal family.[197]

When danger appeared suddenly in the forecourt, Matsumura's agents needed only a few minutes to rush the royals out the back door into the countryside where they could vanish into the population. American and European adversaries could not have recognized the child king or his mother in a crowd of Shuri residents. In fact, Matsumura could have set them in plain sight on the main road to Shuri with a basket of fruit to sell, and Perry would have marched right past them.

Notice that the Okinawans tried to turn Perry away at the gate, but finally let him in after a short delay. The Americans were puzzled that the castle seemed deserted. I suspect that Matsumura used those few minutes to send non-combatants down the back stairs. He wasn't ready to surrender the castle outright, but he "cleared for action" in case of a fight. This was a concept his American naval guests would have understood all too well if they had not been so completely secure in their own superiority.

---

[197] Web site of Shurijo Castle Park: http://www.shurijo-park.go.jp/.

Secret Passage

A back-door escape strategy works against an opponent like Perry, but it would not have succeeded against more subtle enemies from Satsuma. What if someone had attacked the castle who had reconnoitered first? They would have blocked all the gates, bottling up the royals before they could escape. What then?

There is, again, a classic medieval solution to this problem. The solution is an underground passage or gallery reached through a hidden door. The gallery emerges in the basement of an outbuilding, often a tomb, far enough away to outflank the attackers. Such structures were common in medieval Europe.

When I learned that Shuri Castle surmounts a limestone ridge, I suspected that there must be caves beneath the castle. This was confirmed when I read about the Battle of Okinawa, and found that the Japanese commander set up his headquarters in a cave under the castle. He commanded about 100,000 troops, so the cave must have been large enough to serve as a divisional headquarters. (That's a seriously large cave.)

It turns out that the caves under Shuri Castle are well-known, and contain as much as two miles of underground passages.[198] It would be unthinkable that the Sho kings didn't have access to this labyrinth from inside the castle. This was their hidden escape route.

If the Sho kings created an underground hiding place or escape route for the royal family, its existence would have been a secret owned by the king himself and passed down only to the crown prince. Both ends of the escape route would have been concealed in locations only the king could enter. What location might that have been?

The more I studied Shuri Castle, the more my attention was drawn to the Shinbyouden, which was an odd little building in the east end of the castle near the king's living quarters. The Shinbyouden was a morgue. It was a place for the bodies of dead kings to decompose, so that their bones could be recovered for "proper" interment elsewhere.

Would you build a private morgue outside your bedroom window? Doesn't that sound odd to you?

Okinawan nobility had a quaint custom in which they personally

---

[198] http://www.wonder-okinawa.jp/001/002-e/004_02.html

cared for the bones of their ancestors by taking them out and washing them three years and seven years after interment.[199] This was the sacred duty of the head of the household, so it makes perfect sense that only the king could enter the royal morgue. Actually, the king had access to either one of the two royal morgues—one inside the castle and one outside.

The main mausoleum is the Tamauden, a large building outside the castle walls at the opposite end of the hill. Kingly skeletons were carefully preserved in this building, which is about 1,000 feet west of the castle. A Sho king could literally visit his ancestors and meditate on the family curse. Compared to the stately Tamauden, the tiny Shinbyouden was just a temporary resting place.

The Shinbyouden morgue was located in absolutely the most secure corner of the castle. It was in the females-only section where the Satsuma overlords could not snoop. It was surrounded by a 10-foot stone wall. During certain periods of history the gate in this wall was not only locked but carefully guarded. In terms of layered security, this little "morgue" was buttoned up like a bank vault. It was more carefully protected than the king himself.

Why all that security? What was really in there? Even Japanese daimyos with their subtle intrigues wouldn't try to steal a decomposing body! (The treasury, by the way, lies outside the north wall of the castle. Apparently it was not worth defending.)

One interesting idea is that the Shinbyouden contained the secret door to the caves under the castle. If so, then we should view it as a possible entrance to the castle, too. Enemies might sneak in there. No wonder they walled it off and put guards around it!

Did the Shinbyouden contain the entrance to the secret underground escape route? We really don't know, especially after the Typhoon of Steel obliterated the historical castle, sealing off any secret passages that might have existed. If the Sho Dynasty had a deadly secret, however, this was the place they hid it. The location of the Shinbyouden, right behind the king's living quarters, is perfect for either an escape route or a secret vault.

---

[199] Nagamine, 2000, p. 10.

Hidden Armory

There is one last layer to this onion. Imagine that the barbarians have breached the castle gates and escape is impossible. The escape paths and passages are blocked. The slavering hordes have set fire to the buildings around the great square and are cutting the throats of everyone they can catch. Your back is literally against the very last wall. The royals will be killed within minutes unless you can turn the tide of the battle. You look down at that little iron fan in your hand ...

Wouldn't it be better if you had a nice *katana* instead?

Matsumura and Azato, as we know, were expert swordsmen. Okinawans were allowed to study swordsmanship when they were in foreign countries. They just couldn't own a sword at home. Azato was quite confident that he could win a sword duel with any Japanese warrior on the island.[200] Matsumura, of course, was a *bona fide* sword master.

Using swords would be a last-stand strategy for Matsumura. It would be suicidal even if successful, because it would call down the wrath of Satsuma on the survivors. At the time of Perry's visit, Okinawa had been officially swordless for 240 years under penalty of death.

And yet, can we really believe that there was no secret cache of swords in Shuri Castle? Wouldn't the ancient Sho kings have kept something back when they surrendered their weapons to Satsuma? Knowing human nature, I feel certain that the Second Sho Dynasty kept a hidden cache of swords *somewhere*. If they didn't, Matsumura would have arranged it himself.

If there was a secret cache of swords, I would look again in that little morgue behind the king's residence. The cache would have been the Sho family's most deadly secret. They would have guarded it with their lives and kept it in close reach.

How many swords might they have hidden? How many could one pack into a large stone coffin? It would be easy to conceal 200 swords in a small space—enough blades to equip quite a few keimochi bureaucrats in an emergency.

---

[200] Funakoshi, 1988, p. 31.

Conclusion

This chapter gives us a little better image of the situation at Shuri Castle and the defensive options that Matsumura might have entertained. For me, this discussion of escape routes and defensive strategies brings the castle to life. It was a real castle staffed by real people who were often in real danger. We can be confident that they responded to the danger according to their nature, and in much the same way that other people in other castles have met the same challenges.

In the next chapter, we'll look more closely at the problem of getting the king away from a mob of angry opponents during a meeting in the throne room or reception hall of Shuri Castle.

Chapter 6

Shuri
Battle Plan

How does an unarmed bodyguard go about protecting a head of state or other high official in a room full of angry, armed barbarians? How do you prevent your principal from being beaten up, subdued and abducted as a helpless hostage? That is the subject of this chapter.

We have no direct evidence of Matsumura's battle plan, because of his own gift for secrecy and the damage done by the Typhoon of Steel. We are forced to analyze the problem as he did. What is the standard strategy to apply in this situation? How did the Shuri Crucible force Matsumura to modify the standard solution?

Certainly we are speculating, even guessing, at the path Matsumura took in defense of Shuri. Once on that path, however, we can be alert to signs that Matsumura was there before us. We may find his footprints on the path. As we study Matsumura's tactics, we draw ever closer to the applications he drilled with Azato and Itosu.

Combat in the Shuri Crucible

Let us quickly summarize the salient features of bodyguard combat inside the Shuri Crucible. It is important to make these ideas clear, so you can see how linear, hard-style technique developed from them.

- The site of combat is a large reception hall in the castle, as we saw in Figure 3-4. The floor is wide, smooth, and unobstructed by furniture.

- There is plenty of light. We can see the enemy clearly. This is an important prerequisite for impact karate. It is hard to generate momentum toward your target if you are fighting in the dark.

- The fight is a team effort, not individual combat. Our team consists of a dozen handpicked martial artists with formidable abilities but no weapons.

- The opposing team has us outnumbered very badly. When we fight the mob, there are so many opponents that we can turn in any direction and confront a new enemy within arm's reach. In modern terms the Shuri Crucible was a "target-rich" environment.

- Because there are so many enemies, the chief danger is being caught by many hands and forced down to the floor. The enemy is not trying to punch or kick us; they are trying to capture us.

- The other team bristles with weapons. They at least have sabers, and are backed up by riflemen at the edge of the crowd. The rifles have bayonets. Some of the opponents may be wearing holstered pistols. This means we only *begin* the fight unarmed. There are weapons readily at hand if we can take them from their owners.

- Unlike most military ambushes or skirmishes, this is a fight where the opposing commanders are both in the same room. This is a very unusual circumstance, worthy of some creative thought.

- The barbarians win if they capture our principal (the king or regent).

- Our side wins if we can extract our principal from the room and block pursuit by the opposing force.

As a minor comment, notice the remarkable similarity between our karate dojo and the Shuri reception hall. Dojo are spacious, well-lighted, contain no furniture, and have a hard, smooth floor just like the Shuri reception hall. When karate experts assert that a "real" fight never occurs under ideal dojo conditions they have missed something important. In the Shuri Crucible, the bodyguard confrontations did occur under ideal conditions. Today's karate is practiced in halls that exactly replicate these conditions. The Shuri reception hall might actually have shaped our ideas about how to set up a dojo.

When our students perform a kata together, they are unconsciously re-enacting Matsumura's security team leaping to the defense of the king. This is meant more literally than you might suspect.

Standard Tactics

Imagine the president of the United States caught in a room with a mob of angry, shouting people. Suddenly somebody throws a brick, or a shot rings out, and the U.S. Secret Service leaps into action. Imagine how that scene would play out.

Some of the agents, the extraction team, grab the president and hustle him out of the room through the nearest door. They stay with him, shielding him with their bodies, until he is out of danger.

The other agents, the reaction team, turn toward the threat and attack it. It is difficult to hurl a second brick or fire a second shot when a burly bodyguard is sitting on your chest and shoving a gun in your ear.

These extraction/reaction tactics are based on centuries of combat experience. An assassination or abduction is simply an ambush. The only viable response to an ambush is an aggressive counterattack. Otherwise all you can do is to scramble for cover in exactly the place where the enemy wants you to go. That is usually a very bad idea.[201]

Matsumura, the warrior/psychologist, certainly understood extraction and reaction. Unlike the Secret Service, however, he could not hope to control the scene at the end of the fight. If they were attacked, the Shuri fighters would be hopelessly outnumbered. In this situation the only strategy is to rely on a shocking counterattack followed by an abrupt retreat. Matsumura's reaction force had to buy time to get the principal out the door. Then, on a signal, they had no option but to disengage and withdraw at high speed.

Figure 6-1: U.S. Marines with rifles and fixed bayonets in the Shuri Castle reception hall, close-up view. Would you lean on your rifle so casually if it were loaded?

---

[201] U.S. Army Field Manual 7-8: *Infantry Rifle Platoon and Squad*, Department of the Army, 1992.

For example, if a fight had broken out during Perry's visit to Shuri Castle, the reaction team would have had about 30 seconds to get under cover before the surprised U.S. Marines had time to load their Springfield rifle-muskets and fire.[202]

There was one other difference between Matsumura's tactical situation and that of a modern Secret Service. In the reception-hall battleground, Matsumura was only a few feet from the commander of the enemy force. This would have added another goal to his reaction plan. He might well have planned to kill the enemy commander during the fight or abduct him in turn.

In the entire history of karate, Matsumura was the master of turning disadvantage into advantage. Abducting the enemy commander under the noses of his troops is a feat worthy of a bushi. This idea would have intrigued Matsumura.

On a more pragmatic level, Matsumura knew he could not hope to get his entire team out of the battle hall without leaving someone behind. He must have realized that one or two of his men would be taken hostage and tortured for information. He would have seen the advantages of having a hostage of his own to trade for their release. Who better than the enemy commander or one of his officers?

React, Extract, Retreat

Matsumura's rescue plan was very simple, as all such plans must be. The elements were: react, extract, and retreat. He had to disrupt the attack, extract the principal from the hall, and then run for it. We may imagine it this way...

The scene is the reception hall at Shuri Castle. The regent and a few dignitaries face the U.S. commander and his troops. Matsumura and his agents stand stoically among the Okinawa officials, studying their enemies. In Figure 6-2, the agents are the shadowy figures in the background.

The barbarian commander at last grows tired of the fruitless negotiations. He decides it is time to alter the balance of power by

---

[202] The standard wisdom says a well-drilled musket squad can fire three shots per minute. The first shot, however, takes longer. We have to assume that Matsumura had about 30 seconds before the first shots were fired. We know for a fact that Perry's Marines were issued cartridges (13 for each soldier), but even the most hostile witnesses didn't mention any order to preload the rifles.

Figure 6-2: Confrontation in the reception hall, close-up. Regent Sho Taimu bows to Perry, who offers the regent a saber as a gift. The civilian in the center is Dr. Bettelheim, the obnoxious missionary/translator. Matsumura, Itosu, Azato and Choto Kyan are almost certainly among the shadowy figures in the upper left.

taking a few hostages. He points at the regent and barks, "Mister Anders, put that man in irons!" A mob of determined naval officers closes in on the poor, defenseless Okinawans.

Matsumura and his agents step quickly to the front, forming a human wall between the Americans and the elderly ministers. The odds are about 5-to-1, since the ministers are not fighters. They must all be protected and extracted.

The barbarians impatiently lay hands on the agents to drag them aside. At a signal from Matsumura, the struggle begins.

In the first phase of the fight, the American troops seek only to capture and restrain. They want to take prisoners. In fact, they really want only one prisoner: Sho Taimu himself. The barbarians expect that sheer numbers will carry the day, especially against these pitiful islanders who know nothing about weapons and fighting.

In the first five seconds of the fight, the security agents free themselves from the grip of the American officers. The closest troops reel back in shock, with dislocated shoulders and broken elbows.

Three men, led by the bear-like Itosu, grab the regent by the collar and yank him back to the wall. They put their backs against him and face the crowd. Keeping the elderly regent safe against the wall, they struggle toward the escape door. Itosu stuns one sailor with an elbow strike, then spins him around and crushes the man to his chest as a human shield. The struggling sailor cannot break out of Itosu's powerful grip.

The other agents leap directly into the crowd. Their mission is to break the momentum of the troop attack by creating panic and confusion. They slide between the struggling troops, stunning as many enemies as possible in the opening seconds of the fight. Moving like adept swordsmen, they sidestep, parry and avoid the incoming blows. They seek to cripple each opponent with a single strike, if possible.

More troops are pouring into the room from outside, responding to the cries of their fellows. The fight has been in progress for 10 seconds.

Matsumura quickly dispatches the naval officers near him and looks for a new target. Voicing his battle cry, the legendary bushi leaps straight toward the American commander. Each man in the bushi's path goes down with a single, sickening impact. Some of them fly backward so hard that they knock down the men behind them.

Reaching the enemy commander in a few short steps, Matsumura stuns the man with simultaneous blows to the throat and the groin and catches the officer's collapsing body over his shoulder. If circumstances permit, he will carry the enemy commander away as a hostage. If this is not possible, he will break the commander's neck and leave his body behind.

Fifteen seconds have passed.

Itosu and the extraction team have reached the door. They push the regent though the door and turn to face the crowd. Itosu roots himself to the floor in front of the door as a living barrier. When his assistants have herded the last minister through the door, he shouts the signal to withdraw. "To me! Shuri warriors to me!"

At this shout, the embattled agents shift into the second phase of the fight. Their new goal is to fight their way through the crowd to the door and escape. They don't dare be late. They have to reach the door before it closes.

Getting to the door is not easy, however, because the American troops have at last realized that they are outclassed in hand-to-hand combat. Some of them have drawn their sabers. Riflemen are desperately charging their weapons. More soldiers with rifles and bayonets are forcing their way into the room. Matsumura's agents must make haste. Time is running out.

Twenty seconds have passed.

Matsumura reaches the door with his heavy burden. Itosu drops his human shield as Matsumura hands off the enemy commander. Itosu ducks out the door with the naval officer over his shoulder. Matsumura shouts, "To me, Shuri!" The door is about to close.

The agents fight an increasingly desperate battle to reach the door. To win through to safety, the Shuri fighters abandon all caution. They snatch away sabers and use them. They sidestep thrusting bayonets, rip the weapons away from the astonished soldiers, and then drive the weapons point-first into the chests of their owners. They duck, leap, shift, sweep and kick their way through the clutching hands and probing weapons. Some of them use jujutsu throws to hurl one screaming enemy soldier in the face of another, clearing a momentary path through the crowd. They leap recklessly forward, knocking down enemies with pure momentum, until they burst out of the crowd at Matsumura's side.

Twenty-five seconds ...

Reaching the door at last, the senior fighters turn and make a stand. They block the doorway for the few seconds it takes to get the less experienced agents out of the room to safety. One by one they dart through the door leaving Matsumura to exit last, as is his duty and privilege. The bushi glares at the nearby enemies. His ferocious eyes freeze them in their tracks.

Thirty seconds ...

The barbarians are quickly fitting percussion caps to their charged rifles.

Keeping eye contact, Matsumura steps back through the door. The door slams shut. The riflemen raise their weapons but have no remaining targets. One of them fires his weapon at the door in frustration. The hall echoes with the sound of the shot.

There is silence for a few moments as the shocked barbarians catch their breath. A surviving ship captain, cradling a broken arm, straightens up and looks around the room.

"What the hell happened?" he gasps, painfully. No one answers. "And where is the Commodore?"

Reserve Force

Although it has little to do with the development of karate, I feel compelled to point out that Matsumura's battle plan must have had a tactical reserve force. No military officer would overlook this element. Where was Matsumura's reserve force, and how would he have employed it?

I have used the metaphor of the "door closing" in the retreat phase of the plan, but the reception hall doesn't seem to have actual doors. Shuri Castle is an open cluster of buildings among courtyards, gardens, and wide walkways. After extracting their principals, Matsumura's agents would have had to flee in the open, running to more defensible positions within or behind the Seiden. They could easily have been pursued by a mob of attackers.

Picture the Okinawan ministers and bodyguards, fleeing across the striped pavement of the courtyard toward the king's apartments. A crowd of barbarians runs along behind them in hot pursuit, waving sabers and discharging smoky firearms.

Matsumura must have imagined this same scene, and he would have prepared for it. His goal may have been to run for the Keiseimon gate behind the Seiden, and escape into the countryside. Alternately, he might have planned to run to the Shinbyouden morgue or wherever the entrance to the underground passage was concealed. Either way, he would have laid an ambush for the pursuers at the southeast corner of the Seiden to block pursuit. In my mental model of the Shuri security force, this is the part of the plan assigned to Azato, the military strategist and master swordsman.

I can picture Azato at his post near the Keiseimon gate. With him are 200 keimochi bureaucrats, eagerly clutching rusty old swords retrieved from the Shinbyouden morgue. They are the rear guard, assigned to block pursuit while the royals flee.

Matsumura's agents run headlong across the square, leading the herd of troops into the kill zone. I can imagine the surprise on the faces of the Americans as they round the corner of the Seiden and skid to a stop in confusion. Two hundred antique blades flash in the sun. This time it is the Americans who are ambushed. The smoky firearms aren't going to make a very big difference at such close range. A katana is a fearsome close-quarters weapon, after all. (See Figure 6-3.)

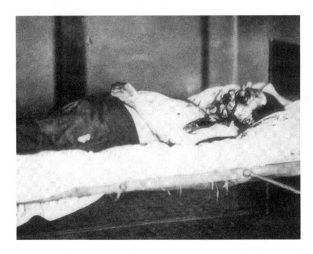

Figure 6-3: Katana attack. The body of Lt. J.J.H. Camus, murdered in Yokohama by an unknown samurai in 1863.[203]

It's a good thing Commodore Perry was hungry and accepted Sho Taimu's invitation to dinner that afternoon. I think Perry stuck his head in a bear trap, and then, quite smugly, pulled it out again and walked away. He narrowly avoided a pitched battle with the most highly trained hand-to-hand combat team in the world. It would have been a vicious and costly fight, for everyone. And it would have meant war between Japan and the United States.

Evaluation

This theory is very colorful, but you must be asking yourself whether it has any historical validity. The answer has to do with the mix of fact and imagination in the theory. I have not gazed into a crystal ball and conversed with the spirit of Matsumura personally, as one Japanese karate guru claims to have done. Given the time, the place, the unique circumstances, the known realities of combat and the exceptional people involved in this situation, Matsumura's actual

---

[203] Bennett, 1996, p. 123 and 142. (Photo courtesy of the Old Japan Picture Library) Camus' right arm was found dangling from his horse's bridle. He had taken two horizontal cuts that cut a wedge from his face, and one cut to the neck that almost decapitated him. The wide black stripe from his neck to his elbow is a gaping wound that opened his chest cavity to the heart and nearly severed his left shoulder.

plan must have had many of the elements I have outlined. The tactical problem is quite clear. If we can agree on the broad outlines of the solution, then we may be on Matsumura's trail.

I used the visit of Commodore Perry as the model for this analysis for two reasons. First, it is the best-documented confrontation between Matsumura and a superior military force. (Perry's invasion of Shuri is the best-documented event in Okinawan history prior to 1945.) There were other confrontations, however. In the 50 years that Matsumura guarded Shuri Castle, there were many confrontations with foreign visitors.[204] Some of them were naval captains with scores of seamen and marines under their command. Some were pirates. Many were whalers. All of them were armed. Considering that karate folklore is completely silent about a major event like Commodore Perry's invasion of Shuri Castle, it is no surprise that we don't know much about the other incidents.

Second, it is significant that Itosu participated in Perry's invasion as an impressionable youngster. For a 23-year-old bodyguard, standing toe-to-toe with 250 armed Americans must have been the experience of a lifetime. Early combat experiences tend to color a person's life, and become a focus of self-esteem in old age. Itosu created or revised most of the shotokan kata in his golden years. It is credible that Perry's invasion was on his mind as he did so. Itosu's kata seem to train the student to fight Perry and his men. They should. Perry was Itosu's "worst case scenario."

The Shuri Crucible provided the fuel that drove Matsumura and Itosu to refine their tactics to make them ever more effective. Matsumura was ruthlessly practical. He drilled the techniques that worked, and abandoned the ones that didn't. He needed the best techniques available in order to execute his rescue plan successfully. We can assume that any technique, any kata, that was personally selected and drilled by Matsumura must have had direct tactical application to the Shuri Crucible. He didn't study karate for the fun of it.

There is one more point to make. Now that you have seen the bodyguard teams at work, let me remind you about Matsumura's bassai kata. "Bassai" does not mean "to penetrate a fortress." It means to extract and to block. When the enemies penetrate the fortress, we have to extract the principals and block pursuit.

---

[204] Kerr, 2000, Chapter 6.

Chapter 7

Bodyguard Techniques

Suppose your life's mission was to prepare for the 30-second fight described in the previous chapter. When you practiced kihon and kumite, what techniques would you concentrate on? High roundhouse kicks? Jumping, spinning back kicks? Floor fighting? Restraint techniques? Chokes?

It is obvious that those techniques do not belong in the skill set of a Shuri bodyguard because they don't fit the situation. What skills did a Shuri agent really need?

Let's break it down by mission and objective. What are we trying to do? What tools do we need in order to be successful? When we finish, we'll have a list of requirements for the creation of a new martial art. For lack of a better name, we might even call this new art "Shuri-te," or "Shuri fist." This is the martial art of the Shuri bodyguards, designed from the ground up for the battle of the Shuri reception hall.

Technique for Extraction

In the fantasy in the previous chapter, sensei Itosu led the extraction team. Remember that in 1853, which is our model, Itosu was not a venerable sensei with a long flowing beard. He was only 23 years old, a student of Matsumura in the seventh year of his apprenticeship, and obedient to his will. It would have been a great honor for Itosu to lead the extraction team. Another thing to remember is that Itosu had the muscles of a circus strongman. He could seize a fit young man and take him prisoner with one hand.

What is the mission of the extraction team? They have to rescue the principal from the U.S. troops and then escort him (or his limp body) out of the kill zone to a safe location. In terms of the Shuri reception hall, the obvious strategy is to get the principal against a wall and fend off the attackers who are trying to reach him. The secondary strategy is to creep sideways along the wall to a convenient door. Once you get the principal through the door, you have won the immediate battle. A doorway is easy to defend. Part of the team blocks the doorway and the other part races away with the principal.

In chapter 8's survey of Okinawan styles and kata an oddity arises. Only the *Shuri* styles practice the naihanchi (tekki) kata. Naihanchi is even more diagnostic of Shuri-te than the pinan (heian) kata are! Naihanchi must have been very important at Shuri Castle. Nobody else studies it.

The legend is that Matsumura brought naihanchi back from China on one of his trips abroad, but we don't really know whether to believe this or not. Any one of these claims that a kata originated in China instead of Okinawa could simply be another example of Japanese racial prejudice against Okinawans. We need to embrace a certain skepticism about such remarks.

If naihanchi really is ancient, the explanation of it has been lost in time. The oldest kanji version of this kata's name is read *"naifuanchi."* You can see it in Shoshin Nagamine's *The Essence of Okinawan Karate-Do.*[205] The translation is *nai* (inner), *fuan* (paw), *chi* (ground). "Inner paw ground?" My Japanese translator assures me that this makes no sense in Japanese and is therefore Chinese in origin. My Chinese translator says it makes no sense in Chinese and is probably Japanese. Whether it makes sense in *Uchinanguchi* (Okinawan) is unknown. Published explanations of this name are all modern guesses by people who have completely missed the point.

We don't really *care* what the original explanation of naihanchi might have been. The critical question is: Why was naihanchi so important to Matsumura? Why did the Shuri bodyguards study naihanchi so relentlessly? Why did Azato force Funakoshi to drill in naihanchi for three years? This is particularly astonishing because the Shuri masters were the champions of tai sabaki (side stepping) and linear impact, but naihanchi doesn't contain *any* sidestepping or linear techniques. On the surface, naihanchi is exactly the opposite of everything Shuri-te stands for.

Consider the tactical situation. There you are, defending the regent from attack. You shove the regent against a wall and put your back against him so you can shield him with your body. Attackers are pressing in on you, trying to get their hands on Sho Taimu.

- You can't leap forward to attack, because that leaves the regent exposed behind you. Therefore, you can't use impact technique.

- You can't sidestep an attack to the left or right, because that would just let the attacker through to the regent. Therefore, you can't use tai sabaki.

- You can move slowly to the left or right along the wall, keeping the regent in the shadow of your body. Otherwise, your only option is to stand still and meet all attacks head-on.

---

[205] Nagamine, Shoshin, *The Essence of Okinawan Karate-Do*, Tuttle, 1976, p. 148.

This sounds like naihanchi (tekki). It may or may not be accurate to say that naihanchi was "invented," "adapted," or "adopted," but it is certainly a good fit to the mission. Naihanchi is the perfect kata for the extraction team to study.

If you have to meet all attacks head-on, wouldn't it be nice to have some kind of shield in front of you? What could you use for a shield in the Shuri reception hall fight? There isn't a scrap of furniture in the room. The only possible shield material is human bodies. And why not?

It is possible to perform naihanchi (tekki shodan) while clutching a weakened opponent to your chest as a human shield. The kata's techniques flow around the body of the enemy. The enemy's torso protects your chest, abdomen and groin from kicks, punches and steel. American naval officers may have carried pistols, but would they have fired through a fellow officer? Given Itosu's great strength, using an enemy as a shield must have been a very effective defensive strategy!

There is no question that Itosu spent years elaborating techniques that are used when your back is against a wall. He spent so much time walking around the castle in *kiba dachi* (horse-riding stance) that people started calling him "the horse." He passed the techniques down to us in *tekki nidan* and *tekki sandan*, and told us to study them. Figure 3-4 depicts huddled Okinawan ministers in the southeast corner of the reception hall. These are frightened men with their backs to a wall. Given the date, the place, and the situation, Itosu is almost certainly one of the figures in this historic picture.

Technique for Reaction

What martial arts techniques would be useful for the reaction mission?

The goal of the reaction mission is to create "shock and awe" among the attacking troops for about 30 seconds, and then disengage and retreat. This gives the extraction team a chance to complete their mission. It is about the amount of time it takes to load a Springfield or Enfield rifle-musket. This does not seem to be a coincidence. Shuri-te kata are very short compared to mainland Chinese kata. There must be a reason, and this could be it.

To deliberately plunge into a mob of angry enemies seems suicidal to the layman. The trained martial artist knows that the mob gets in its own way. A fight in a dense crowd of bodies has its own rules. For instance, if you keep moving the bad guys can't converge on you. If you use low, shotokan-like stances, the mob has trouble even seeing you unless you are within arm's reach. Then it is too late.[206]

You can accomplish this mission either by plunging straight through the crowd or by standing in one spot and striking north, east, south, and west in rapid succession. Every enemy who flies backward becomes a missile to impact his fellows. Every enemy who falls to the ground becomes an obstacle they trip over.

You can strike in every direction, but members of the mob have to be careful not to hit each other. They can't swing their sabers for fear of cutting each other. They can't shoot at you without hitting one another. Jumping into the center of a mob has tremendous tactical advantages provided, that is, that you can stun or kill each opponent with a single blow.

If you jump into a crowd and try to *grapple* with them, you are doomed. Your goal is to put eight men down in 15 seconds and then run for it. Your punch has to destroy a man as if he had been shot. That's ikken hisatsu.

What techniques are especially useful for the extraction phase of the fight?

- You must be able to shake off enemies who are trying to subdue and arrest you. This means breaking holds on wrists, clothing, and body, including attempts to tackle you or grab you by the hair. Let's include the common choke holds, too. One way to subdue a person is to choke him.

- It would be helpful to practice techniques to burst through the front line of the mob into the interior of the crowd. If you are outside the mob, they can shoot you. Inside the mob, they don't dare shoot.

- You need to be adept at tai sabaki to sidestep attacks and change direction quickly inside the crowd.

- You need techniques to stun, maim or kill each opponent in the shortest possible time. You have about two seconds to stun or cripple each new opponent. There is no time to "wear him down."

---

[206] One might picture Matsumura's agents cutting through the crowd like velociraptors in the elephant grass *(Jurassic Park II)*, and with much the same effect.

Technique for Retreat

From the standpoint of karate theory, the retreat phase is the most interesting part of the Shuri reception hall battle. At this point the reaction team has beaten up the crowd for 15 to 20 seconds, and the extraction team has dragged the principal out the door to relative safety. Someone gives the signal to retreat. What skills should we study to move as rapidly as possible toward the exit?

There are four things that make this part of the fight different from earlier phases:

- We have lost the element of surprise. The enemy knows he can't prevail by numbers alone, and weapons are coming into play.

- Our own success has thinned the mob that provided cover for us. The enemy soldiers can see us now, and they have more room to swing sabers and lunge with bayonets.

- The escape door is swinging shut. We have to get there in time, or be left behind.

- We don't have the luxury to change direction like a rabbit. We have to bore straight through the crowd like a charging bull.

Our goal in this phase is not to create confusion or to inflict damage, but to cover ground quickly through a room of awakened enemies. What skills do we need for the retreat phase?

- To make our way through the gauntlet of swinging weapons and sprawling bodies, we need some special acrobatic skills. We need to leap over obstacles and duck under slashing sabers. Maybe we'll need to dive to the floor once or twice to avoid being shot. Some of those 1853 naval officers had efficient cap-and-ball revolvers.

- In this phase there is a premium placed on the ability to knock people out of the way. We don't need to kill them with one blow; we need to make them sprawl headlong as we clear the path.

- Blocked by a stalwart opponent we cannot quickly overcome, we need to be able to bypass an enemy by sliding or leaping to a position just beyond him. This is the most difficult type of tai sabaki.

- Faced with armed opponents, we need to be able to steal their weapons. Once we steal a weapon, we will use it to force enemies out of the path.

- Confronting edged weapons, we need techniques to put the tessen to effective use.

- Having reached the door, we need skills for holding the enemy at bay for a few more seconds while the other agents escape.

- If the escape route runs up a staircase, we need techniques for blocking pursuit on the stairs.

In shotokan, we don't normally think of ourselves as fighting our way through a crowd so we can flee, but that is exactly the skill demanded by this phase of the conflict. It opens up entirely new avenues of bunkai interpretation.

Technique for Abduction

Let's explore the idea that Matsumura might try to abduct an enemy officer from the reception hall, not because there is any good evidence for it but because we can learn things while exploring. Besides, the idea is audacious and fun.

First of all, have you realized that the only difference between rescue and abduction is the attitude of the principal? Otherwise the techniques are the same.

We can assume that the regent is happy to be rescued and will cooperate with the extraction effort. He'll run straight toward the door. A wounded Matsumura agent is doubtless happy to be rescued, but perhaps is unable to cooperate. You have to pick him up and walk off with him. The enemy commander, I think, would not be happy to be abducted, so you have to stun him, pick him up and walk away.

How much technique do we need to play out this part of the scenario?

- For the uncooperative subject, we need techniques to stun a person helpless but not really injure him. There is no point in having a dead or paralyzed hostage.

- For the unconscious or stunned subject, we need technique for lifting and carrying a limp body.

If you have a black belt in shotokan, you have performed these techniques a thousand times in empi kata. Itosu wanted to be sure we knew how.

Firearm Techniques

In 1853, when Perry's Marines marched into Shuri Castle, military firearms had been present in Okinawa for about 300 years.[207] Gunpowder itself was invented in China and is almost as old as Shaolin boxing. Our modern idea that karate arose before the advent of firearms is completely wrong. Matsumura certainly studied how to shoot rifles and pistols during his trips outside of Okinawa, just like he studied sword fighting. This was an obvious requirement of his position.

One thing that caught me by surprise was Sells' revelation that Azato was a *jukendo* expert.[208] Jukendo is a sport like kendo, but it simulates bayonet fencing instead of sword fencing. The jukendo bayonet (the *mokujyo*) is a six-foot bo carved in the shape of a long-barreled rifle.[209] Knowing Azato's obsession with disarming a swordsman, we might suspect that he studied jukendo to learn how to disarm a rifleman. That would be a very useful skill in the reception hall fight.

We might even find the bodyguards leveling a gun at someone in a kata. Most karateka will find that idea quite astonishing. It isn't. Shuri's enemies carried firearms. The bodyguards trained to meet this challenge.

Inappropriate Techniques

One of the extraordinary things about hard-style karate is the surprising number of traditional martial skills that are *missing* from it. Hard stylists grudgingly acknowledge that karate has surprising holes in it, and often mumble something apologetic about "knowledge that has been lost over the centuries." Nothing could be farther from the truth. Much of the support for the Shuri Crucible theory rests on these missing techniques. They are missing for a reason.

Picture a fight where the field is so crowded that there are always three of four opponents within arm's reach, and most of them are trying to grab you. What common martial skills would not be useful in the Shuri reception hall fight?

---

[207] Henshall, 1999, p. 46. Ieyasu Tokugawa used a company of musketeers when he took over Japan in 1600. The Satsumas used guns when they took over Okinawa in 1609.

[208] Sells, 2000, p. 58.

[209] See http://www.bogubag.com/Bogu/Jukendo/jukendo.html.

- **No ground fighting:** In the Shuri reception hall, trying to take an opponent down and pin him is just going to get you killed. If you hit the floor, six angry enemies will kick you to death. You have to stay on your feet or die. Therefore, we have no jujutsu ground fighting in hard-style karate.

- **No chokes:** Judo fighters know that it takes about ten seconds to make a person unconscious with a blood choke, and over a minute with an airway choke. Matsumura's agents didn't have that kind of time. They couldn't spend more than a couple of seconds on each opponent. In karate, we have defenses against chokes, but we never practice choking an opponent.

- **No restraint holds:** What would be the point of applying a restraint hold in the Shuri reception hall? You would have to release it immediately to keep fighting. In our kata, the few restraint holds twist the opponent into a vulnerable posture for an immediate finishing technique. (The human-shield technique of naihanchi may be an exception.)

- **No vital-point strikes:** The chuan fa taught by Sakugawa included sinuous techniques that struck multiple vital points in turn, disrupting ki energy to weaken the opponent. Shuri-te abandoned the *dim-mak* pressure points because they take too long to apply. Hard-style karate is based on one-punch knockdown instead.

- **No high kicks:** You can't launch those flashy kicks when there are people jostling you on all sides. Standing on one foot with your knee up and your crotch wide open is not a good idea in a real fight. There are no fancy kicks in hard-style kata; in fact, there are very few kicks of any type. The front-snap and side-snap kicks are used as short-range, infighting techniques that keep the groin covered.

- **No night fighting.** Chuan fa contains specific techniques for fighting in the dark when you cannot see your enemy. These techniques were very practical for pedestrians on the dark forest roads of Shuri, but they had no application in the well-lighted reception hall. There is no point in including these skills in the training regimen of the Shuri bodyguards.

Conclusion

In this chapter we have generated a requirements list for a Shuri bodyguard fighting system. We know what must be included, and we have some idea of what should be left out. Both are important.

This list of techniques is a *prediction* implied by the Shuri Crucible theory. In the next two chapters we will test the prediction. Do we see the bodyguard fighting system in the shotokan (Shuri-te) kata? If we do, what does it tell us about the bunkai?

Chapter 8

Analyzing the Shuri Kata

In the previous chapters we have attempted something unique. We have written a requirements document, or proposal, for a new martial art designed to meet the needs of the "Shuri Secret Service." We assume that Matsumura implemented this new martial art to fit his needs, and that linear, hard-style karate is the result.

One way to test this theory was to go looking for bodyguard applications in the Shuri kata (which is the subject of the next chapter). We can also compare Itosu's modified kata with their more primitive ancestors. By determining what Itosu added to these kata, what he removed, and what he left alone, it might help us see into the minds of the Shuri bodyguards.

Where will we find the Shuri-te kata? The Shorin styles that received their kata directly from Itosu (shotokan and Mabuni shito-ryu) practice remarkably similar kata with the same emphasis on linear technique. The Matsumura orthodox style performs the familiar Itosu kata as if they were soft Chinese kata. Shoshin Nagamine's Matsubayashi-ryu practices "Shorin" kata that Itosu would not recognize. (Chotoku Kyan took out the linear techniques before passing the pinan to Nagamine.) As the hardest and most conservative of the hard styles, shotokan and shito-ryu can make a reasonable claim to be Shuri's most direct descendents. The kata passed on to us by Funakoshi and Mabuni are as close to Shuri-te as we are likely to get. The fact that the shotokan and shito-ryu kata are almost identical is the evidence that these styles have independently preserved Itosu's teachings.

In this chapter we will compare three of Itosu's kata with allegedly more primitive versions of the same kata. This teaches us some very interesting things about the difference between Shuri-te and earlier martial arts.

Kata Analysis

When I first began this chapter, I had in mind a simple comparison. I wanted to contrast certain shotokan kata with the ancient forms they sprang from, hoping that the differences would show us Itosu's fingerprints. This would help us see what techniques and strategies were important to the Shuri bodyguards. I was confident that I could always look to Naha-te for the original, Chinese versions of Shuri's kata. That was before I had a good look at Naha-te.

There is virtually no overlap between the Shuri kata and the Chinese styles practiced at Naha. (This is one of the reasons I began to suspect Shuri's kata *didn't* really come from China.) In fact, Naha and Shuri have only one kata in common.

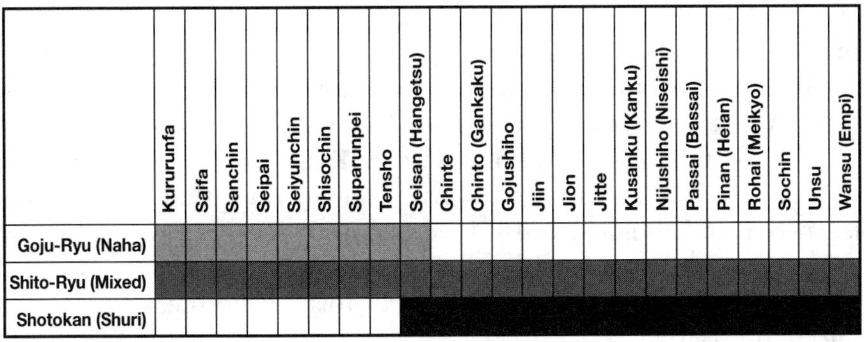

	Kururunfa	Saifa	Sanchin	Seipai	Seiyunchin	Shisochin	Suparunpei	Tensho	Seisan (Hangetsu)	Chinte	Chinto (Gankaku)	Gojushiho	Jiin	Jion	Jitte	Kusanku (Kanku)	Nijushiho (Niseishi)	Passai (Bassai)	Pinan (Heian)	Rohai (Meikyo)	Sochin	Unsu	Wansu (Empi)
Goju-Ryu (Naha)	■	■	■	■	■	■	■	■	■														
Shito-Ryu (Mixed)	■	■	■	■	■	■	■	■	■	■	■	■	■	■	■	■	■	■	■	■	■	■	■
Shotokan (Shuri)									■	■	■	■	■	■	■	■	■	■	■	■	■	■	■

Figure 8-1: Kata shared by goju-ryu, shito-ryu and shotokan. Showing kata shared by at least two of the styles. Shuri-te (Shorin) styles and Naha-te styles have almost *nothing* in common. (Shito-ryu was Kenwa Mabuni's attempt to combine both extremes in one style.)

After some feedback from my fellow San Ten sensei, however, I realized that a comparative kata analysis would require a little more effort. I therefore obtained videos of 119 kata from shotokan, isshin-ryu, Matsumura orthodox shorin-ryu, Matsubayashi shorin-ryu, Okinawan goju-ryu, Mabuni shito-ryu, and white crane chuan fa. The performers were Angi Uezu, Anita Bendickson, Gary McGuinness, George Alexander, Hirokazu Kanazawa, Issac Florentine, Jim R. Sindt, Joel Ertl, John Sells, Keiji Tomiyama, Kenneth Funakoshi, Mario Higaonna, Shinyu Gushi, Takayoshi Nagamine and Toshiaki Gillespie.

I spent several weeks analyzing these tapes. I collected tables of data, and generated many graphs showing the similarities and differences among the various styles of Okinawan karate. I wrote a long, boring chapter full of charts and statistics. Fortunately, I had an attack of good judgement at the last minute and threw that chapter away. I narrowed the focus to just three kata of special interest: kanku, naihanchi, and chinto. They all teach us something about the Shuri Crucible.

Before-and-After Views

One way to test our Shuri-te "design" is to examine the kinds of changes Itosu made to existing kata when he created the Shuri-te curriculum. For this we need before-and-after versions of the kata for comparison. This isn't easy, however. Itosu's modified kata have overrun Okinawa and most of the rest of the world. It is difficult to find the original kata anymore.

By a quirk of fate, we have one window into the kata of Itosu's youth. We can compare Itosu's revised kata with the similar kata taught to Tatsuo Shimabuku by Chotoku Kyan. Kyan, as you recall, learned virtually every Okinawan kata ever known. Kata that Matsumura learned from Sakugawa in 1811 were passed on to Kyan when he was a boy in 1878. Kyan passed some of these pre-Shuri kata to Shimabuku in the 1930s. In the 1950s, Shimabuku formalized these fossil kata into isshin-ryu.

This is why isshin-ryu seems so different from both Shuri and Naha styles. Isshin-ryu is a kata time capsule. Of course, we know that Kyan and Shimabuku changed a few things, but we just have to live with that. Funakoshi made a few changes too. Even so, there are fundamental differences between the shotokan and isshin-ryu versions of these same kata, and some of that is due to ideas introduced by Itosu. It's worth looking into.

We are fortunate to have detailed theory and applications for the isshin-ryu versions of kusanku (kanku), naihanchi (tekki), and chinto (gankaku) kata, published by Javier Martinez of Puerto Rico.[210] The Martinez publications are particularly valuable because they present detailed bunkai based on Fukienese grappling techniques such as those that Kusanku might have used to throw Tode Sakugawa into the creek. Martinez has researched multiple Chinese arts in order to achieve this perspective.

It is clear from Martinez's own comments that his interpretations of the isshin-ryu kata do not reflect modern isshin-ryu practice. Martinez places his emphasis on the ancient techniques, which were a mix of grappling, locking and striking. The bunkai he envisions

---

[210] Martinez, Javier, *Isshinryu Kusanku Kata Secrets Revealed*, San Juan, 1998; Martinez, Javier, *Isshinryu Chinto Kata Secrets Revealed*, San Juan, 1998; and Martinez, Javier, *Isshinryu Naihanchi Kata Secrets Revealed*, San Juan, 1999.

don't seem to have much in common with the current isshin-ryu bunkai demonstrated by Angi Uezu, for instance, which are of the modern punch/strike/block variety.

Angi Uezu, by the way, was the son-in-law of Tatsuo Shimabuku, the founder of isshin-ryu. Until recently, Uezu was the head of isshin-ryu in Okinawa. I was fortunate to obtain Isshinryu kata videos prepared by Uezu to serve as references for power and timing issues. Some things you can't get from a book. These kata are the "before" picture, which we may contrast with the shotokan "after" kata.

For orthodox shotokan technique and bunkai we can turn to Ertl and Bendickson, whose shotokan instructional videos are second to none. Several of their tapes penetrate the bunkai of specific kata to great depth. In addition, the San Ten sensei and I have suggested a number of new approaches to shotokan bunkai based on the Shuri Crucible (in Chapter 9). These applications are part of the "after" view.

Kusanku (Kanku Dai)

Kusanku is a special kata for Shuri-te styles. It is especially pertinent to the present study because it was created by Matsumura's teacher, Sakugawa, so we can reasonably assume that Matsumura learned the original kata from its original author. Matsumura's modified form of the kata was passed on directly to Itosu. Itosu modified it again before teaching it to Funakoshi.

Kyan's version of kusanku is supposed to have come from Chatan Yara, who was another direct student of Kong Su Kung.[211] It is not clear how much Kyan modified the kata he taught to Shimabuku. In any case, the isshin-ryu version of kusanku seems fairly soft, circular and antique compared to other versions. It seems reasonable that it is still pretty close to the techniques taught by Kong Su Kung.

The remarkable thing about kusanku is its reputation as a "night-fighting" kata. In my experience, shotokan stylists don't know this part of the kusanku legend, and there is a reason for that. Shuri's long-range impact techniques require light to see by, so it might be more correct to say that shotokan's kanku dai *used to be* a night-fighting kata. The Shuri Crucible changed the rules of engagement, and one change was turning on the lights.

---

[211] Nagamine, 2000, p. 84.

What do I mean by "night fighting?" I'm not talking about skulking ninjas. Night fighting is fighting in the dark. It has three goals: (1) to avoid being caught by the enemy; (2) to locate and attack the enemy in the dark; and (3) to remain in control of the enemy until he has been defeated. You have to touch him before you can strike him. You can't let go until you finish him off. If that sounds like an opportunity to apply those ancient Fukienese grappling techniques, you may be correct.

Let's compare the first 10 moves of kusanku with the corresponding moves in shotokan's kanku dai.

In the opening of isshin-ryu's kusanku, Martinez executes four moves to dislodge, weaken, unbalance and throw a single opponent who has grabbed the lapels of his jacket. He jabs his fingertips into the opponent's testicles, breaks the lapel grip with a wedge block, jabs fingertips into the opponent's carotid sinuses, and then twists the opponent's head 270 degrees to throw him on the ground (or break his neck).

The next five moves dislodge, unbalance, weaken and throw a second opponent who has pinned Martinez's arms from behind. Martinez breaks the opponent's hug with a move that resembles manji uke, then reverses the move to the opposite side to capture the opponent's right arm. He controls the right hand while doing a back elbow strike to break ribs. Still holding the hand, Martinez breaks the arch of the opponent's left foot by stomping on it with his heel. Finally he grips the attacker's right arm with both hands and executes a shoulder throw.

Yet another attacker jumps in to pin Martinez's arms from behind. Martinez again controls the opponent's right arm and again uses his elbow to break ribs. He locks the wrist to pull the opponent off balance as he turns to face him. Then Martinez does a *mae geri keage* to the femoral nerve to set up the final uraken to the temple.

Notice that these applications use several moves against each of three opponents. The performer fights one enemy at a time. This is the classical picture of monkish self-defense using chuan fa.

In shotokan, the parallel series of moves (from the beginning of kanku dai to the first kick) involves half a dozen opponents holding your arms and jacket (see Chapter 9). The first few moves of kanku dai involve an eye poke, wrist and clothing releases, a couple of wrenched shoulders and backs, two arm breaks, a groin kick and (if we follow Ertl's lead) perhaps as many as three throws. These moves put at least four opponents out of the fight and do damage to at least two others. We fight more enemies than in the isshin-ryu kata, and we fight multiple enemies at the same time. In the Shuri-te tradition, the shotokan techniques are ruthless and instantly devastating.

The details of the techniques are not really important. The critical difference is the mindset. The ancient applications used multiple techniques to reduce one attacker. Itosu's linear interpretation provides weapons against *many simultaneous enemies*. In fact, there are applications in kanku dai where a single technique injures multiple attackers (see Figure 9-10). Again, this is completely consistent with the difference between the world view of the Shaolin monk and that of the keimochi bodyguard.

Naihanchi (Tekki)

There are all kinds of rumors about the origins of the naihanchi (tekki) kata. The sideways motion of the kata, neither advancing nor retreating, has been weakly explained in a dozen ways. My suggestion that the naihanchi performer has his back to a wall because he is shielding someone appears to be completely unexpected. That may not be the original purpose of the kata, but it goes a long way toward explaining why naihanchi was so important at Shuri Castle. It is a natural kata for the extraction team.

To a shotokan stylist the naihanchi kata of isshin-ryu has several unexpected features. It resembles tekki shodan superficially, but the isshin-ryu version of the kata is the mirror-image of the Shorin version. It starts by stepping to the left instead of the right. (This is the kind of change that Kyan might have introduced to assert his independence of Shuri.)

Angi Uezu's performance of naihanchi uses a special, upright stance with the toes and knees turned inward, similar to the feeling of shotokan's *sanchin dachi*. There are two explicit *fumikomi* (downward kicks using heel or edge of foot as striking surface) kicks to the opponent's knees, which have been blended into the sideways steps in shotokan. There is a horizontal nukite (spear hand) to the ribs with the palm facing upward, where a shotokan stylist performs a hook punch. There are six *nami-gaeshi's* where a shotokan student would expect only four. The moves of the kata are generally similar to tekki shodan, but the isshin-ryu version includes upward elbow strikes, ridge-hand blocks, and a surprising "knuckle block" where you stop a punch by hitting it head-on, fist-to-fist. This last move looks rather improbable and painful. (However, one might think differently if they had knuckles like Chotoku Kyan.)

The naihanchi kata demonstrated by Martinez is almost identical to the Uezu version. The bunkai presented by Martinez are quite remarkable, however, and are very much in the ancient Chinese tradition. The performer and the opponent stand face-to-face. Using the standard naihanchi gestures, Martinez strikes the opponent's testicles with his fingertips and then applies a painful grip to the opponent's right triceps muscle, holding it like a suitcase handle. He applies an elbow strike to the right upper arm to paralyze the arm, then yanks on the arm to break the opponent's posture at the waist. He uses nami-gaeshi against the inside of the opponent's right leg to stun the femoral nerve or wrench the knee, shifting the opponent's weight to the left foot.

At this point the opponent is bent over at the waist with his head near Martinez's right hip. Martinez does a right downblock into the back of the head and grabs the man's hair in his fist. He uses the hair grip to twist the head around and lock the neck. He casually slips in an arm lock on the weakened right arm, rendering the opponent helpless, immobile and unable to offer further resistance. At this point, Martinez demonstrates a knee lift under the man's chin to hyperextend and break his neck.[212] This sequence is a typical example of the applications Martinez suggests for naihanchi.

Notice again how much of the kata is devoted to subduing a single opponent.

An even more extreme set of naihanchi bunkai is offered by Nathan Johnson, a student of Zen Buddhism, who believes that the original naihanchi kata contains no blocks or strikes whatsoever, but represents a complete joint-locking system instead. Johnson explains that the brutal bunkai of shotokan and isshin-ryu are not very Zen-like, and would not have been used by Shaolin monks.

Johnson lets his opponent grasp his crossed wrists. He quickly reverses the hold, places the opponent in a wrist lock, and flips him

---

[212] Martinez, 1999, p. 93-99.

over on his back on the floor. Then, using familiar naihanchi motions and postures, Johnson plays with his opponent like a cat would with a mouse. Every time the enemy gets his feet under him, Johnson reverses the twist on the wrist lock and flips him back the other way. This adaptation of naihanchi is extremely clever, to say the least.[213] If it is historically accurate, Shuri-te has traveled a *long* way from its roots at the Shaolin Temple.

Once again, the bunkai uses many moves to subdue a single opponent.

Joel Ertl offers an orthodox shotokan interpretation of tekki shodan, similar to most of the tekki sessions I have seen over the years. The opening cluster dislodges a wrist hold, followed by one or perhaps two devastating elbow strikes to the ribs or solar plexus of the opponent on the right. There is an optional throw before Ertl turns his attention to a second opponent on the left. The bunkai of the kata proceeds as a series of block/counter moves designed to deal with a flurry of kicks and punches from three simultaneous opponents. The performer fends off punches and kicks left, right and center in rapid succession.

The significant thing about the shotokan bunkai of tekki shodan is that the performer shifts his attention rapidly from one opponent to another, and does not have the luxury to toy with a single enemy. That's quite consistent with Shuri-te evolution. The ancient Zen monks could concentrate on one opponent at a time, but Matsumura's men didn't have time.

Chinto (Gankaku)

When the chinto (gankaku) kata is examined for before-and-after differences something disappointing arises. Chinto is actually not suitable for a before-and-after comparison. Chinto was created by Matsumura himself. It was *always* a Shuri kata, so there really isn't a viable "before" picture to examine. I considered dropping chinto from the analysis completely, but then I found several interesting things. There are some special secrets hidden in chinto, and they tell us something about the Shuri Crucible.

The stories about the origin of chinto kata are fairly consistent.

---

[213] Johnson, 2000, p. 182-209.

Sometime during Matsumura's career a Chinese sailor, possibly a pirate, was stranded on Okinawa in the vicinity of Tomari. This is hardly surprising because Tomari was Okinawa's second seaport after Naha. There is a legend that the sailor, named Chinto, was a thief and the Tomari villagers petitioned the king to have the royal bodyguards put him away.

Matsumura, and possibly others, tried to arrest Chinto. They found him in a cave by the beach. Matsumura's legend says he never lost a fight, but he didn't exactly win this one. Matsumura could not arrest Chinto. In the end Matsumura befriended the sailor and offered to feed him in exchange for lessons! Other Tomari residents struck the same deal with Chinto, and all received a few weeks of exotic martial instruction from the pirate.

By one means or another, these lessons became formalized as the chinto kata. As usual, it is very hard to figure out who taught what to whom, but Matsumura is usually credited as the author of the kata. The contending author is Kosaku Matsumora, who was involved in the same episode and later taught his own version of the kata (the one we find in isshin-ryu). If Matsumora was there, then Oyadomari was involved, too. I would not be surprised if all three masters collaborated on the new kata. Today, the isshin-ryu and Matsubayashi shorin-ryu versions of chinto are very similar, and are often credited to Matsumora of Tomari, while the other Shorin styles, including shotokan, perform a kata that looks just like Gankaku and is credited to Matsumura at Shuri. The two kata are about 60 percent similar in sequence and technique.

When a shotokan stylist looks at isshin-ryu's chinto kata, two items stand out. The first is that the kata is performed along a *diagonal line* extending to the northwest of the origin (presuming all kata to begin by facing north). The angled *enbusen* (lines for performance of fight techniques) must be symbolic, because no one can suggest a practical explanation for it. Furtermore, the isshin-ryu version doesn't make you balance on one foot like a "crane on a rock." Those very difficult stackups are simply not in the isshin-ryu version of the kata.

On the whole, chinto is a bizarre kata demanding a logical explanation! We have only the faintest of clues. We know that Matsumura had a hard time defeating Chinto, so apparently we ought to find *something* in the kata that was outside of Matsumura's experience. He went back to study it. He created the kata to immortalize it. It was something special and important.

There is a persistent rumor that the kata shows how to fight on treacherous ground, which might mean slippery mud, soft sand, or possibly uneven, rocky terrain where neat dojo stances don't work very well.

Let's combine these limited clues with an awareness of Matsumura's situation at Shuri, and see what comes to mind. Shuri Castle is a very civilized environment—graded, paved and polished. There is no "treacherous ground" to be found there. When would a Shuri bodyguard need to fight on "uneven ground?" What could that angled enbusen symbolize?

There is one circumstance that might fit. Turning back to Figure 1-8, the throne room floor plan, the escape route from the raised dais to the second floor goes up a narrow staircase. This is the natural bottleneck in the escape route. In order to delay pursuers, the Shuri bodyguards must have studied how to block this stairway. Chinto's angled enbusen might symbolize a sharply-sloping ramp, hillside, or staircase.

Martinez presents an elaborate analysis of chinto, complete with a floor plan, to show that the performer is deliberately piling up bodies in specific places to obstruct a narrow bridge or hallway.[214] Like a bridge, a stairway is a narrow passage where you can make a stand and buy time for your principals to get away. Enemies have to come at you from below. This gives you tactical advantages that make stairway fighting attractive, but you need special techniques to make it work. Fighting on a stairway is very different from fighting on a flat dojo floor.

Matsumura might not have realized this before he confronted chinto the first time. The stories about chinto often mention a seaside cave. Seaside caves have sandy, rocky, or slimy footing. If Matsumura had to fight uphill within a confined passage, the pirate Chinto might have given him serious trouble. Matsumura relied on impact technique for quick victories, but you can't use impact technique uphill. This could be the factor that was outside of Matsumura's experience. He went back to the cave to study how to attack and defend on a steep

---

[214] Martinez, 1998, p. 14.

slope. Apparently he saw some use for this skill.

This is pure speculation, of course, meant to be explored and learned from. If you were to execute some light kumite on a staircase, you would find that the environment seriously constrains your tactics and technique. After a few minutes, you'll start to figure out how to do it. Generally speaking, you must attack the head and hands with short, sharp kicks when facing downhill, and use your hands to attack the opponent's feet and knees when facing uphill.

For instance, if you need to bring down a person above you on the stairs, you can do it by squatting low because that lets you catch his feet while ducking under most of his kicks. Use *juji-uke* (X-block) to capture his forward foot; then yank on it to drop him on his back. There are three X-blocks in gankaku, one of which is kneeling.

Matsumura and Itosu have also shown us the complimentary technique. If you are trying to hold the passage against someone below you on the stairs, don't give him an easy shot at your forward foot. Pull back into crane stance, raising the lead foot into a kicking posture. If he reaches for it, he's going to get kicked in the teeth and knocked down the stairs. That's the classic gankaku pose.

If you are blocking the stairway against a mob of attackers, one tactic is to deliberately knock them back down the steps, mowing down the people below like dominoes. This blocks the passage by causing many injuries and piling up bodies on the landing below. You could hardly do better than to leap down the stairs with a jump kick, bowling over the first rank and sending them rolling down the stairs into their companions. A jump kick at a downward angle builds up awesome momentum.

Does that sound too dangerous to you? Remember, to a keimochi bodyguard, victory was more important than mere survival. Shuri-te is not self-defense; it is defense of *someone else*. It is permitted to sacrifice yourself, as long as you win.

If you would hesitate to leap down a flight of steps at a horde of enemies, here is another interpretation. The double jump kick in gankaku is also a defense against having your foot grabbed from below. If your first kick is caught, you might want to launch the second one into the opponent's face before he spills you on your back. Several pieces of gankaku seem to link up in this fashion, which promotes one to question whether there is a complete stair-fighting system hidden in this kata.

Do we have any objective evidence that the staircase bunkai is really the original purpose of the kata? Let's assume that the kata begins at the top of a staircase. When we move away from the origin of the kata, we are moving downhill. When we move back toward the origin, we are moving uphill.

Most kicks, punches and blocks against the enemy below us on the stair would probably contact him above the waist. After all, his legs are out of reach below us. Turning uphill, most kicks, punches and blocks with the opponent above us on the stairs would probably hit the lower half of his body. If the kata was originally performed on a slope, we ought to see some sign of this in the bunkai.

I watched the tape of Angi Uezu performing the bunkai for chinto with half a dozen of his isshin-ryu black-belt assistants. I recorded which part of the assistants' bodies (upper half or lower half) was involved in each exchange with Uezu, tallying the data into downhill and uphill exchanges from Uezu's point of view.

For this performance, at least, Uezu's portrayal of chinto bunkai struck at the upper body (or blocked hand attacks) 87 percent of the time when facing downhill, but blocked the legs or punched the groin 62 percent of the time when facing uphill. Most of the encounters occurred in the downhill direction, as if he was defending the top of the stairs. These results are consistent with the idea that the original author was fighting on a slope.

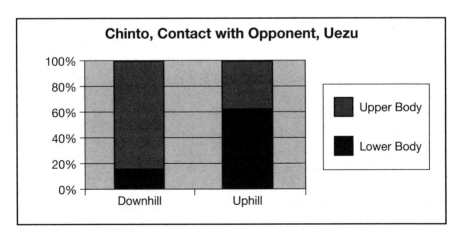

Figure 8-2: Bunkai contact level (upper or lower body) for chinto performed by Angi Uezu, versus the direction the performer was facing. Facing downhill, most applications strike the opponent's upper body. Facing uphill, most of the contact is with the opponent's lower body. This supports the idea that the original kata was performed on a slope.

I certainly cannot make all of chinto or gankaku fit into the stairway theory, but the fit is good enough to give us some ideas for research and teaching. When was the last time you had your students work on stairway fighting? It could be a life-saving skill, especially for women. It is important to hold the "high ground," and this kata shows us how.

What Itosu Added

When comparing the isshin-ryu kata of Martinez and Uezu with standard shotokan doctrine, we see dramatic differences in technique, power, embusen, and bunkai. From these differences we can draw additional support for the theory of the Shuri Crucible. The changes Itosu imposed on the kata match the bodyguard style of fighting.

Motion

After viewing those 119 kata, it was quite apparent that Itosu's Shorin kata are full of motion. Impact technique is fueled by momentum, so the body has to be moving toward the opponent at the moment of contact. In comparison, white crane's *hakutsuru* kata is practically standing still, and goju-ryu's sanchin kata is like a glacier melting slowly in the sunlight. Itosu emphasized motion.

Power

The techniques of linear power generation were not visible in the Isshinryu kata I examined.[215] These techniques, building toward mastery of *ikken hisatsu*, absolutely *dominate* shotokan kata.

The difference in raw power between shotokan and isshin-ryu kata is immediately obvious to a shotokan stylist, although I suppose the isshin-ryu stylist might not see it. It isn't just a question of making "jerky" start-and-stop motions instead of smooth, circular ones. For one thing, the basic principles of impact karate demand that the fighter maintain a straight and erect backbone when focusing technique. This reduces disk-rupturing injuries caused by the intense shock of contact with the target. Shuri-te kata demand upright posture in nearly every move in order to generate and transmit this power without injuring one's own spine. In

---

[215] Note that my remarks refer to the kata only. One surprise of my kata research was the discovery that soft-kata stylists often do hard-style technique when they demonstrate bunkai or kumite. They didn't learn that from their kata.

the isshin-ryu version of kusanku, however, the performer's lower back is bent out of the vertical more often than not.[216] It is clear that linear impact was not an issue when this kata was developed.

Multiple Opponents

One of the things Itosu added to his kata was multiple opponents. We can see this clearly in the mind set behind the bunkai. Older bunkai deal with one opponent at a time. Newer bunkai shifts from opponent to opponent quite rapidly, and sometimes deals with several opponents at once.

In a one-on-one fight, you can evade an attack by using tai sabaki. In a many-on-one fight, you can evade multiple simultaneous attacks only by leaping directly toward one of your opponents and jamming his technique. By jamming one person's attack, you can move out of range of the kicks, punches and grabs launched by his friends. The rapid motion of shotokan kata is an effective strategy for evading multiple attackers.

Impact Bunkai

As we have seen in the previous sections, there is also a dramatic difference in bunkai when you compare the isshin-ryu versions and the shotokan versions of naihanchi (tekki) and kusanku (kanku) kata. Martinez's step-by-step interpretations of isshin-ryu bunkai are fundamentally different from their shotokan counterparts.

If Martinez's interpretations are close to the original bunkai, it looks as if Itosu substituted high-impact interpretations for the original grappling applications. In shotokan we are *hitting* people, not squeezing their muscles and twisting their thumbs.

Standard Enbusen

The enbusen is the floor plan of the kata, as if you had marked it on the floor with tape (as we often do with beginners). Itosu's kata are variations of a standard enbusen. In shotokan we think of this as having the shape of a capital "I" or "H" but in the original pinan kata the standard enbusen looks more like a double-pointed arrow (↔).

---

[216] In Martinez's treatment of kusanku, his lower back is visibly bent in about 70 percent of the photographs.

This implies that Funakoshi flattened out the arrowheads to create the "H" of the heian kata. Why is a mystery.

The significance of Itosu's standard enbusen is that it serves as a sort of signature. At the very least it says, "Itosu was here." It also makes it possible to see a standard tactical plan in the kata, a theme we'll explore later in this chapter.

What Itosu Discarded

The Shuri Crucible theory predicts that certain classes of martial techniques would be useless to the Shuri bodyguards (see chapter 7). For the most part, the missing elements relate to techniques that take too long to apply, or that tie up the performer's hands in attempts to restrain the opponent, making him vulnerable to attack by other enemies. Can we see this pattern in the revised kata? What techniques did Itosu reduce or remove?

Fewer Pressure Points

Martinez's isshin-ryu kata contain elaborate sequential strikes to pressure points on various acupuncture meridians. Martinez strikes the opponent three or four times to weaken him and set him up for a final blow or throw. Vital-point striking is a common practice in soft-style karate and chuan fa, inherited from the "pecking" attacks of white crane.

This kind of tap-tap-tap attack is simply absent from the Itosu kata. You don't poke the enemy in four vital areas to "set him up." In shotokan you create a split-second opening and then strike him once. The blow may or may not strike a vital point such as the philtrum or solar plexus, but if so it is a point on the centerline of the body where the enormous force will be absorbed and won't just spin the opponent around. It looks as if Itosu abandoned the venerable theory of acupunching in favor of the one-punch knockdown. This is certainly the way he fought on the street.

This is an important distinction because it explains how the vital-point knowledge of chuan fa was "lost" to hard-style karate. The military bodyguards of Shuri had no use for a strategy that required them to hit each opponent several times. Their goal was to hit the opponent once and be done with him. This rendered most of vital-point theory useless to them.

Fewer Nukite Strikes

As a direct effect of abandoning the vital points, there has been a general reduction in the number of finger-poking strikes in the Shuri kata. There are still a few nukite strikes in shotokan, but not nearly as many as you see in isshin-ryu. There appear to be a total of seven nukite attacks in naihanchi, chinto and kusanku, compared to a total of two attacks in tekki shodan, gankaku and kanku dai.

It is sobering to notice that two of the nukite strikes that Itosu preserved are clearly presented as "bad examples." He seems to be saying, "If you try this, the other guy will catch your arm and twist it." Those would be the nukite techniques in *heian sandan* and near the end of kanku dai. He was warning us not to do this.

No Submission Techniques

The isshin-ryu kata of Martinez emphasize applying a hold and controlling the opponent until you can finish him off. The shotokan kata take hold of an enemy only momentarily to amplify the impact of a technique. You don't see shotokan bunkai where you apply a wrist lock or ankle break to an opponent who is already on the ground, like you do in some isshin-ryu bunkai. In shotokan you might crack the prostrate opponent's skull with your heel, but you wouldn't grab his foot and twist it to control him.

No Night Fighting

Itosu seems to have removed an entire class of night-fighting techniques from the Shuri kata. (I refer to the techniques intended to deceive the opponent about your position, and the techniques that let you silently search for an opponent in the dark.) The Angi Uezu video of kusanku describes these techniques explicitly. In one, the performer thumps his left foot on the ground to make a noise, while leaning over to the right to keep his body out of line with the sound. The technique is intended to draw an attacker in. This technique does not appear in the shotokan kata at all.

Searching for an opponent consists of slow, silent sweeping with the lead hand and foot, rather like radar. The emphasis is on silence. The performer moves forward slowly until he touches an opponent. In Shuri-te, this technique has been converted into triple and quadruple *shuto uchi* (knife hand strike) sequences such as you see in heian nidan. The Shuri bodyguards didn't need to fight in the dark. Their "searching hand" does blocks and chops instead.[217]

Another aspect of night fighting is the awareness of light and shadow. If there is one strong source of light, it is a good idea to get it behind you. This bathes the enemy in light while casting your face and hands in shadow.

Itosu, Funakoshi and six other students were attacked on the Naha-Shuri road one night after a moon-viewing party (almost certainly on a night with a full moon). It was just before dawn, so the moon was setting in the west. Confronted by a hostile gang in the moonlight, Itosu shouted, "Stand with your backs to the moon! Your backs to the moon!" Funakoshi thought Itosu had lost his mind. He couldn't understand why the old man was shouting about the moon![218] This story demonstrates that Itosu understood the principles of night fighting, but had never discussed them with his closest students. He trained them for the well-lighted Shuri reception hall, not for the shadowy streets.

What Itosu Left Alone

And what about the techniques and skills that Itosu left alone? He added linear technique and discarded vital-points, but what did he decide to preserve?

Shuri technique still looks a lot like its Chinese relatives when the performer is stepping backward, standing still or turning. Techniques that depend on body rotation and a solid foundation are equally valid across the board. The concepts of blocking, sidestepping and counterpunching go back at least as far as white crane, and are probably universal.

When you sidestep and retaliate with your shotokan *gyaku zuki* (reverse punch), you are applying techniques and tactics that come directly from the Chinese heritage. The karate styles are all very similar in this regard.

Naihanchi contains many techniques that Itosu passed along to us unaltered. The nami gaeshi (returning-wave kicks) are a major

---

[217] Nagamine, 2000, p. 90 shows *sagurite no kamae* (knife hand block), "searching hand fighting posture" from patsai (bassai) kata. It is very close to *shuto uke*.

[218] Funakoshi, 1975, p. 49-50.

feature of the kata, as is the supported backfist strike. The double blocks are present in Naihanchi, although some of them are open-hand blocks. The elbow-strike into the palm of the opposite hand is identical to the one we do in Shuri-te. The double punch that punctuates the midpoint and end of the kata is ancient, although no one seems really clear about its function.[219]

Chinto, too, contains a number of familiar moves. The opening X-block that catches the opponent's wrist is there, and you can see a version of manji uke used as a throw. The jump kick and subsequent X-downblocks are almost identical to shotokan. The downward knifehand block is present, followed by two techniques that use double shuto strikes. The details of these sequences are quite different from those in shotokan, however. After that, chinto departs from gankaku almost completely. There are repeated clusters of block/elbow/kick techniques, but they bear no resemblance to the crane-on-a-rock poses and spins of shotokan. (It looks as if Matsumura and Matsumora got only halfway through Chinto's kata before the pirate vanished, leaving them each to finish the kata on his own.)

Kusanku begins with the same upraised hands as kanku dai, which is a posture inherited from white crane. The crane is spreading its wings, so to speak. The twisting punch/block combinations are visible, but are performed in the opposite sequence (block/punch). The classic sidekick with uraken to the south is present, although isshin-ryu and most Shorin styles use a front snap kick here. (The sidekick is a Funakoshi innovation.) Kusanku includes the shuto to the neck followed by front snap kick almost as we do it in shotokan. In the following move, the kusanku performer actually kneels on the ground to catch the opponent's leg and yank it out from under him. The kusanku performer dives to the floor twice, not once. The jump kick at the end of the kata looks very familiar.

In all, Itosu's kata are about 50 percent similar to their isshin-ryu "ancestors." Another 40 percent looks familiar but distorted by different basic principles and new bunkai. About 10 perecnt of the techniques just don't cross the boundary in either direction.

---

[219] Shihan Philip Skornia of zendo-ryu showed me an effective application for the double punch in tekki shodan. It involves a block, an arm bar and a throw using the left hand only while the right is busy elsewhere.

Old and New Bunkai

In short, the differences between the isshin-ryu kata and their Shuri counterparts are consistent with the needs of the Shuri bodyguards. If the technique takes too long to apply, it won't work against multiple assailants. Night-fighting techniques just didn't apply. Itosu edited these techniques out of the system and substituted linear applications that had a similar look. It seems that he was trying to preserve the "look and feel" of the traditional kata while still converting them to linear impact. We should not be surprised if some of the substitutions turned out to be a little awkward. This kind of revision forces one to make difficult compromises.

This conversion process left us with the very confusing bunkai situation we all struggle with in shotokan and related Shorin styles. Itosu didn't obliterate the old bunkai entirely. We see the linear-impact bunkai on the surface of the kata, but just below it we sense the earlier interpretations where we grapple with people, poke their vital points, and twist their joints.[220] No wonder we have such a hard time figuring out Itosu's bunkai. Whenever we look at our kata, we get double vision.

Once you realize that the Shorin kata contain two independent sets of applications, you can start to exploit them both. We can study impact technique *and* grappling technique. The confusing bunkai isn't a curse, but an opportunity.

Tactical Themes in the Kata

No one would suggest that any hard-style kata is a literal battle plan for a real fight. Itosu's kata are too symmetrical and artistic to be taken literally. Even so, you can see the shadow of the Shuri battle plan in Itosu's H-shaped kata. Itosu's organized mind forced a certain imprint on the kata, presenting the Shuri battle plan in a series of distorted images, like snapshots that are slightly out of focus.

Remember that Itosu was 23 years old when he confronted Perry

---

[220] Abernethy, Iain, *Karate's Grappling Methods*, NETH Publishing in association with Summersdale Publishers LTD, England, 2000. Available from http://www.iainabernathy.com. This is a very interesting look at the grappling system that lies beneath Itosu's linear bunkai.

and all those Marines. He thought about that experience for 50 years before releasing the pinan (heian) kata. We should not be surprised that Perry's visit had an impact on Itosu's kata.

Our shotokan kata begin with the karateka stepping warily up to a mark on the floor, as if stepping through a door into a hostile arena. (Where are we? Where is this door?) There is a feeling that there are many enemies in front of the fighter, but few behind him. (Why would that be?) He seems to be facing a hostile gang or mob. (Who are these people? Why are they angry?)

There is a tradition in karate that the kata begin with defensive moves, symbolizing that karate is non-aggressive. The karateka stands still with hands extended or clasped in front of his body, gathering his resolve. Then he launches a series of moves against nearby opponents to the left, right, back and front. These opening moves look like blocks to beginners, but advanced students can see very effective wrist-release and escape techniques here.[221]

It looks as if the karateka has been grabbed and held by the mob. (Why would they *restrain* him instead of beat him?) He spends several seconds breaking these holds and clearing some space to move in.

Then a very odd thing happens. If karate is truly non-aggressive, the kata might start at the front of the room and work backward in a series of morally-correct evasions and counters. This isn't what we see.

Instead of defending or escaping, the hero of our kata *attacks the crowd*. (Why would he do that?) He plunges headlong into the gang of enemies, applying crippling punches and joint breaks in all directions for about 15 seconds.

In the first half of the kata, these techniques are relatively conservative and offer few openings to opponents. Most of the time the karateka keeps his feet on the ground and fights with his hands. The karateka darts rapidly from one target to another in an apparently pointless campaign to stun multiple opponents rapidly. It is as if he is trying to panic the crowd. (Why panic the crowd?)

About halfway through the kata, the performer suddenly shouts. We all know that this is the *kiai* that helps focus a finishing blow. There is no mystery about why he shouts. The mystery is, why doesn't

---

[221] See Figure 9-1 to Figure 9-4, for instance.

he shout sooner? Why doesn't he shout on every move? Why use focused blows on multiple parties for 15 seconds and *then* shout? If this happened in real life, we might assume that the shout was a signal. The first phase of the fight is over. Responding to this signal, the karateka suddenly turns and fights his way out of the crowd again.

To me, the second half of Itosu's kata seem much more deadly than the first half. During this exit phase, the karateka brings his most powerful weapons into play to clear a path back to the door. He stomps legs and feet. He sweeps, leaps, ducks and kicks. He throws opponents bodily into the crowd—always in the direction of his goal—as he fights his way home. He snatches weapons from his enemies and strikes them down. He takes desperate chances, as if the exit door is about to close. There is another shout as he applies a finishing blow to the last enemy who blocks his way. Is it another signal?

The kata ends with the karateka turning to face the bruised and battered mob as he brushes off the last attackers. At this point, there is a feeling that the enemies are all in front of him again, and none are behind. He steps backwards, away from the mob, as if backing warily through a door, and the kata comes to a close.

I'm sure you recognize this pattern. It is visible in all of the beginning and intermediate shotokan kata: the *taikyoku* kata, the heians, bassai dai, empi, kanku dai, and the temple kata (jion, jiin, and jitte). Most of Itosu's kata last about 45 seconds when performed esthetically. At combat speed, however, most of them can be completed in about 30 seconds.

Tekki shodan is the exception to this pattern. The tekki artist seems to step through the door and face that same mob, but he doesn't plunge into it. One plunges into the mob in the other shodan-level kata, so why would it be important to keep the wall behind you when performing tekki? At this point it seems the answer should be clear: The tekki performer is shielding the principal.

The basic kata of shotokan, hammered into the Shuri-te mold by Itosu, are quite consistent with the tactical goals of the Shuri battle plan. It is as if Itosu had a bigger picture in mind when he crafted these mini-battles for us to practice. You don't have to twist or distort the kata in order to see the Shuri extraction/reaction missions in them. *The kata fit the plan.*

Chapter 9

Bodyguard
Bunkai

In the previous chapter we examined how the Shuri kata differ from their ancestors, and found that the differences are consistent with the predictions of the Shuri Crucible theory. The next step is to use the Shuri battle requirements in another way: as a bunkai checklist. We have created lists of techniques that should be required by each of the three missions: extraction, reaction and retreat. Now we'll look for these techniques in the kata.

This is the unique approach to bunkai offered by this book. Starting with a list that describes a complete bodyguard fighting system, can we find all the required applications among the techniques we have practiced all these years? Does hard-style karate, embodied as shotokan, contain the complete Shuri bodyguard system?

Finding all of the required techniques in the shotokan kata does not necessarily prove the validity of the Shuri Crucible theory. That's not the point. Instead, it proves that most of us know very little about shotokan bunkai. The bodyguard list is a remarkable tool for prying unexpected bunkai out of the old familiar kata.

Note

Traditional karate students learn bunkai haphazardly over many years, with no way to know how much progress they have made or what they have overlooked. This chapter presents the list of fighting skills you *should* have learned from the kata. These are the skills your students must learn to be competent Shuri bodyguards.

Don't teach random bunkai as if you were finding shells on the beach. Learn and teach a complete self-defense system.

Sugiyama's 25 Kata

To discuss bunkai in the shotokan kata, we need a standard system of reference so that you and I can be, literally, on the same page. The San Ten senseis have solved this problem by adopting sensei Sugiyama's *25 Shoto-Kan Kata* book as our standard reference on kata. This book is simply the best job anyone has ever done on documenting a system of kata. The book contains hundreds of meticulous drawings of each step in the kata, as if each move was drafted by a mechanical engineer. It also contains parallel explanations in English, Spanish and Japanese.

When I tell you to do heian shodan, step 3, I'm looking at Sugiyama. You should own this book. You can get it from http://www.amazon.com.[222]

Required Bunkai List

Our analysis of the extract/react/retreat battle plan shows that it requires agents with the following list of skills:

- Break out of simple holds on wrists and arms.
- Break out of restraining holds on clothing.
- Break out of arm locks and wrist locks.
- Break out of holds on hair.
- Break out of body restraint holds (hugs, with arms free and also with arms pinned).
- Counter attempts to tackle.
- Throw off choke holds.
- Burst through a line of enemies to penetrate the crowd.
- Rapid-fire body shifting inside the crowd.
- One-hit stun/maim/kill techniques for targets in the crowd.
- Rapidly clear a path through alert enemies.
- Use an enemy as a weapon by throwing him at another enemy.
- Use an enemy as a shield against other enemies.
- Jump and dive to avoid weapons.
- Leap past a blocking enemy.
- Snatch and use enemy weapons.
- Abduct an enemy.
- Block and strike with tessen.
- Fight on a stairway.

---

[222] Oddly, Sugiyama left out jiin. On the other hand, the new edition of the book includes the new kitei form.

In this chapter we will go through this list to see if the shotokan kata teach these skills. That's the academic question. The practical question is whether the image of the Shuri reception hall makes new and interesting bunkai pop out of the kata.

Dinglehoppers

You are aware of "bunkai," and may have heard of "*oyo.*" I want to call your attention to a third term that should be as well-known as the first two: "Dinglehopper."

A "dinglehopper" is a kata application that is pathetically wrong. The word comes from the Disney movie *The Little Mermaid*, where Ariel the mermaid brings a fork to Scuttle, the seagull, and asks him to explain it. Scuttle, full of false wisdom, says the fork is a "dinglehopper" and is used to comb and curl your hair.

Well, you *could* use a fork to comb your hair, but in fact Scuttle's explanation is horribly wrong. Similarly, many of the applications we see demonstrated for shotokan kata are sadly impractical and unrealistic. Some of our greatest masters are guilty of promoting dinglehoppers. All of our lesser masters do it.

The real bunkai of the Shuri-te kata is so vicious it quite takes your breath away. It breaks necks. It breaks arms. It incapacitates multiple people in a single move. It rips out eyes. It crushes throats. It destroys knee joints. It targets and breaks critical bones. It ruptures vital organs. People hiss and flinch when you demonstrate.

This chapter is a glimpse into the "real" bunkai of Shuri-te. When I look at the kata, this is the kind of fighting I see. It seems so obvious once you understand what Matsumura and Itosu were up against.

Break Wrist and Arm Grips

The first requirement is that Shuri-te should help you break simple holds on your wrists and arms, the kind of thing an untrained person would use to restrain you. This is obviously a primary self-defense skill, especially for women.

If you are a bodyguard in the Shuri reception hall, it is natural that the enemies will try to grab you and restrain you. They are European or American sailors, marines and naval officers, and not Asian martial artists. They are inept at restraint. They will grab your wrists, arms, clothing and hair. How can you break free?

Do the shotokan kata contain simple wrist releases? Any beginner will immediately think of heian shodan step 4, where you rip your captured right wrist out of the opponent's grip (against the thumb) and then complete the circle by striking down on his head or collarbone with your fist.

And what else? Imagine that people keep trying to grab your arms as you move through the kata. Can you recognize other let-go-of-me techniques?

Figure 9-1: Wrist release, heian shodan, step 1. The opponent grasps both of your wrists. All you do is stack up for a downblock, and your wrists come free.

The next time you are in the dojo, have your senpai stand in front of you and grasp both of your wrists. Perform the opening move of your favorite kata and watch what happens. In most cases, senpai won't be able to maintain his grip on your arms.

People say that the kata all begin with blocks, but it is equally true to say that they all begin with wrist releases. All of the basic blocks begin with exaggerated stackups. The stackups have a hidden agenda. The stackups are remarkable wrist releases. There are wrist releases *everywhere* in the kata.

For instance, the first move of heian shodan is a downblock, *gedan barai.* The stackup for this block puts the blocking fist up near the opposite ear, and the pullback hand extended out toward the enemy. This brings your elbows together in front of your body as you stack up.

Prepare to open heian shodan. Have senpai grab your wrists. Step forward a little so that you are crowding senpai's personal space, and then do the full gedan barai stackup. As your elbows come together, both wrist grips are cleanly broken.

Heian sandan opens with an inside block, *uchi ude uke.*[223] The pullback hand withdraws through the bent elbow of the blocking arm. The left arm, launching the block, rips the senpai's hand off your right wrist. The blocking arm usually comes free at the same time because the stackup levers against the senpai's thumb. The subsequent double blocks (heian sandan steps 2 and 3) make it impossible for the senpai

Figure 9-2: Wrist release, tekki shodan, step 1. The opponent grasps both of your wrists. Drop your weight to drive your arms through his grip, forcing his hands open.

---

[223] The naming of the inside block vs. the outside block is a perennial point of confusion in Shotokan. The block that sets up next to the ear is called *soto uke, soto ude uke,* outside ude uke, or outside block by Nakayama, Nishiyama, Kanazawa, Enoeda and Ertl; uchi ude uke (inside forearm block) by Okazaki and Sugiyama; and *uchikomi* by Funakoshi. The block that sets up next to the opposite shoulder or hip is called uchi uke, uchi ude uke, inside *ude uke,* or *inside block* by Funakoshi, Nakayama, Nishiyama, Kanazawa, Enoeda and Ertl, and *soto ude uke* (outside forearm block) by Okazaki and Sugiyama. I use the conventions of Nakayama's ubiquitous *Best Karate* series to avoid confusion. By this convention, heian sandan begins with uchi ude uke, inside forearm block.

to maintain any remaining grip on your wrists at all. The double inside/downblock is a general-purpose let-go-of-my-arm tool.

The opening move of tekki shodan (naihanchi) doesn't look like a wrist release, but it works as one. You place your open hands together, fingertips pointed at the floor, as if guarding your groin. Then you drop your weight in the first step. If you are close to the senpai and drop your weight far enough, this move drives your arms down through his grip to the point where he has no control. Do what you will after that. (This works best if the senpai is a few inches taller than you are. In real life, a restraining opponent is usually taller than the victim.)

Figure 9-3: Wrist release, bassai dai, step 1. Bring the clasped hands (1) under the opponent's right forearm (2) and up to the outside. Leap forward and drive his crossed wrists back against his chest (3). He will often stagger backward and fall.[224]

---

[224] I first saw this technique in a class with Kyoshi Robert Stevenson, Technical Director of the International San Ten Karate Association. His senpai was knocked completely off his feet.

The opening of bassai dai is a dramatic wrist release and attack (See Figure 9-3). The senpai grabs your wrists as you prepare for the opening move of the kata. You rotate your forearms to the left and up to your shoulder, then jump in and slam your combined forearms into the senpai's chest. His arms get so twisted that he can't defend himself, and he often winds up sprawling on the floor as a result.

The opening of kanku dai can be interpreted as an elegant wrist release. It is sad that so many sensei write off this move as a symbolic or empty gesture. It is actually very practical.

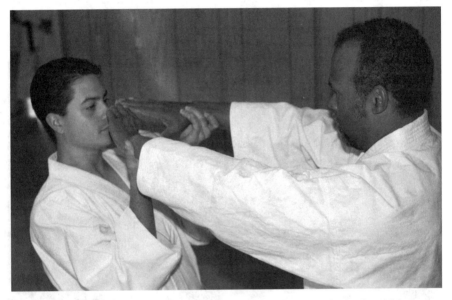

Figure 9-4: Wrist release, kanku dai, step 1. The opponent grasps both of your hands. The opening move of kanku dai breaks his grip. If he tries to hang on, poke his eyes.

Stand with your hands together in position to open kanku dai. Have the senpai grip your wrists as before. You will find that it isn't very difficult to raise your hands as prescribed by Itosu, especially if you keep your elbows close to your body. When your hands reach eye level, pretend to drive your fingertips at the senpai's eyes to break his concentration. He won't be able to prevent you from driving your fingers into his face. Then snap your arms up and outward to break his grip on your wrists (against the thumbs), exactly as in the kata.

How do you manage a wrist release when the enemy is just too big and too strong? Let's turn our attention to heian godan, step 15.

In this move we extend the left hand at full length and then smack the hand with a right crescent kick. The kicking leg drops into horse stance and we finish the move with a right elbow strike to the palm of the hand.

Have your senpai grip your left wrist with his right hand. Let the crescent kick pass above the hands, not striking anything, and then stamp downward into horse stance. This catches his forearm beneath

Figure 9-5: Wrist release, heian godan, step 15. When the attacker's grip (1) is just too strong, try this. Perform the crescent kick to loop your leg across his forearm (2), and drop your weight on his wrist to break free (3). You can follow through with the elbow strike as in the kata (4).

your right thigh as you stamp down, using the weight of your whole body to break the hold. If he manages to hang on anyway, this technique bends him forward so deeply that the following elbow strike catches him right in the ear.

I could go on at length. The kata are full of wrist releases. But are these bunkai practical? They are simple, easy to remember, and they work. What could be more practical than self-defense skills that make you difficult to hold?

Break Grips on Clothing

I'm sure every shotokan student knows that a person who grabs your jacket is asking to be punched. In the Shuri reception hall, Matsumura's billowing jacket would have been grabbed and held by barbarian hands. The kata include many devastating responses to a grip on your uniform jacket. This is a class of bunkai that is neglected entirely in most karate schools.

Let's begin with the lowly downblock, gedan barai, which is the first technique many of us learn in shotokan. Stand as if ready to begin a kata. Have senpai stand in front of you and grasp your right lapel with his left hand. Step back with your right foot into front stance, pulling his arm out straight, and do a standard left-hand gedan barai. Just swing your whole arm into the back of senpai's elbow, but be careful. Elbow breaks work on the first try.

Figure 9-6: Clothing release (arm break), heian shodan, step 1. This is a reminder that even the simplest techniques can be devastating. The opponent grasps your shirt with his left hand. Step back to straighten his arm and downblock the back of his elbow to break it.

Itosu's kata make use of a position called *koshi kamae*, where we stack one fist on top of another beside the hip. In my dojo we call this the "cup and saucer" position. The first place we see this kamae is in the seventh move of heian nidan, the instant before the side-snap kick. It reappears in *heian yondan* and kanku dai.

Figure 9-7: Clothing release, heian nidan, step 7. When grabbed in the area of the chest or shoulder (1) use koshi kamae to break his posture (2) before launching the kick and backfist strike (3).

Ertl and Bendickson have documented some very practical applications for this innocent-looking stackup.[225] For instance, you can have senpai grasp your jacket with either hand just about anywhere in the vicinity of the right chest or shoulder. Raise your arm to the outside, higher than the senpai's arm. Now do the cup-and-saucer stackup, with focus, to your left hip as in Heian Nidan step 7 (See Figure 9-7).

---

[225] *Shotokan Karate Applications*, Volumes 1-3, Ertl/Bendickson Productions, 1998. http://www.karatevid.com.

Your right forearm strikes sharply down into the fold of senpai's elbow, buckling his arm, forcing him to bend forward at the waist, and pinning his arm to your chest. He winds up in a very awkward and vulnerable position. In the kata the next move is usually a strike to the face and a kick to the groin.

There is a similar move in tekki sandan, where a person who grabs your jacket really regrets it an instant later (See Figure 9-8). Stand in horse stance and have senpai stand on your right. Senpai grabs your jacket at the right shoulder, using his left hand. You execute a slow *kake-te* with your right hand (tekki sandan, step 29), and rest the edge

Figure 9-8: Clothing release, tekki sandan, steps 29 and 30. Using the exact motions of the kata when grabbed at the arm (1), grasp the opponent's upper arm at the elbow (2). Twist the arm in against your hip as you launch the hook punch to the head (3).

of your hand in the fold of the senpai's elbow, grasping his upper arm firmly. Maintain this grip on his elbow as you execute the left hook punch (*kage zuki*, tekki sandan step 30). As your pullback hand draws back to your right hip, senpai's shoulder gets wrenched very painfully. To save his shoulder, senpai will bend forward and down, placing his head directly at the focus of the hook punch.

Kakiwake uke (wedge block) is no mystery to anyone. (See Figure 9-18.) We first encounter it in heian yondan, step 12. The opponent grasps the lapels of your jacket. You drive your fists up under his chin to break his concentration, and then strike down into the fold of the elbows to break his posture. Grip his wrists to hold him steady as you kick his belly out through his backbone.

Multiple Attackers

There are two places in kanku dai where enemies regret grabbing your jacket, and they illustrate the Shuri-te theme of dealing with multiple attackers. In the opening of kanku dai you raise your hands

Figure 9-9: Clothing release against multiple attackers, kanku dai, step 1. When grabbed by two opponents (1), take your arms over (2) and behind (3) the opponents' arms, then finish the move as in the kata. Watch the opponents spin and arch to avoid damage to the shoulder joint (4).

185

toward the sky, separate them, and then swing them down and forward until they meet in front of your abdomen (kanku dai step 1).

Have senpai and another student stand beside you and grasp the cloth of your jacket at the shoulder to restrain your arms (See Figure 9-9). Reach for the sky, separate sharply, and then draw your arms far to the rear and down so that you encircle the arms of the enemies to the side. Bring your hands together in front of your abdomen again, as prescribed by Itosu, and watch the contortions of your assistants as they spin around to avoid dislocating their shoulders!

Later in the kata there is a move where you raise your knee, bring your forearms together in front of your face, dive at the floor and then spring up again (kanku dai step 39). I had never seen a satisfactory bunkai for this move, in spite of stories about evading bo sticks and swords, until I tried this move while four of my students were hanging on to my jacket. All four yelped and landed on their backs on the floor. The dive is a very effective four-person throw (See Figure 9-10).

Figure 9-10: Clothing release against multiple attackers, kanku dai, step 39. Multiple opponents grasp your jacket (1). Trap their arms between yours (2) and dive to the ground (3). Spring back up immediately (4). (To avoid injury to your assistants, follow the directions in the text.)

This is how you do it. Have two assistants stand to your left. One grasps the cloth at your left shoulder with his left hand. The second assistant grasps your left lapel with his left hand. Now have two more assistants grasp your right shoulder and lapel using their right hands. This symmetrical arrangement is very artificial, but it helps the students roll out safely. If somebody uses the wrong hand, he's going to land on his face instead of his back. You also have to be sure that the students' elbows are bent, not locked, before you drop to the ground. Otherwise you are going to injure someone in your demonstration.

Swing your arms to the rear and then up in a circular motion so that you can catch their arms between yours as you slam your forearms together before the dive. Done correctly, this creates a "bouquet" of six elbows, all tightly pressed together in the same spot in front of your chest. Raise you knee and dive forward as prescribed by the kata. The four assailants cry out and sprawl on their backs. I have had no difficulty springing back up afterward. They are only too happy to let go of my jacket at that point.

A person who grabs your clothing has set himself up for a damaging response. Techniques like these *must* have been part of the Matsumura arsenal. Those haori topcoats they wore were just too easy to grab and hold.

Break Arm and Wrist Locks

It should come as no surprise that the shotokan kata show us how to break out of a hammer lock, where your arm is twisted up behind you.

Every beginner recognizes the escape from the hammer lock represented by heian sandan step 9. The enemy catches your extended right hand and applies a wrist lock, rotating your right wrist counter-clockwise from your point of view. This painful twist forces you to spin to your left into a hammer lock, which is a classic playground restraint hold. Unfortunately for him, you continue the turn to the left, using your hips to yank the captured arm straight (relieving your pain) as you whip an uraken into his temple.

Itosu liked to take a system of related moves and spread them out in multiple kata. Kanku dai step 50 shows us how to handle the parallel situation where the enemy twists the captured arm in the other direction as if setting up a classic wrist lock and throw. This time you duck your head under the captured arm as you spin, and then give

Figure 9-11: Arm lock release, heian sandan, step 9. You grab an opponent's lapel (1) and he applies a counterclockwise wrist lock (2). The pain forces you into a hammer lock (3), but you use your hips to yank your arm straight and follow through with an uraken into his temple (4).

him a hammerfist in the ribs for his trouble.

Shotokan makes use of a very limited number of linear kicks, as you may have noticed. These are the powerful kicks that transfer energy directly from your center to the opponent's center in a straight line. This kicking tool kit contains front snap kicks, front thrust kicks, side snap kicks, side thrust kicks, and back kicks. Using these few kicks (and either foot) you can stand in kumite kamae and kick directly to any point of the compass without turning the body. This makes it very difficult for an enemy to apply a wrist or arm lock to a shotokan fighter. No matter how the attacker twists you around, his pelvis and knees are never out of reach of your feet.

For now it is sufficient to note that the shotokan system includes responses to wristlocks and hammerlocks, as required by our analysis.

Break Hair Grips

In a rough-and-tumble situation, grabbing the other person's hair is a natural and powerful technique for taking control of his posture. A person who grabs a shotokan stylist is asking for a beating, of course, and nearly any strike or kick can effect a release from a hair grab. Let's look a little more deeply.

There are two obvious places in the shotokan kata where we grab an opponent's hair and use it to destroy him. Everyone will think of heian yondan, step 23, where we grab the opponent's hair with both hands before yanking his head down into our rising knee (step 24). The grip on his hair breaks his posture and pulls his face into position for a powerful finishing blow.

The other place is step 7 of empi. We perform a rising punch under the chin, grab the hair, and then yank the opponent's head toward our left shoulder as we spring in and punch into the bowl of the pelvis above the pubic bone, rupturing the bladder. In the following move, step 8, we turn away and do a downblock while still holding the hair.

Remember that the context created the karate. Nineteenth-century Okinawan men wore beards. Step 7 of empi works better if you grab the opponent's beard instead of his hair. Yank his chin over your shoulder as you strike his bladder with your left fist, and then use the

Figure 9-12: Breaking away from a hair pull, heian yondan, steps 9 and 10. Hold the attacking hand against your head to reduce the pain, and strike with the other hand. If he can reach your head, then you can reach his.

"downblock" to yank his chin down to knee level as you turn away. Given that he is collapsing in agony anyway, the extra yank on the beard can flip him into a somersault. Empi is called "the dumping kata" because it is full of throws.

All of that is beside the point, of course. What can you do when the opponent grabs *your* hair? *Yama-zuki* is a good candidate. Look at bassai dai, step 35. The opponent grabs your hair and pulls your head forward. You respond with a "mountain punch," driving your left fist into his face and your right fist into his groin. If he doesn't let go on the first try, do it a couple more times like we do in the kata.

The best counter to a hair-pull is to grab the opponent's hand and hold it firmly against your head while you counterattack. Let's look at steps 9 and 10 in heian yondan (See Figure 9-12). Have senpai stand in front of you and grab your hair with his right hand. Use your left open-hand upblock to grab his wrist and anchor his hand against your head. Then do shuto-uchi to the neck and kick him in a painful place. He'll let go.

Break Bear Hugs

A "bear hug" means to wrap your arms around a person and pin his arms. Does shotokan show you how to break a bear hug? Matsumura's agents would have needed this technique to avoid being caught and held by their opponents.

Figure 9-13: Rear hug release, heian sandan, steps 20 and 21, classical interpretation. In the classical interpretation of this move, the attacker gets an elbow in the ribs and a fist in the face.

190

Four applications come to mind immediately for breaking the front or back bear hug. The first comes at the end of heian sandan when you drop into horse stance and perform punches and elbow strikes to the rear (heian sandan, steps 19 to 21).

Have senpai pin your arms to your sides from behind. To escape, drop your weight suddenly into a low horse stance and execute the punch/elbow combination. It is very hard for senpai to prevent you from sliding down out of the hug.

Having said that, shotokan experts may have misunderstood the end of this kata. Perhaps we have one of those troublesome translation problems here.

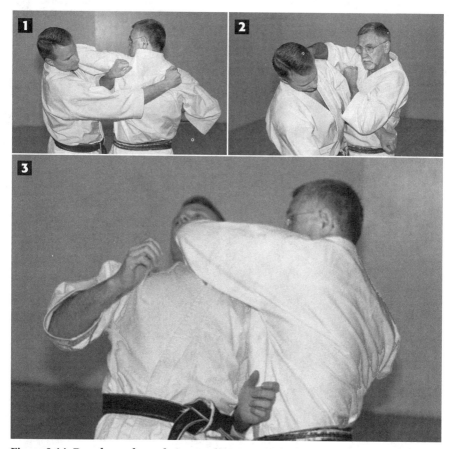

Figure 9-14: Rear hug release, heian sandan, steps 20 and 21, alternate interpretation.
You spin to face the opponent (1), and then use fists and elbows on him (2). The final elbow smash to the head has the whole weight of the body behind it (3).

Try this simple experiment. Perform heian sandan up to step 19. This is the left oi-zuki just before you spin around and drop into horse stance. Stop in that position and have senpai step up *behind you* (on the "north" side of you) and attempt to encircle your shoulders with his arms.

Now do movement 21. Spin around to face senpai, and as you turn you can strike him in the face with the back of your left elbow, your left hammerfist, right forefist, and right elbow in rapid succession. Rat-tat-tat-tat! All four blows use powerful body momentum as you shift to your left and drop into horse stance. This is the classic Matsumura use of momentum.

In movement 22, you shift sharply to your right and repeat the same set of blows in the opposite direction. Note that the final strike, the left elbow to the side of senpai's head or neck, is a lethal finishing technique worthy of a kiai. You don't have to modify the kata at all to achieve this bunkai. Just move the enemy to a different position.

Matsumura and Itosu liked to hit very hard. If you can't figure out the application of a technique in one of their kata, follow the body momentum to see where it leads. Momentum was their weapon.

Figure 9-15: Bear hug release, tekki nidan, step 1 and 2. Drop weight and spread elbows to break the hold, then use you knee and fists.

The opening to tekki nidan is a classic bear-hold release (tekki nidan steps 1 and 2). Your arms are pinned to your sides by a hug. Drop your weight and force your elbows up and to the sides to slide out of the hold. Then you drive your doubled fists sharply upward in front of you and fling off the attacker's arms as you step out of the hold.

Sensei usually say that the enemy who pins your arms is standing behind you. This release works even better if the enemy is in front. Those doubled fists come up right under his chin.

There is another bear-hug sequence in Hangetsu (steps 7-9). Someone pins your arms with a hug from behind. You force your elbows up to get some room, then push your thumb knuckles into the back of his hands to weaken his grip. Try it with senpai. You can't argue with those sharp knuckles (See Figure 9-16).

There is an outstanding escape from a rear bear hug in chinte, (steps 27 and 28). Senpai embraces you from behind, leaving your arms free. You bend forward at the waist and strike behind using both fists in a pincer movement, striking both sides of the opponent's rib cage using the sharp first knuckle of the fist. This is a very effective releaser. In the next movement you spin to the left to face the enemy

Figure 9-16: Rear hug release, hangetsu, steps 7 to 9. Sharp thumb knuckles pressed back into the attacker's hands, toward the chest break the attacker's grip.

and perform a second pincer. One fist strikes the center of his back at the same time as the other fist strikes the solar plexus.

Hangetsu contains one of the most elegant bear-hug releases. Have senpai embrace you from the front, arms pinned. Step forward in *hangetsu dachi*. Slip your foot between senpai's legs, and then around behind one of senpai's calves, so the back of your knee is against the back of his knee. Once in this position, a very slight motion of your hips sends senpai sprawling on his back. He always lets go as he falls.[226]

Finally, the opening move of empi is *very* close to a classic jujutsu throw that breaks a bear hug from the rear (empi step 1). From the opening *kamae*, with your hands at your left hip, you suddenly step to the left and kneel on your right knee. Your right arm appears to downblock, and the left fist winds up in front of your chest. Then you spring back up and continue with the kata.

The throw is called *seio otoshi*, the kneeling shoulder throw.[227]

Figure 9-17: Rear hug release, empi, step 1. It opens with seio otoshi, the kneeling shoulder throw. The opponent hugs you from behind, pinning your arms (1). You drop your weight, yank on his arm, and follow through to the final position (2).

---

[226] Australian sensei Gary Simpson is the master of unexpected bunkai from simple stances.

[227] Tegner, Bruce, *Complete Book of Jujitsu*, Thor, 1978, p. 97. See http://home.online.no/~thom-hal/Seio_otoshi_bilde.htm for a good set of photos, or any book on advanced judo/jujutsu technique.

Senpai hugs you from behind, pinning your arms. Drop your weight, yank on his arm, and over he goes.

Oddly, it doesn't seem to matter which of the opponent's arms you pull. If you yank on his left arm, as in the kata, he falls over your bent knee and your final position is very similar to the kata. If you yank on his *right* arm, as most jujutsu students would do, he pitches over your right shoulder instead. In this case, your final position after the throw is exactly the same as in the kata. Either way, it is clear that shotokan gives you tools to deal with front and rear hugs.

Break a Choke Hold

One easy way to take a person prisoner is to choke him unconscious. Judo players do it every day. You can choke a person with your hands, from the front or the rear. You can wrap your arm around his throat

Figure 9-18: Front choke defense, *kakiwake uke*, with takedown. (Based on heian yondan, step 12, and jion, step 2.) Pull your opponent's arms (1) while driving your knee into his groin (2). Once his posture is broken, step in for the hip throw (3) and *coup de grâce* (4).

from the rear for either an airway choke or a blood choke. Do the shotokan kata show us how to deal with these threats?

First we should mention that the bear-hug releases illustrated in the previous section are also excellent for countering an arm choke from the rear. Heian sandan, steps 20 to 21 (Figure 9-13) is made to order for the attacker who wraps his arm around your neck from behind. Applying the choke forces the attacker to place his face next to your ear where you can punch it easily. The opening throw of empi, step 1 (Figure 9-18), will hurl a choker right over your shoulder and onto the ground in front of you.

When the enemy stands in front of you and reaches for your throat with both hands, the standard shotokan response is kakiwake uke, the wedge block from heian yondan, step 12, or jion, step 2.

Figure 9-19: Choke release, nijushiho, step 17. The finger choke from behind (1) is easy to dislodge using this technique from nijushiho. Spin counterclockwise with arms extended to dislodge his hands from your throat (2). Capture his arms so he can't block the ridgehand strike to the temple (3).

Shotokan students often practice the wedge block followed by *hiza geri* and a takedown.

We see a similar response to a front choke in bassai dai, step 23. The enemy reaches for your throat or hair, and you respond by knocking his hands upward with *jodan awase-uke*.

One of my favorite choke defenses is the spinning "helicopter" move in nijushiho (step 17, just before the first kiai). Have senpai grasp your neck from behind with both hands, as if trying to squeeze your throat. Spin around counterclockwise to face him, swinging your left arm high as you turn to rip his hands off your throat and trap them under your left arm. Use the momentum of the sudden turn to power the ridge-hand strike to the temple.

Of course, for someone who can wield shotokan power, these special techniques are almost beside the point. Front snap kick and back kick tend to disrupt most attempts to choke us.

Stop a Tackle

Our barbarian enemies in the Shuri reception hall are American naval officers and Marines. They are not really trained in any sophisticated combat art, but they are brave as bricks. One of these guys is going to try to tackle you, knock you on your back, and sit on your chest. In the Shuri battle, it is death to lose your footing and sprawl on the floor. Therefore, Itosu's kata must show us how to deal with a tackler. Do they?

My first thought was that the shotokan kata are built on tai sabaki to a much greater extent than you see in the corresponding soft-style kata. Shotokan kata sidestep, shift and change direction constantly. Any one of these moves could evade a diving tackle.

The classic defense against a front tackle is hiza geri (knee kick). The enemy tries to tackle, and you knee him in the face as he comes in. There it is in Heian Yondan, step 24. Another defense is to strike strongly downward with *tettsui* (hammerfist) into the back of his neck as he tackles. There is a splendid opportunity for this in sochin, step 1.

Any one of us would think of *otoshi empi uchi*, of course. Most of the *soto ude uke* moves in the kata could also be downward elbow strikes if you stretch a point.

The most interesting tackle defense in shotokan, however, is the opening move of heian yondan.

Figure 9-20: Tackle release (neck lock), heian yondan, step 1. Stun the attacker with *teisho uchi* (palm-heel strike) (1). Trap his head between your palms (2). Twist counterclockwise to peel him off and drop him on his back (3).

In heian yondan you slap your hands down sharply toward your right hip, step to the left in back stance, and slowly execute a double, open-handed block to the upper left. This is one of the most enigmatic moves in shotokan. In 80 years nobody has published a convincing bunkai for it. I have searched widely. This move is so enigmatic that there aren't even any dinglehoppers for it.

Have senpai simulate the front tackle, turning his head to his left so that he hits you in the belly with his right shoulder (See Figure 9-20). Have him hug your hips. Look down at him. His head is by your right hip. Your first move is to strike the back of his head/neck with the heels of your open hands. If you drop your weight into it and use *kime* (focus), the enemy will be stunned by this blow.

Wrap your left hand around the back of senpai's head. Place your right hand underneath his face so that the heel of your right hand is against the right side of his jaw. Now, keeping very close to the motion prescribed in the kata, *slowly* twist his head 180 degrees counter-clockwise so that his nose points toward the ceiling. He'll let go of your hips to save his neck.

- If you execute this move slowly and powerfully, you'll peel the tackler off your body and move him into a very vulnerable, unbalanced posture. *This is the only way we should practice this move with a partner.*

- If you execute the move with more vigor, you can throw your enemy over on his back. You will do damage to his neck in the process. *Do not practice this vigorously.*

Briggs Hunt, the Olympic wrestling coach who was my first sensei, taught me this move in his dirty-fighting class at UCLA in 1971. You have to practice it very slowly because it is lethally dangerous... which might have something to do with the fact that Itosu wanted us to practice this move in slow motion. That idea is worth some thought. If true, it implies that other slow-motion steps in Itosu's kata are *also* joint locks of some kind. This often appears to be the case.

The opening double-block cluster in heian nidan (steps 1 to 3) can be used for this same purpose with a vicious addition. This time let's assume that senpai has a topknot and beard, as Okinawan gentlemen did 150 years ago. He tackles you; his head is by your right hip. Your left hand grips his topknot. You right hand grips his beard at the chin. Note that your hands are in the classic cup-and-saucer koshi kamae!

Do the double block very gently and watch senpai rotate his body to relieve the deadly pressure on his spine. Holding on to the topknot and beard, slowly explore the next two moves of the kata and watch what they do to senpai's neck. At combat speed, these moves would very nearly tear his head off. When I demonstrate this application, people look shocked. It's a murderous technique.

Practice this technique like you were working with a loaded gun. Don't be careless with senpai's spinal cord.

Are these the "real" bunkai of the openings of heian nidan and heian yondan? The applications certainly work. They are very practical. They might be bunkai, or they might be oyo. In either case, if you perform this neck-wrenching move at combat speed, your opponent will spend the rest of his life on a gurney. What could be more real than that?

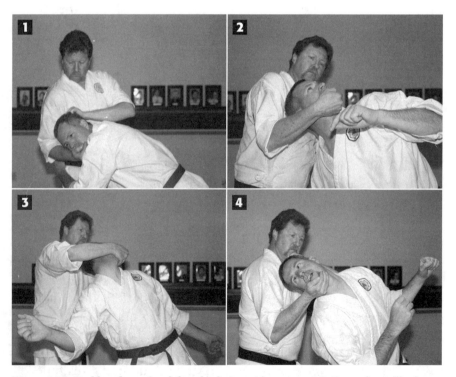

Figure 9-21: Tackle release (neck break), heian nidan, steps 1-3. Grasp the tackler by his topknot and beard (1). Rotate his head strongly to the left to spin his body (2) and arch his back. When his nose points directly to your left (3), snap his head back around 180 degrees to break the neck (4).

Burst Into the Crowd

Part of the Shuri battle plan involves plunging into the crowd of barbarians and sowing panic inside the mob for half a minute. How do you break through that first rank so you can disappear into the mob?

Any shotokan black belt will immediately think of the opening move of bassai dai, which is usually credited to Matsumura himself. The performer of bassai dai is supposed to feel like he is "bursting through the wall of a fortress." Sounds appropriate, doesn't it?

In bassai dai you perform the wrist release described earlier and then leap straight at the person who had been holding your wrists, striking him in the chest with your reinforced block (bassai dai, step 1, Figure 9-3). It is pretty simple to knock senpai straight over on his back with this move. That lets the warrior through the first rank, into the interior of the mob. I think it is significant that the performer turns around and attacks the first rank from the rear in the following move. He seems to be saying, "Hey! Don't look at the *regent*, gentlemen. Look at *me!*"

We see the same kind of explosive aggression in gankaku (chinto), another kata originally created by Matsumura. After a few clearing moves to break free of clinging enemies, the performer executes *nidan geri* straight into the front rank of the mob, landing inside (gankaku, step 7). Again, we momentarily spin around and engage the first rank from the rear before proceeding.

The knife-hand blocks in steps 8 to 11 of heian nidan provide a vicious technique for driving an opponent backward at high speed (backing him into the crowd). The first three steps are knife-hand blocks, but the secret lies in realizing that it is the stackup for the block that sweeps his arm aside. Knock the arm to the side with the stackup, and then strike shuto-uchi to the face, neck or collarbone. Immediately step in and do it again with the other hand, knocking his other arm to the outside with the stackup and then striking at the head with the block. The only way he can avoid the blows to the face is to backpedal rapidly. Three steps into the crowd, you use your left hand to deflect his left punch again, but this time you grab his wrist, push it down, and drive a nukite into his throat with a kiai.

Bassai, gankaku and heian nidan are all credited to Matsumura as the original author. Matsumura was very aggressive.

Rapid Tai Sabaki

To survive as the lone fighter in a crowd of enemies, you must be hard to follow and hard to catch—like a rabbit dodging a pack of coyotes.[228] This implies many rapid changes of direction. Does shotokan teach us how to do that?

Shotokan uses rapid stepping, shifting and turning as an engine for generating raw power to put into technique. Naturally we must change direction quite a lot in our kata because otherwise we'd run right out of the room. This is just a fact of life in shotokan.

If you need documentation, take a look at the opening moves of kanku sho (steps 1-4) where the performer shifts east/west/south/north in rapid succession. You'll find the same pattern in hangetsu (steps 13 to 21). Sudden changes of direction are built in to the enbusen of all of the H-shaped kata, too.

Shotokan (Shuri-te) is shifty. We don't just root like a tree and fight it out in one spot, except in the tekki kata and one or two others that Funakoshi selected for us to study.

Stun/Maim/Kill with One Strike

You can't fight a crowd of military officers barehanded for very long unless you can put each person out of the fight in about two seconds. If you can deal with each opponent that swiftly, you can shift quickly from one man to another and keep on moving through the crowd. After each engagement you spin around, select a new target, strike him *once*, and move on. This ability is a requirement of the Shuri battle plan.

How do you disable a person in two seconds or less? There are four general ways to do it:

- Hit him *very* hard (ikken hisatsu).

- Break a joint.

- Break a bone.

- Maim him. Destroy his eyes, ears or throat.

---

[228] Or a thescelosaur dodging a velociraptor. See Figure 3 of Hamilton, E.L., et al., *Pursuit-Evasion Games in the Late Cretaceous*, Calvin College, 2004. http://www.mathmodels.org/problems/21831/solutions/001/body.html

Any one of these four approaches can make a fighter helpless in two seconds or less. Do the shotokan kata teach these techniques? Yes, undoubtedly.

Breaking Joints

The shotokan kata are full of elbow-breaking techniques. If you break a man's elbow, he stops fighting. Most of the inside blocks (uchi ude uke) in the kata work nicely as elbow breaks. For instance, many of the inside blocks in bassai dai work as elbow breakers.

It's widely heard that heian nidan step 2 is an elbow-snapper. In fact, elbow breaks are so common in Itosu's kata that the obvious need not be harped upon.

What about knees? Does shotokan teach us how to attack knees?

Actually, shotokan is remarkably quiet about attacks to the knees. The knee is the primary self-defense target, yet we rarely practice attacks to knees in the kata and almost never in the dojo. Why? Because knee attacks are incompatible with the *do*. You can't follow the path for a lifetime if you let your students practice knee attacks. Sooner or later one of your students will cripple you. Then you'll be sidelined for life.

Have senpai step back and downblock, showing you a nice, deep front stance. Sit on the floor in front of him and take a look at his knee. Warn senpai that when he feels pain, he should immediately relax and sit down on the floor. Now place your hand against the inner side of the knee joint and press slowly outward. Move the knee gently sideways to the outside of the stance. You can move the knee only a couple of inches before senpai abruptly cries out and collapses.

The knee is very delicate and vulnerable. This is another one of those "loaded gun" experiments. Don't be careless with senpai's knees. If you kick a person's knee to the outside in this fashion, you'll rip his knee apart and cripple him for life. In fact there are sensei who hobble around in knee braces because of this injury.

The few places in Itosu's kata where we make some sharp, circular motion with a foot can be made to fit this model without difficulty. Nami gaeshi, for instance, the returning wave kick in tekki shodan (steps 29 and 32), is a brutal knee-buster. Many sensei say that the returning wave kick is an attempt to block a front snap kick to the groin. However, I personally believe this is an inaccurate application.

Once you are sensitized to the potential of sweeping the opponent's knee to the side—a move you must *never* do in kumite—you'll start to see opportunities appearing in the kata. You'll find nami gaeshi knee sweeps in stackups for other moves, such as steps 12, 14 and 16 of heian sandan, and steps 37 and 39 of bassai dai.

Be very careful experimenting with knees. Orthopedic injuries are permanent. The knees of our partners are so vulnerable to our slightest mistake that hard-style karateka avoid the knee entirely in contests, in class and even in the kata. Itosu practiced karate for almost 70 years. He saw people crippled by knee kicks. We don't want to see it in our classes.

Breaking Bones

If you can take a person out of the fight in two seconds by breaking a joint, you can also do it by breaking a bone. You can break almost any bone in the body if you try hard enough, but the easy targets are the neck, collarbone, jaw, ribs, hand and foot bones. Did Itosu show us how to attack these targets?

Shotokan's deadly shuto uchi to the side or back of the neck is in plain sight in heian yondan (step 9), and in several parts of kanku dai. Those combinations of shuto uke and shuto uchi at the end of heian shodan and the middle of heian nidan can easily be interpreted as strikes

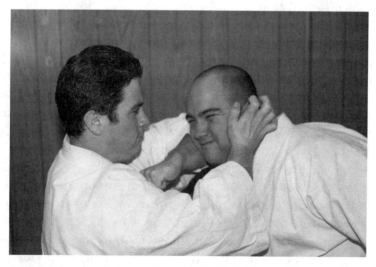

Figure 9-22: Jaw breaker, heian yondan, step 6. Catch the mandible between the elbow and the palm-heel strike. It breaks at the corner of the chin.

to the collarbone or neck as you prefer. We stamp on the opponent's feet regularly in several kata, breaking delicate metatarsal bones. We attack the metacarpal bones in the back of the opponent's fist in tekki sandan, step 10. What about attacks to the jaw and the ribs?

Have you ever broken a "wishbone" from a chicken or turkey? It's a U-shaped bone. Children pull the ends apart until the bone breaks, and the child with the biggest fragment gets his wish. You can also snap a wishbone by squeezing the tips of the bone together. It breaks at the top of the arch. U-shaped bones are easy to break if you compress the free ends together. The mandible (jawbone) and ribs are classic U-shaped bones.

To break a man's jaw, place the heel of your left hand against the corner of his jaw below his right ear (See Figure 9-22). Now apply a powerful elbow strike against the opposite side of the jawbone, beneath the left ear. Use the technique you have practiced countless times in heian yondan (step 6 and step 9), where you do a head-level elbow strike into the palm of your hand. Catch his jaw between the palm and the elbow and the bone will break next to the chin.

It works the same way on a rib. Place your right hand on the opponent's back below his left shoulder blade. Direct the left elbow strike at the front of the chest, about two inches below his left nipple. Ribs crack under the arm. I usually think of this in terms of tekki shodan, step 3. You do a backhand block to open him up, slip your hand behind his back, and slam your other elbow into his chest. A person with a broken rib doesn't even want to breathe, let alone fight.

In our previous discussion of the knee, we talked about sweeping the knee to the outside for a crippling joint attack. Of course you can also sweep or kick the knee in the other direction, from the outside toward the inside of the stance, which forces the enemy to kneel abruptly. This can destroy the knee also, but is rendered much worse by stamping down on the back of his calf while he is kneeling. This breaks one or both lower leg bones, or at least damages the knee joint, ankle, toes and foot. This is a brutally effective interpretation of the horse-stance sequence in the second half of heian sandan. Kick his knee to the inside and then stamp down on the back of his calf. People with broken legs don't chase you around the room.

The special technique found in tekki sandan, step 10. Begins with a lower-level block (*oshi-uke*) with the right hand. The opponent grabs your wrist. You free your wrist by making a large, circular motion, putting pressure against his thumb. The finish occurs when you whip your knuckles sharply downward against the back of his hand. This strike breaks a metacarpal bone in the back of the hand. This injury, seriously interferes with one's fighting ability.

It is safe to say that Itosu showed us how to immobilize a man in two seconds by breaking a bone. In fact, most of these techniques don't require even one second.

Figure 9-23: Leg breaker, heian sandan, step 16. Sweep the knee from the outside to collapse his stance (1). Stomp down on the back of the calf to break the fibula, wrench the ankle, sprain the toes or cause a variety of other injuries (2, 2a).

Figure 9-24: Metacarpal break, tekki sandan, step 10. This was a favorite technique of Kanryo Higaonna, Itosu's friend from Naha.

Figure 9-25: *Nihon nukite* **attack to the eyes. Chinte, step 23.** If you put shotokan power behind it, this is much more than just a finger in the eye. There is no reason that it cannot penetrate the eye socket.

Maiming Soft Tissue

Finally, let's take up soft-tissue injuries, especially maiming attacks to the eye, ears and throat. These are soft-tissue targets that can abruptly end a man's ability to fight. We ought to find them in the kata.

Any punch can be an attack to the eye, but the two-finger poke to the eyes (nihon nukite) is the classic attack. We don't see eye pokes in the beginning and intermediate shotokan kata, but you'll see it when you learn chinte (step 23). Jam your finger into a person's eye and he won't think about anything else for some time. It is possible to make the finger rigid and put shotokan power behind it, and actually burst through the paper-thin sheet of bone behind the eye, into the brain cavity.

Briggs Hunt, my first combat teacher, says he did this to a Japanese soldier on a Pacific island in World War II. The attack killed the soldier but broke one of Hunt's fingers. He spent weeks crawling through the jungle with his finger tied to a crude splint. Hunt used to wave his crooked finger at me and warn me never to try that stupid technique!

Attack the ears by slapping them with your open palms—as in heian yondan, step 23. At the end of the kata, first clap your hands against the opponent's ear canals, *then* grab his hair and knee him in the face. This attack does damage to the balance mechanism, inducing violent vertigo. The victim can't walk for hours or days, not to mention causing permanent damage to his hearing. However, don't slap senpai's ears unless you want to give your house to lawyers.

The throat is one of the most vulnerable targets on the human body. A solid blow to the trachea or larynx can be lethal because the airway swells shut. We generally avoid practicing this attack in the dojo because it is so dangerous. There's a surprise ridgehand strike to the throat in jitte (step 3).

It's common knowledge that the testicles are an effective soft-tissue target. Even so, it is worth mentioning that many senseis identify heian godan steps 22 and 25 as a grab at the opponent's testicles. You slip past his punch, grab the package, and yank on it. Then you downblock the package with the other hand to add insult to injury.

Did Itosu show us how to attack the soft-tissue targets? Yes, they are all there, but you'll notice one odd thing. The eye and throat attacks are not in the beginning or intermediate shotokan kata, which Itosu taught in public schools. He thought the kids might get into trouble. We should follow his lead and reserve the eye/ear/throat attacks for the advanced students, or for students who have an immediate need for self-defense skills, such as young females. We don't want to see those techniques used on a playground by young children. They work too well.

One-Punch Stops

To stop a person with only one punch, you must hit him in exactly the right spot or you must hit him *extremely* hard.

Hard stylists don't do kata where you pretend that you are standing in a rowboat and can't move. We *move*. Compared to soft-style kata, hard-style kata are very dynamic. Hard stylists use long, low stances to take big steps rapidly around the floor. There is a fundamental reason for this: it generates momentum and momentum creates impact. This was Matsumura's big contribution to karate.

Linear momentum techniques are everywhere in the shotokan kata. There is no need to belabor the obvious.

Force a Path Through the Crowd

Until I worked out the requirements of the Shuri reception hall plan, it never occurred to me to use karate to scythe a path through a dense crowd. How would you use karate if your goal was simply to knock people out of the way?

It seems to me you would want your opponents to sprawl headlong to the left and right, perpendicular to your line of advance. That way they can't grab your feet from the ground as you pass, and you don't have to walk on their bodies.

There is a way to do this, and it is visible in several of the kata. It is usually in the second half of the kata, which is where we would expect to find it.

There are three historical points to bear in mind here. First, Kanryo Higaonna, Itosu's friend from Naha, was a master of unexpected kicks to the legs and knees. Itosu would have been interested in this unusual skill. Second, Chotoku Kyan knew a technique for cutting through an angry crowd without using his hands. Third, shotokan is amazingly silent about attacks to the knees. The subject is simply taboo in many dojo.

But wouldn't the Shuri bodyguards have attacked knees? Knee attacks must be somewhere in the inventory.

Have you ever wondered what *kiba dachi* (horse stance) is really for? Horse stance is a general-purpose platform for launching a variety of vicious attacks on knees. These attacks send the enemies sprawling out of your path. You can use your hands to help, but you don't have to.

Warning! These techniques are not practiced in shotokan dojo because the risk of permanent orthopedic injury is high. Do not attempt these techniques at full speed. Do not allow students to practice these techniques unsupervised.

How do you cut through a crowd? Suppose you were to step forward aggressively in horse stance like we do in heian sandan, jion, jiin, and jitte. Time each step to impact the lead knee of the next opponent as you force your way through the crowd.

In some cases, you can use your knee to drive the opponent's knee to the outside of his stance, breaking his balance and throwing him to the ground. Sometimes you can impact his knee from the outside inward, collapsing his front leg so that he has to kneel. You can also simply step in and hook your leg around behind his lead knee in a deep kiba dachi stance. In that position, simply turn toward the opponent in front stance and watch him collapse on the floor. See Figure 9-26, Figure 9-27 and Figure 9-28. These are elegantly simple moves to apply. This solution would be especially effective if it caught the fighters by surprise, and it only needs to work very briefly to satisfy the exit phase of the battle.

At this point let's take another look at the story of Chotoku Kyan at the cockfight. He fought his way through an angry crowd so effortlessly that he never had to let go of his fighting cock. Arakaki and Shimabuku were astonished. The knee attacks described here are so devastating that you hardly need to use your hands in the fight. This may be the explanation of Kyan's effortless passage through the mob.

Oddly enough, there is another karate application that can be used to quickly and economically hurl opponents out of your way as you advance across the room. It is easy to apply, and requires almost no strength. The warrior who was punching at your face one second finds himself lying on his back behind you the next second. This technique, too, is encountered in a triple sequence in gankaku, marching resolutely back toward the finish line. It is manji uke. It is a throw. It is probably not the throw you are thinking of.

Manji uke is the double block we first encounter in steps 23 and

Figure 9-26: Forcing a path through a crowd. In the first encounter of this series (1), the fighter pushes the opponent's knee to the outside (1a), breaking her stance and forcing her to fall on the ground (2).

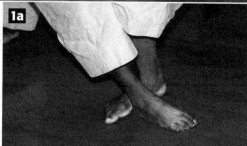

Figure 9-27: Forcing a path through a crowd. In the second sequence (1), the fighter breaks an opponent's stance by forcing the lead knee to the *inside* (1a), then finishes off the opponent with teisho uchi, as in jion (2).

Figure 9-28: Forcing a path through a crowd. In the third sequence (1), the fighter uses kiba dachi (side stance) to slip his foot inside and behind the opponent's lead knee (1a). Then he shifts into front stance and steps forward (2). That's all it takes to throw the opponent out of the path.

26 of heian godan. Settle into a back stance with your left foot forward. You left hand will downblock, so stack up next to your right ear. Your right hand will do a high forearm block to the rear, so stack up by reaching forward at middle level. To execute the block, pull your hands apart in a "ripping" motion. That's the advice of Funakoshi.

Have senpai step forward and punch oi zuki (front punch), right foot forward and right punch extended. Slide into position so that your left knee presses against the outside of his right knee. Pretend you just blocked his punch with a left outside forearm block. There you are, punching and blocking with knees touching.

Move your right hand forward and grip his right wrist. Lift his arm slightly so you can stack up for the downblock beneath his arm. Now you're all ready to do the double block. It seems as if you are going to yank on his arm while striking his body with your downblock, doesn't it?

This is exactly correct, but with one tiny difference. Lift his captured arm up above your head and bring his forearm around against the back of your neck. Now straighten your back and do a picture-perfect manji uke, just like in the kata. Senpai will flip sideways over your extended left leg and land on his back behind you. The path ahead is clear.

This throw is very easy to set up, and can be applied virtually any time you can catch the opponent's right wrist with your right hand. Of course, the symmetrical throw (left wrist, left hand) works just as well.

Throw an Enemy at His Friends

Shotokan stylists have a very strange relationship with throws. The few throws we practice are always one-on-one competition techniques that put an opponent on the ground without hurting him. From the point of view of the bodyguards, any throw that fails to do vicious injury is a dinglehopper. You don't throw an opponent on the ground. You throw him *at another opponent*. This is another Shuri technique that is too dangerous to practice.

There are places in the shotokan kata where we open a gap in the crowd by hurling an enemy soldier through the air toward two or three of his friends. This would be a throw in the exit phase of the kata, where the victim's body flies in the direction of the exit door (the finish line). We have a real-life example in which shorin-ryu karate

Figure 9-29: Manji uke as a throw, heian godan, step 23. Catch your opponent's right wrist in your right hand (1) loop it *behind* your neck and slip in behind his right knee with your left foot. Straighten your back. The opponent flies out of your way (2).

master Yabu Kentsu, a student of Itosu, broke up an attack by a gang of robbers by throwing one of them at the others.[229]

We have an obvious example in the exit from empi, where we pick up an enemy and throw him toward the finish line using a shoulder wheel throw (*kata garuma*, empi, steps 35 and 36). I propose that we are hurling his body into two other soldiers who are blocking our escape. Then we leap over the pile of struggling bodies and back out the door. It seems like this might be a useful technique for exiting a bar fight. (Toss the bartender at the bouncers, jump over the bodies, and run for the car.)

A similar situation plays out at the end of kanku dai (steps 56 to 60). You catch an enemy's wrist and spin around with his arm locked over your left shoulder. This puts you in position for an over-shoulder-lock throw.[230] Very well, let's throw the enemy's body straight toward the finish line, knocking down our next opponent. Then we'll jump over the two prostrate bodies to engage a third opponent. This interpretation exactly fits the moves of the kata.

Iain Abernethy points out that heian sandan steps 19 and 20, usually

---

[229] Kim, 1974, p. 66.

[230] Tegner, 1978, p. 128-129. Tegner didn't include the Japanese name of the throw, but the photos issued make the application quite clear.

interpreted as breaking a bear hug (See Figure 9-13 and Figure 9-14), is precisely correct for a simple hip throw.[231] This would be a case where we grab the last enemy who is blocking the door and hurl him into the crowd.

Itosu allowed only a handful of judo or jujutsu throws to appear in the hard-style kata. Notice that none of them are *sutemi waza* (sacrifice throws). This is another place where a missing class of techniques reinforces our image of the Shuri battle plan. We're drilling for a battle that we can't win on the floor. We do all our techniques standing up.

Use a Human Shield

This idea comes from an analysis of naihanchi (tekki shodan). In this kata, hugging an injured enemy to your chest as a human shield feels like a very natural thing to do, particularly if you are outnumbered, unarmed and have to meet every attack head-on. It also explains some of the mysteries of this kata, such as why the performer doesn't seem concerned about protecting his groin. When you hug an enemy to your chest, your groin is covered. With your back to a wall, only your head and your feet are vulnerable. (Tekki shodan aggressively defends the head and the feet.) And again, using this interpretation makes unexpected bunkai pop out of the kata.

Assume that you have your back to the person you are protecting, and a crowd of enemies is pressing upon you from the front and sides. Most of them are trying to grasp your jacket and drag you away from your principal.

From position 3, the elbow strike pose, pull senpai across in front of you, with his back to your chest (See Figure 9-30). Step 6, normally considered a hook punch, wraps around senpai's chest and hugs him tightly. The back of the thumb knuckle digs deeply into senpai's newly-broken ribs. In real life, this would be excruciating. Given Itosu's great strength, he would not have had much trouble supporting and controlling his human shield in this fashion. Itosu could have compressed the man's chest to the point that he could not breathe at all.

From step 6 on, you have senpai clinched tightly to your chest. The rapid blocks and strikes of steps 8 through 10 flow perfectly

---

[231] Abernethy, 2000, p. 39.

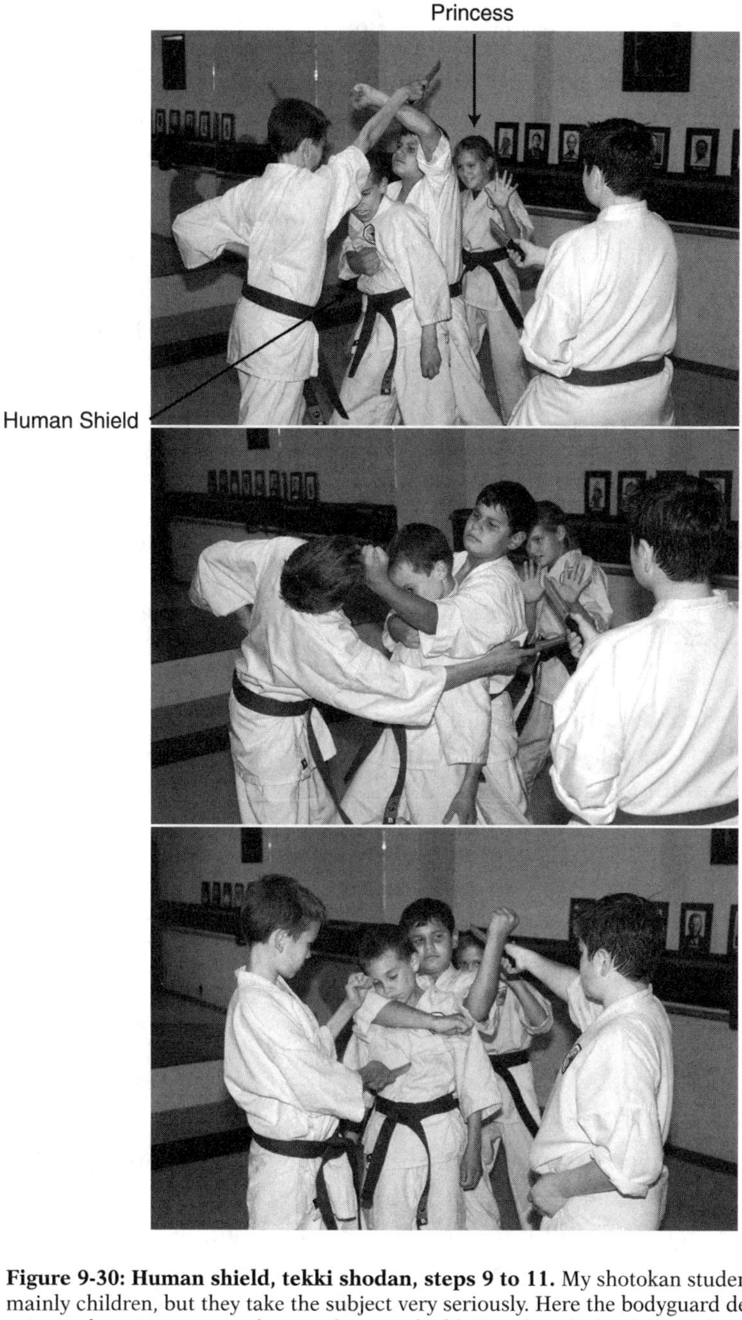

Figure 9-30: Human shield, tekki shodan, steps 9 to 11. My shotokan students are mainly children, but they take the subject very seriously. Here the bodyguard defends the princess by using one attacker as a human shield. Note how little of the performer's body is exposed to attack.

around the trapped body. The downblocks in this section release senpai's body for brief moments. They need to recoil instantly to catch senpai's body again, but that's not difficult at full speed.

Notice how steps 11 through 16 (the nami gaeshi kicks and supported blocks) jerk senpai's torso left and right with ease, maneuvering him into the path of incoming attacks. This is the most sensible bunkai I have ever seen for this sequence. The traditional explanation, that the horizontal supporting arm is "protecting the solar plexus" is very weak, and begs the question of why the performer's groin is left wide open to a kick? With the human shield in place, both the solar plexus *and* the groin are covered.

The nami gaeshi kicks can be used either to defend the feet against stomping attacks from the side, or as sweeps to pull an opponent in close enough to strike him in the face with that supported block. There is no need to attempt the improbable feat of blocking a kick from the front. The shield prevents that attack from occurring.

This interpretation of the kata really startled me when I reached step 20, which is the second elbow strike, just after the first kiai. At this point senpai is held tightly in the crook of your right arm. Your left hand reaches out and hooks behind the head of another enemy on your left. Now perform the elbow strike as required by the kata. You'll find that it bangs their heads together very sharply! For someone with Itosu's strength, that would be a very satisfying application.

The human shield is a special technique that probably doesn't have much application in modern self-defense, but it is worth exploring now and then with your students. For one thing, it turns tekki shodan into a practical fighting kata instead of a mysterious dance whose meaning has been "lost in the mists of time." The moves are the same as before, but in the Shuri Crucible the moves make sense.

Jumps and Dives

Jumps and dives are not subtle. Sometimes a weapon comes at you in a horizontal sweep that you can't sidestep. You have to employ vertical tai sabaki—straight up or straight down—to avoid being cut. In the case of diving to the floor, we might be avoiding a bullet. Never forget those Marines in the corner of Figure 3-4. Their rifles can be primed and ready about 30 seconds after the fight begins. If you glance up and see the muzzle of a Springfield rifle drawing down on you, it's time to throw yourself at the ground.

Even though our power comes from the floor, we'd don't want to lie down on it. Notice how quickly we bounce up again after touching the ground in the kanku kata. People debate the meaning of these dives to the ground. They have missed the point. The lesson of kanku is not how to dive; it is how to spring up again before someone jumps on your back.

Leap Past a Blocking Enemy

When we discussed clearing a path through the crowd, the idea was to knock people rapidly out of the way so you could make forward progress toward the exit. Suddenly you're faced with Sergeant Brutus, the man-mountain. His legs are like tree trunks and his wrists are so big and sweaty you can't get a grip on them. For some reason, this guy always shaves his head.

You can't take him out because he's just too big and too stupid to understand that he's been killed. You have to bypass him instead. He hauls back his right fist and swings at your head.

The solution to this problem lies in the *sankaku tobi* (triangle jump), formerly shotokan's most top-secret technique (See Figure 9-31). It is the jump at the end of *meikyo* (steps 31 to 33). Funakoshi taught this move to very few people.

You are in left front stance, standing on a narrow ledge on the face of a cliff. The cliff rises as a sheer wall to your left, and falls away in a drop to certain death on your right. There is an opponent in front of you, blocking your way. Behind you other enemies are approaching, so you can't retreat. What do you do?

The enemy in front attacks to the head with a right oi-zuki. You block the attack with your left hand and grab the attacker's arm. Your right hand strikes his head or neck with a hammerfist, and you keep your right forearm pressed tightly against his neck/shoulder as you leap past his left shoulder. As you leap, you turn 180 degrees in midair so you land in right back stance facing his back. By maintaining your grip on his arm and shoulder, you have spun him halfway around into an awkward, off-balance position. A slight additional pull on the arm and push on the neck spins him over the edge of the cliff.[232]

---

[232] Based on personal communication from sensei Ricardo Llewelyn, 6th dan, President of the International San Ten Karate Association.

Meikyo is Funakoshi's personal adaptation of one of Itosu's three Rohai kata, which are thought to have originated with Matsumura. The triangle leap comes straight from the Shuri master of changing disadvantage into advantage. We should not be surprised.

Figure 9-31: Triangle jump, meikyo, steps 31 to 33. You are trapped between enemies on a narrow ledge, indicated by the white line on the floor (1). You have to leap past the blocking enemy (2) before the other one strikes (3).

Stealing Weapons

For unarmed fighters facing a mob of armed opponents, the ability to steal weapons from the enemy is very desirable. In aikido these techniques are referred to as *tachi dori* (sword stealing) which will functiion as a general term for stealing any type of weapon.

Warning! Practicing with live, edged weapons can result in severe injury. It is recommended that you use a rubber knife, a *shinai* (practice sword), and a bo stick for your practicing.

"Karate" is known as the fighting art that uses no weapons. If you pursue the *do*, this is all you need to know. If you pursue the *jutsu*, (skill or technique) however, karate is the art that *steals weapons and uses them*. A karate man with a weapon is the equal of 10 karate men with empty hands.

Is there historical evidence that the Shuri protectors were adept at stealing weapons? There is the story of Azato disarming the sword master, and a somewhat unsavory story of Itosu taking a sai from an assailant and then driving the point through his heart.[233] Both men were acquainted with Kosaku Matsumora, the master of wet-towel disarming. The Shuri bodyguards had some good mentors in tachi dori.

The shotokan moves for arming yourself with an opponent's weapons are almost all on display in heian godan. That makes heian godan a very special kata.

Steal One-Handed Weapons

Here comes an angry naval officer, running at you with his saber upraised above his head. Give senpai some harmless object like a yardstick to swing. Have him hold it in his right hand and stand in right zenkutsu dachi. Have him swing the yardstick in a vertical cut (straight down) toward your head.

You have to leap in with your left foot forward and intercept senpai's descending forearm using an open-handed X upblock, as in heian godan, step 9. (Always block the arm, never the weapon.) Using the exact motions of the kata, grasp senpai's wrist with your right hand

---

[233] Kim, 1974, p. 30.

Figure 9-32: Catching a saber, heian godan, steps 9 through 12. Use the X-block to catch the attacker's wrist (1). Pull the arm down and break the elbow (2). Slide the hilt out of the attacker's nerveless fingers (3). Step forward and thrust with the point (4).

(See Figure 9-32). Pull his arm down and back to your right hip, while twisting his arm so that the back of the arm and elbow are facing up. (Sugiyama illustrates this very clearly in step-by-step illustrations in heian godan step 10.)

The next step in this technique, which is widespread in self-defense classes, is to use your left fist to hammer down on the opponent's elbow, breaking his arm. (Be careful with senpai.)

Once the arm is broken, it is child's play to let your grip slip down his wrist to the hilt of the saber. You'll find it isn't difficult to take a natural grip on the hilt and pull the weapon from his nerveless fingers. It comes out of his grip with the point already aimed at his chest. The final move of this cluster (heian godan, step 12) is to lunge forward, thrust to the chest and kiai. No wonder. The saber goes right through his heart.

This move works for other one-handed weapon attacks such as swinging a club or stabbing downward with a knife. Or you can catch a simple punch with it and break the elbow.

The other dramatic weapon-stealing technique occurs at the end of heian godan (and reoccurs in other kata). In step 22, we lunge forward in a long left zenkutsu dachi, sweep an attack aside with the left hand, and reach deeply forward with the right hand as if trying to grab the other person's belt. Shotokan sensei usually say that this is a strike to the groin, or that we are grabbing the enemy's leg so that we can yank it off the ground and throw him on his back. These interpretations are all right, but they shortchange a very exciting and versatile technique.

Have senpai stick the yardstick through his belt at the left hip, is if it were a sheathed saber or wakizashi. Then have him attack you with

Figure 9-33: Stealing a saber, heian godan steps 22 and 23. You can sweep the punch, reach in deeply, and pluck a weapon from the opponent's belt.

a right oi-zuki. Sweep the punch aside with your left hand and reach deeply forward with the right. Grasp the hilt of the saber and pull it from its sheath as you jump back. It comes free with the point directed at the enemy.

In the next move of the kata, we perform the same technique on the opposite side, but pay attention to the stackup in heian godan, step 25. As you pivot to the left, you can't help making a horizontal cut across senpai's throat with the saber. Then you block his next attack by cutting his forearm, and finish by slashing his thigh, in step 26. If you want to show off, you can have senpai carry two swords, like samurai warriors did, and steal them both in quick succession with this maneuver.

If you can steal a saber from a scabbard, you can steal a pistol from a holster—even a shoulder holster. Matsumura knew about pistols and holsters.

Steal Two-Handed Weapons

You can use this same technique to steal a bo or a rifle/bayonet out of the hands of a soldier who tries to jab you in the chest with it. I first recognized this technique years ago while thumbing through a World War II Army manual on unarmed combat.[234]

Give senpai a bo or jo stick and tape a rubber knife to the end just for fun. You need a vivid idea of where the bayonet is in order to appreciate the technique.

Have senpai stand in a left front stance, pointing the rifle at your chest in bayonet-fighting fashion See Figure 9-35). (If he were to raise the rifle to fire it, he'd have his right index finger on the trigger.) Have him lunge forward as if trying to stab you in the chest with the bayonet.

Slap the bayonet to your right with your left hand, performing heian godan step 22 again. Reach in deeply with your right hand and grasp the buttstock of the weapon immediately *behind* senpai's right hand. Use your left hand to strike the forearm[235] of the weapon up and back toward senpai's face. This sharp strike often pops the weapon out of senpai's left hand entirely. Shove the barrel of the rifle toward senpai's face with your left hand as you yank the butt of the rifle

---

[234] Basic Field Manual, *Unarmed Defense for the American Soldier,* June 30, 1942, FM 21-150, p. 202-218. The Army got the hand positions reversed, but the principle is there.

[235] The wooden grip that supports the barrel is known as the forearm of the rifle.

Figure 9-34: Basic bayonet drill. Modern armies don't do much bayonet drill because their weapons are too short and are made of plastic instead of hardwood. Stab with the point (1). Strike to the head with the butt (2). Pull back (3). Smash the face with the butt (4). Rake the face with the blade (5). Begin again at step one. (This drill is excellent for use with a kitchen broom.)

toward your right hip with your right hand. The rifle spins 180 degrees and ends up under your control. The barrel of the rifle hits senpai in the face pretty sharply, too, which helps break his grip. An instant later the bayonet slices down the length of his face and chest. When you finish in the manji uke pose (step 23), you have the rifle raised over your head with the bayonet pointed straight at his heart. You can skewer him easily, but in terms of the Shuri battle there is no need. He's out of the fight anyway. The gun-barrel impact on the face is a stunner.

If you can avoid the opponent's initial lunge, the rest of the technique is very easy to perform. This is a place where *sen no sen* timing is crucial.

This same technique can also be used against a vertical cut with a

Figure 9-35: Stealing a rifle/bayonet, heian godan, steps 22 and 23. Slip past the bayonet and lunge deeply forward, slapping the weapon to your right with your left hand (1). Catch the neck of the rifle in your right hand (2). Yank the butt of the rifle toward your hip as you strike the forearm of the rifle into the enemy's face (3). Pull the weapon free and use it (4).

Japanese katana, although it is more risky. The vertical cut at the head begins with the swordsman raising the weapon over his head. Then he steps forward and brings the weapon down on the victim's head or shoulder using a two-handed grip.

Take another look at Figure 6-3, and set aside all thought of trying this with a real katana. Have senpai use a padded *chanbara* (sword fighting) sword. Have him lift it up with both hands and cut vertically down at your head.

Timing is everything. Leap in as before (heian godan, step 22) and deflect the descending sword to the right using your left hand and forearm. If you slap the blade to the side with the palm of your hand, you must keep your thumb tucked in *tight* or it will protrude into the path of the descending blade.[236]

Use your right hand to reach in deeply to grasp the very end of the sword hilt, below senpai's hands. This gives you tremendous leverage against his grip.

Yank on the hilt with your right hand, pulling it back using *hiki te* (pull-back hand) to your right hip. The sword will rotate 180 degrees quite rapidly, and the blade will strike senpai in the face. You end up in manji uke pose, heian godan step 23, with the katana raised overhead in your right hand, the point aimed at his head. As you perform the finishing moves of the kata, you'll slice his neck and leg with the katana.

Jitte kata contains some clear bo-stealing techniques in steps 14 to 19. These are well-known in shotokan circles. In jion we have another bo-stealing sequence in steps 23 to 25, where we use palm-heel strikes against the opponent's elbows to break his grip on the weapon. Any of these bo-stealing sequences could just as well be rifle-stealing sequences.

In bassai sho, we return again to the theme of stealing the rifle and bayonet. Standard U.S. Army bayonet drill (World War II vintage) requires a lunge with the point at the enemy's throat, then a swinging buttstroke to the side of his head, then a direct smash into the face with the butt, and finally a slash across the face or neck as the point

---

[236] If you don't keep your left thumb tucked in very tightly during this technique, you will lose it. This might be the reason Shuri-te curls the thumb tightly into the hand in *shuto* techniques. The bodyguards must have practiced how to disarm a Satsuma swordsman, and their expert teacher on the subject *was missing a thumb*.

Figure 9-36: Stealing a katana, heian godan, steps 22 and 23. Deflect the opponent's *hands* to the side with your left hand (1). Grip the tip of the hilt with your right hand (2). Yank on the hilt suddenly to rotate the blade into the opponent's face to break his concentration (3). Pull the blade free and use it (4).

swings to the front again. (See Figure 9-34.) If the bayonet is not mounted, or is broken, the buttstroke becomes the primary fighting technique. Bassai sho, step 3, appears to be a sophisticated defense against the buttstroke.

This time let's assume that senpai has not mounted the bayonet. This reduces the overall length of the piece to about four feet. Use a jo stick or shinai.

Put senpai in left zenkutsu dachi, holding the forearm of the rifle in his right hand, and the neck of the stock in his left hand. Senpai launches the buttstroke. The butt of the rifle swings toward the left side of your head.

In step 2 of bassai sho, you turn toward senpai, shift under the buttstroke, and seize the weapon in your hands. Your right hand catches the neck of the stock behind the lock and your left hand grabs the barrel. Senpai is in a very weak position to resist when you twist the rifle clockwise and pull it out of his hands. The butt of the rifle comes to your right shoulder, and the muzzle comes up against his chest. Cock the hammer with your thumb. Pull the trigger. *Bang!*[237]

The heian godan techniques for stealing a sword or rifle from an enemy are elegant, sophisticated and effective. Who invented them? Remember that Azato was famous for disarming swordsmen, and he was also a master of bayonet fighting using a wooden rifle. These

Figure 9-37: Stealing and firing a rifle, bassai sho, step 3. The attacker attempts the buttstroke to the left side of your head. Duck under it and catch the stock with your right hand (1). Grasp the forearm of the weapon with your left hand (2). Exactly as in the kata, twist the rifle clockwise and pull it out of his grip (3). (When using a real Civil War rifle as we did here, it is clear that the attacker cannot maintain his grip.) Level the gun and use it.

---

[237] This application suggested by Gary Simpson, sixth dan, Zanshin Kai Karate Do (Shotokan) and Kobudo of Perth, Australia, in personal correspondence.

techniques are an unrecognized gift to us from Azato, by way of his best friend, Itosu. Maybe Azato left us a legacy after all.

Tachi dori, in this general sense, is alive and well in hard-style karate. We take weapons away from people and use them.

Abduct an Enemy

This requirement is icing on the cake. Matsumura was very aware of his own reputation, and would be attracted to a grandstand play like abducting the opposing commander under the very noses of his officers. There are also enormous tactical and diplomatic advantages to having the enemy commander under lock and key. There he is in the Shuri reception hall, only four steps away. The fight starts, and Matsumura's agents leap into the crowd, creating pandemonium. This is his chance to kidnap Commodore Perry. How would he do it?

The perfect combination of moves for an abduction is right there in empi (steps 35 and 36, without the leap). The usual interpretation is that we strike to the throat and groin in step 35, then scoop the enemy up on our shoulders for a wheel throw as part of step 36.

The blow to the throat is the tip-off. Nakayama shows this as an inverted Y-hand strike that grasps the jaw.[238] Inverted or not, the Y-hand strike to the throat is the classic technique for situations where you want to knock the opponent out but leave him unharmed. Does that sound like an abduction technique to you?

The throat is full of vulnerable structures, and most karate blows to the throat and neck are nothing less than attempted murder. The Y-hand strike, however, shocks both carotid arteries (where you feel the pulse under the angle of the jaw) without breaking the neck or lethally crushing the larynx and trachea. This has two interesting effects. The victim's body reacts to the artery strike by instantly reducing blood pressure to the brain, and the victim faints.[239] Also, the compression of the larynx, light as it is, stuns the voice and leaves the victim choking… unable to call for help or issue orders to his men.

Your other hand, of course, slaps the victim's testicles in step 35, which is yet another way to make a man helpless and gasping without

---

[238] Nakayama, Masatoshi, *Best Karate: Jitte, Hangetsu, Empi,* Kodansha, 1981, p. 141.
[239] Mashiro, 1978, p. 32.

230

putting his life at risk. This strike also makes him bend forward at the waist, which helps you pull him up on your shoulders.

Warning: You can kill your senpai if you drop him from this height and he doesn't know how to fall properly. It's a skull-cracker. For karate classes it is better not to complete the throw.

As your opponent folds forward, you can squat under him and roll him across your shoulders. If you let him roll all the way across and drop him on his head, you've done a wheel throw. If you stop halfway through with the enemy commander draped across your shoulders, it's called a "fireman's carry". This is the technique firefighters use to carry unconscious people out of burning buildings. The exit door is a short distance away, guarded by your own extraction team.

It is no accident that this move occurs at the end of the kata. Nabbing the enemy commander is the very last thing you would do before leaving.

You may find this to be quite a novel application of empi, steps 35 and 36, but give it some thought. This isn't a dinglehopper. Every bit of it works as if it were designed by a master. Perhaps it was.

Figure 9-38: Abducting the enemy officer, empi steps 35 and 36. Blows to the throat and groin stun the enemy (1). If you do only half of the throw, you can walk away with the opponent (2).

Iron Fan Technique

If the only weapon Matsumura could carry into the throne room was his tessen, then perhaps Itosu's kata also contain tessen techniques.

There are several designs of iron fans, but we can deduce that Matsumura's agents carried solid steel truncheons disguised to look exactly like real fans. Such tessen are readily available even today. Matsumura needed an iron fan that would turn a katana blade, and it had to be as innocent-looking as possible because he was in daily contact with suspicious Satsuma overlords.

So, you should picture a tessen as an iron rod about a foot long and as thick as your thumb. How do you use it in combat?

Not to belabor the obvious, but a tessen is an iron club. It is heavy. If you hold it in your right hand and start doing your kata, you'll find yourself swinging the club at heads, hands and legs. You'll punch and strike with both ends of it. You'll break bones with it.

If you have sai training, you'll block an overhead sword attack by laying the shaft of the tessen along your forearm to deflect the incoming blade. Grab the hilt of the sword with your other hand and

Figure 9-39: Tessen used like a sai to deflect a blade.[240]

---

[240] This tessen is from http://www.e-budostore.com/special.htm

Figure 9-40: Tessen used to trap or break a forearm (bassai dai, steps 19 and 20). The same grip can strangle or break a neck.

use the tessen to break the opponent's wrist. You'll end up holding the iron fan in one hand and the sword in the other.

The tessen makes its unique contribution, however, when you hold it with both hands while your wrists are crossed in *juji uke* position. Held this way, the tessen can be used very effectively to block kicks. The attacker's shin strikes the iron bar, with very painful results. We use this position in several shotokan kata.

Combining the tessen with juji uke hand position creates a triangular opening behind the bar and between your wrists. This opening is a powerful vise. You can use it to catch and hold a person's arm, as in bassai dai, steps 19 and 20, when you bring your doubled fists to your chest while kicking the opponent's leg. This hold is extremely painful when applied gently, and it snaps the forearm bones like wet sticks when applied with vigor.

There is one more tessen-related observation to make. The iron fan was carried in the belt at the right hip. When we do *koshi kamai* (cup-and-saucer stackup), we may be about to pull the weapon out and use it. X-downblocks often stack up in koshi kamae at the right hip.

It is not definitely known whether there are indisputable tessen techniques in the shotokan kata, but there are places where the tessen turns a weak or inexplicable move into a powerful statement. Since we know that the author of bassai carried a tessen in real life, it isn't too great a stretch to assume that some of this is deliberate.

Stairway Fighting

Fighting on a stairway or steep slope requires special techniques. They are not difficult, but they need to be practiced ahead of time.

When facing downhill, trying to hold the stairs against attackers from below, use gankaku's crane stance to keep your lead foot out of reach, while snap-kicking any hands or heads that come within reach. If the opponent catches your foot, use the other foot to jump-kick his face. This is the perfect application for *yoko tobi geri* (flying side kick).

When facing uphill, trying to force your way up the stairs, duck down low and use X-blocks to catch the opponent's lead foot. Grab his ankle and pull, dropping him on his back. Finish him off with a downward punch.

Figure 9-41: Stairway fighting is a battle for the uphill fighter's front foot. Keep it out of reach. Gankaku, steps 18 and 24. ("Gankaku" means "crane on a rock." Here we see the crane about to strike at the frog in the water.)

Playing the Bunkai Game

As your skill level rises in karate, you start to see more kinds of bunkai in the kata. Some of it is good and some of it is not. A lot of them are "dinglehoppers" masquerading as applications.

"Good" bunkai is practical, effective and satisfying. When you demonstrate it to people, they look suddenly pleased and excited. "Bad" bunkai is strained and improbable. When you demonstrate it, people look disappointed in you. We've all seen this look, we've all worn this look.

The following is an informal list of clues and tests that make it easier to find the good bunkai and avoid the bad. We all develop such rules, but sometimes writing them down helps us see them more clearly.

1. Good bunkai is easy and natural to apply. It does not require great strength, extraordinary speed, miraculous timing or paranormal insight. Those are all signs of dinglehoppers.

2. Good bunkai can be applied gracefully from some familiar entry point such as an upblock or downblock, or some standard self-defense scenario such as having your arms pinned from behind. You should not have to do something awkward and unnatural in order to apply the technique.

3. Remember that the enemies are not all kicking and punching. Shotokan kata are absolutely full of wrist-releases, clothing releases, and elbow-breaks. Check those options first. Blocks are awesome elbow breakers.

4. Pay attention to the stackups and the motions between the numbered poses in the kata. Often the stackup is the important part of the application.

5. Don't get seduced into the idea that the enemy is a karate fighter. Matsumura's enemies were not karate fighters. Look for what the move does to someone who is fighting stupidly.[241]

---

[241] McCarthy, 1999b, p. 101. McCarthy says, "To this day, in fact, self-defense applications work best against those who are completely unaware of the techniques being used to counter their assault."

6. If you can't figure out a bunkai for a move, try moving the enemy to a new location. The opening move of heian nidan seems to be addressed to an enemy on your left. The tackle defense demonstrated in this chapter uses the heian nidan opening to destroy an enemy who is standing in *front* of you.

7. Whenever you turn your back on an opponent, it means you have stunned, maimed or crippled him somehow. Figure out how. Alternately, sometimes you do turn your back as you throw him over your shoulder. That's an exception that proves the rule.

8. To stay close to the spirit of Shuri-te, always assume that there are plenty of opponents. There are bunkai that attack three or four opponents at a time. Don't limit yourself to one enemy. Throws hurl one enemy at another one, for instance.

9. Look for bunkai and tactical lessons in the steps and turns themselves. Turns can be throws, for instance. Turns can also be evasions. If six people step in to punch you on the first move of heian shodan, five will miss and the sixth will be lying on the floor with the print of your fist on his chest. Motion and change of direction have bunkai, too.

10. The direction of travel is a clue. Stepping backward is usually defensive. Charging forward usually isn't. Charging forward doing upblocks in heian shodan is not an attempt to protect your face.

11. Follow the momentum. Your body momentum tells you where the enemy is. You are moving toward him so that you can hit him with power.

12. Punches are often blocks; blocks are often strikes. If the first shuto is a block, then the second one is a strike. We never just block, block, block, block. (In the heian, almost none of the knife-hand "blocks" are blocks. The stackup is the block. The shuto is the counterblow.)

13. Look for interpretations where you pull the enemy with hikite while punching him with *zukite* (punching hand) as we see in the tekki kata. You hit twice as hard that way.

14. Slow moves are special. In the "advanced" kata the slow-motion moves provide a platform for practicing breath control. In most of the Shuri kata, however, slow moves usually signal joint locks.

15. There are brief grappling techniques in the kata, but they always have a sharp, immediate payoff. For instance, we use both hands to twist an opponent's arm in bassai dai, step 19. Then we kick his legs out and let his falling weight rip his shoulder right out of its socket. Look for the payoff.

16. Using *kakushi-te* (hidden hands) to explain bunkai is not acceptable. Don't make up "hidden" moves that are not part of the kata. Anybody can explain bunkai by making up extra moves! When you play the bunkai game, you have to work with what is there.

17. When you are really stumped, get a new perspective by watching a video of the same kata from a different style of karate. Sometimes the meaning of the move is crystal clear in the other style.

18. Never argue about the "best" bunkai for a move. The best bunkai will be self-evident. If there is something to argue about, you haven't found the best one yet.

Above all, never forget that our search for kata applications often uncovers multiple legitimate bunkai for the same motion. They aren't all dinglehoppers. By adding a new idea about an application, you can acquire a brand new weapon that you have already practiced thousands of times. In fact, you may have had that experience while exploring this chapter.

Conclusion

This chapter summarizes a series of karate applications that sprang out of the requirements of the Shuri Castle security plan. There were certain skills the bodyguards needed, so they created a martial art to fulfill that need.

In the future, if a student asks you the meaning of a move and you don't have a good answer, don't try to bluff. Students can tell when we are covering up. Swallow your pride and tell the truth. Say, "I'm sorry, but Itosu didn't tell us the meaning of that move."

It's only the honest truth. Itosu didn't tell us the meaning of *any* of the moves.

The question is: Why not?

Chapter 10

The Bunkai Mystery

Shuri-te is the most deadly fighting art ever invented. Why don't we know how to apply it?

When you examine Sugiyama's kata book, *25 Shoto-kan Kata*, you could easily catalog 7,000 specific facts about the correct way to perform the shotokan kata. The knowledge is precise, voluminous and rich. Most of it came directly from Itosu. The shotokan masters have tried to document and preserve every detail of this information. Masters of other Shorin styles have been equally careful to preserve every fragment of Itosu's and Kyan's kata heritage.

Where is the corresponding information on the Shuri-te applications? There should be, at a minimum, 200 to 300 officially sanctioned kata applications, preserved in meticulous detail by these same masters. These are the vicious applications Matsumura taught his bodyguard agents. Where are they? Why don't we know them?

I have studied shotokan karate for 30 years, and I am the most junior of the San Ten Sensei. We have been to the classes, attended the seminars, listened to the masters, interviewed the experts, read the books, survived the summer camps and viewed the expensive videos. The authoritative knowledge of the shotokan bunkai simply isn't out there. What we have instead is a babble of conflicting guesses.

Itosu created quite a number of our shotokan kata, and extensively modified the rest. He was a ferocious fighter when the need arose. Can you believe his kata are just dance steps with no meaning? I can't. Itosu had a deep knowledge of fighting. When we compare his kata to the Shuri battle plan, we see vicious and appropriate bunkai everywhere we look. There is simply no doubt that Itosu's head was full of sophisticated, practical, effective kata applications.

But Itosu's direct students, including Gichin Funakoshi, struggled with bunkai the same way we do.[242] None of the karate styles descending from Shuri-te can explain the bunkai of Itosu's kata any better than we can in shotokan. What lesson can we draw from this observation?

We *know* that Itosu understood the bunkai. We know that his students, who founded the Shorin family of karate styles, did not

---

[242] McCarthy, 1999b, p. 126. Choki Motobu publicly derided Funakoshi for being unable to explain the bunkai of Itosu's kata. (Of course, Motobu didn't know the bunkai of Itosu's kata, either.)

understand the bunkai. There is only one conclusion to reach: *Itosu was deliberately silent about the applications.*

Why? Logically, there are only a few possibilities.

- Itosu actually didn't know the bunkai of his own kata.

- Itosu was satisfied with the superficial interpretations.

- Itosu thought the applications were unimportant, or perhaps he was ashamed of them.

- Itosu thought it was better for students to discover the bunkai on their own.

- Itosu was sworn to secrecy.

Did Itosu Know the Bunkai?

Now and then you see a comment in the karate literature indicating that Itosu did not have a complete knowledge of the bunkai, or that he told someone that certain moves were "just for show." These stories usually have a critical tone. They seem to say, "Itosu wasn't so great. He didn't know the moves either." We find these rumors easy to believe because they mirror our own experience. Some of the moves are so baffling that they really seem meaningless.

On the other hand, sometimes a sensei is not altogether truthful with an unreliable student. I once had a student who was so dangerous that I simply didn't teach applications while he was in the room. I froze him out. Eventually he faded away. I think of this episode when I read tales about Itosu telling Chotoku Kyan or Choki Motobu that he did not know the meaning of a move. He may have been unwilling to tell them.

There might well have been some moves that Itosu couldn't explain. He might even have had a few dinglehoppers of his own. That idea misses the point. Itosu knew many effective applications for the kata, but he didn't teach them to his students. Even if Itosu was partially ignorant of the applications, partial ignorance would not explain complete silence. There was some other mechanism operating.

Are the Bunkai So Obvious?

Itosu's major contribution to the Shuri kata was to phase out circular technique and replace it with linear technique. He seems to have discarded most of the vital-point strikes, locks and throws in favor of elegantly powerful punches, kicks and strikes. When he converted a kata to Shorin style, he often painted over the original applications with a bright new coating of white-belt bunkai.

In white-belt bunkai, a punch is just a punch and a block is just a block. There are no deep and sophisticated applications. There are no hidden techniques. What if the simple-minded, obvious bunkai is exactly what Itosu wanted us to study?

It is very disturbing to think that there might be no Shuri-te bunkai beyond the obvious blocks and punches. I would reject that idea out of hand except for one nagging doubt.

The San Ten Sensei have shown me the internal skills of karate (the "basic principles") which I had not understood prior to meeting Hanshi Cruz. I now realize that it can be a satisfying lifetime challenge to perform even the first two moves of heian shodan correctly. Technical mastery of a single move can be a *do* in its own right.

I have seen sensei Randhir Bains teach a two-hour class on the internal skills of *gyaku zuki* (reverse punch), from the ground up. We literally started with the toes and moved upward through the skeleton one joint at a time. We didn't get to the knuckles until the second hour. I have seen sensei Armando Jemmott do the same step-by-step analysis of putting power into *mae geri kekomi* (front thrust kick). Sensei Robert Stevenson makes it clear in his seminars that a simple shift-and-jab attack (*kizami zuki*) involves dozens of internal skills that must be conquered one at a time.

If you follow the path toward technical mastery, the simple white-belt bunkai are all you need. The Shuri battle plan and the advanced bunkai are a pointless distraction. Your attention should be directed inward. Maybe this is what Itosu was thinking. Itosu might have adopted this attitude as he converted the jutsu into the *do*.

I don't personally believe that this is the whole story, but it might be part of the explanation. If you study karate for self-improvement, the internal horizon is vast indeed.

Was the Bunkai Unimportant?

When viewing a video by Karl Lowe called *Rifle Fundamentals*, I expected to see demonstrations of gun safety, maintenance and cleaning, sighting in, firing positions, using a sling, iron vs. telescopic sights, caliber selection, and how breathing interacts with trigger control. I was completely wrong.

Lowe's tape is entirely devoted to twirling, spinning, tossing and catching the rifle in time to music, as if it were a baton. It is a training tape for Color Guard groups, a popular high school performance activity. The kids train relentlessly, have great fun, get good exercise, and never think of their rifles as weapons. The fact that rifles fire bullets is irrelevant to their performances. These kids never see a cartridge.

When Itosu converted the jutsu into the *do*, he handed us the rifles but kept the cartridges in his pocket.

By this theory, Itosu didn't tell us the bunkai of the kata because that information just wasn't important anymore. The 20th century had dawned. The bodyguards had retired. The fairy-tale castle had become a dilapidated ruin. The Shuri Crucible was like a bad dream, fading into history. The devastating technique of "one fist, certain death" had no remaining purpose.

The vicious kata applications were irrelevant to health and character development, and would probably just get someone into trouble. You can almost picture the elderly Itosu saying, "Do the dances; get the exercise. Forget about fighting the world. Those days are gone." He might even have been a bit ashamed of the viciousness of his art. Shuri-te destroys the opponent through vicious neurological and orthopedic injuries. This might be embarrassing to an elderly gentleman in a culture where martial artists usually followed a Buddhist value system.

When we expend such great effort trying to rediscover the bunkai, we are fighting the flow of history by recreating the jutsu from the *do*. It is a fascinating study, but it probably means that we don't understand the true path at all. If you are on the true path, the kata applications just don't matter. Itosu might have thought that explaining them was completely pointless.

Is Self-Discovery Better?

There are sensei who say it is better for us to discover the bunkai ourselves as our skill level increases. This produces a natural increase in expertise over the years and, after all, we benefit the most from the things we discover on our own. No doubt this point of view has its merits, but it is often a rationalization for the speaker's own lack of knowledge.

The virtue of learning bunkai by self-discovery is that it eventually trains you to improvise new martial-arts techniques on the spur of the moment to meet changing situations. The person who simply memorizes specific responses to specific situations cannot achieve the same level as one who improvises on the fly. Struggling to interpret the kata trains your imagination to see the possibilities inherent in each situation.

The drawback is that self-trained means half-trained. Your progress is self-limited by your own experience and imagination. This is a severe handicap. Left to our own devices, we can never determine how big the task is. After 30 years of effort, have I found even half the bunkai? I don't know. I don't know how much there is to find.

This is why the Shuri Crucible theory is so important. We finally understand what Matsumura and Itosu were trying to do. The bunkai checklist in Chapter 9 is a theoretical breakthrough because it tells us what we *should* be able to learn from the kata. It gives structure and direction to our studies. The list shows us how to explore the bunkai so that our mastery, even if incomplete, is at least well-rounded.

Was Itosu silent because he thought it was better for us to figure things out on our own? That is doubdtful.

In fact, we probably haven't found the real reason yet.

Oath of Secrecy

During the height of the Shuri Crucible, Matsumura's agents acted like a resistance group or an organized crime ring. They lived double lives. They met in secret in the middle of the night. They kept their karate hidden from public view (and doubly hidden from the Satsuma overlords). If their activities had been discovered, they might have paid with their lives.[243]

---

[243] Funakoshi, 1975, p. 4.

In his 30 years with Matsumura, and the 20 years following, Itosu must have attended or led about 15,000 karate practice sessions. People who train together for years usually become good friends with many shared experiences. They have many stories to tell about one another. I could show you wonderful dojo stories from the Shotokan,[244] for instance, but karate historians can tell us next to nothing about the 20 years of training conducted in Itosu's home. We know the Shuri masters practiced in secret, but why were their students still silent about the training half a lifetime later?

Wouldn't Matsumura have sworn his agents to silence? Severe vows of silence were a part of Okinawan karate tradition.[245] "I swear on my family honor to protect the house of Sho and to keep all its secrets." The oath would affirm fealty to the king. They would have sworn never to reveal their security plans, and never to let their secret techniques become public. It would have been a binding oath and a blood oath, and they would have kept it. That explains most of the silence. The bodyguards promised not to talk about their work, and they didn't.

In this context, let's return to the story of Itosu and Choki Motobu. Every time Itosu taught Motobu a new technique, Motobu would pick a fight with someone on the street to try it out. Itosu expelled Motobu from his class. The usual explanation is that Itosu would not tolerate an irresponsible brawler. The question is, was Motobu expelled for brawling, or was he cast out for disregarding the vow of secrecy? Itosu's other students were very careful not to demonstrate Shuri-te in public, even if it meant walking away from a fight.[246]

Why, then, did Itosu suddenly start teaching karate in public in 1902? Doesn't that contradict the whole idea of a secret oath? He went from secret practices to public classes almost overnight.

Here's an abbreviated timeline of events following the end of the Sho dynasty:

- 1879 – King Sho Tai forced to abdicate.
- 1880-1900 – Itosu teaches secretly for 20 years.
- 1902-1906 – Itosu teaches karate in public schools.

[244] Nicol, C.W., *Moving Zen*, William Morrow & Co., 1975.
[245] Haines, 1995, p. 90-91.
[246] Funakoshi, 1975, p. 49-51. After the moon-viewing party, Itosu and his students retraced their steps and took the long way home to avoid the gang that wanted to fight them.

For 20 years after Sho Tai left, Itosu treated karate as a secret art to be practiced only in the dead of night with just a dozen hand-picked students. Then suddenly in 1902 Itosu reversed this policy and went public, teaching karate in broad daylight to large classes of public-school students. This was a stunning turnaround that demands an explanation.

What does this have to do with a secret oath? Let me reissue the timeline with one more date inserted.

- 1879 – King Sho Tai forced to abdicate.
- 1880-1900 – Itosu teaches secretly for 20 years.
- *1901 – King Sho Tai dies in exile.*
- 1902-1906 – Itosu teaches karate in public schools.

Itosu kept his oath of secrecy until the king he swore to defend had died. Then he went public. That coincidence is too forceful to ignore. The death of the king changed the rules. Itosu acted differently afterwards—as if he was released from his oath.

Evaluation

Why did Itosu keep the bunkai a secret from his students?

Itosu was clearly conflicted, and making some sort of compromise in his own mind. Shuri-te was a secret art developed by the Shuri bodyguards for a very deadly reason. You don't just share a secret like that. Itosu had sworn that he would not reveal the art except to Shuri bodyguards. No one else had a "need to know."

And then Sho Tai was deposed and the bodyguards were all fired. They hoped, no doubt, that Sho Tai would one day return. They waited to see what would happen to the king.

If Sho Tai had somehow been reinstated as king of Okinawa in the 1890s, where would he have found a dozen highly-trained, unarmed security agents? Itosu continued in his duty by training the next generation of bodyguards in his home. Itosu prepared them in all the necessary skills, but he never told them their mission. He taught them the kata and the basic skills, but held back the vicious bunkai. Since he could not explain the mission, he really couldn't tell them the bunkai, either. That would have given away too many secrets.

In 1901, Sho Tai died in exile. The king would never return. The bodyguards would never be needed. Two things must have happened at that point.

One, Itosu decided that the health benefits of karate meant that he had a duty to share it with the public. He started teaching grade-school students in broad daylight.

Two, he must have decided to bury the bunkai. It would be irresponsible to teach it to children in school. It would be like handing them knives and guns. We know he was worried about this because he removed the eye gouges from the heian kata. He didn't want his young students to injure each other.[247]

As for the fledgling bodyguards, 20 years in training at that point, Itosu simply ended their training and sent them into the world as teachers. These men would never be needed by Shuri, so Itosu never completed their training. They would never face sabers and bayonets as he had done, and therefore they didn't need the deadly bunkai. They didn't need the *jutsu*. He sent them forth to teach the *do*.

Funakoshi and his brethren never witnessed the kind of confrontations that Matsumura and Itosu lived through. They didn't know about extraction and reaction. They thought karate was for health and character development only. They studied kata designed for a battle they couldn't envision. All they knew was that doing 50 kata per day was a recipe for long life and good health.

And then these students became our masters and our teachers. That means that *our* training is incomplete, too. In all humility, we must acknowledge that we knew that already. Now, at least, we have a theory about what happened.

This has been the state of the art for 100 years. With great respect, I now suggest that it is time to put the missing pieces back into karate.

---

[247] McCarthy, 1999b, p. 106.

Chapter 11

The Future
of Shuri-te

The Shuri Crucible is a theory. In Western science, a theory must do two things. It must provide a single, consistent view that explains the known facts. The Shuri Crucible provides a much more consistent view of hard-style karate history than anyone has proposed before. Second, a theory must lead us into new developments and new discoveries. The Shuri Crucible awakens many new interpretations of kata bunkai, but what else does it offer? How does it lead us into the future of karate?

According to Funakoshi, with a nod to Sun Tzu's *The Art of War*, "Know your enemy and know yourself; in a hundred battles you will never be in peril." We have known neither the enemy (visiting barbarians at the Shuri court) nor ourselves (Matsumura's secret security force), and therefore we have blundered again and again. In particular, we have tried to teach the spiritual *do* while searching for the combat jutsu. This mistake has cost us dearly. It has come close to killing the art. Traditional karate is all but dead, and those of us who love it are desperate to bring it back.

The Shuri Crucible explains karate's past, and also points the way to karate's future.

Why 99 Percent of Students Quit

The Shuri Crucible theory exposes karate's weaknesses as well as its strengths. We now know why we have so many problems teaching Shuri-te and its many derivatives, including shotokan, shito-ryu, the shorin-ryu styles, wado-ryu and even taekwondo. We can see exactly why most of our students quit after a few months.

We promised them self-defense (the *jutsu*), but gave them Japanese character development (the *do*). They came to us to learn how to fight. Instead of that, we trained them to endure injustice, pain and hardship without complaint. That's not the same thing. In fact, that's the exact *opposite* of what they expected.

The Character Development Myth

"The ultimate aim of karate lies not in victory or defeat but in the perfection of the characters of its participants." So said Gichin Funakoshi, a person of unquestioned good character. Is this statement honne or tatemae? Is it true, or does it conceal the truth?

Most of us have never stopped to wonder what Funakoshi's "perfection of character" actually means. We have a vague idea that it means to have the courage of your convictions; to speak the truth; to live according to a higher moral standard; to resist temptation; to defend what is right and oppose what is wrong; to stand up for the weak and the helpless. These are all very noble ideas, drawn straight from our Judeo-Christian heritage. (Think of the chivalry of King Arthur and the Knights of the Round Table.) In fact, these western ideals are the *opposite* of the Japanese idea of "good character."

Japanese cultural values are drawn from a completely different heritage. The Japanese people are quite unconcerned about our quaint Western concepts of good and evil. Their idea of personal integrity is to close ranks with their neighbors to keep the truth (honne) hidden and leave the falsehood (tatemae) unchallenged. The idea that an individual would follow his conscience instead of going along with the crowd is horrifying to them. The very idea upsets the *wa* (the Japanese sense of harmonious communal unity).[249]

The Japanese don't acknowledge a Supreme Being or a higher moral standard. They are skeptical about the sanctity of human life. Finally, they sincerely believe that they are a superior race surrounded by inferior races. They casually regard all lesser races, peoples and cultures as gaijin, barbarians. If Japan's historical treatment of conquered nations is any guide, gaijin occupy a position somewhat below livestock on the social scale.

"Character development" to a samurai meant to suppress all sense of personal responsibility and instead give his superiors instant, blind obedience.[250] A samurai was expected to seek his own death in the service of his lord, and therefore learned to "push through" pain, injury and hardship to the point that death in the line of duty could be attained. Well-trained samurai were expected to behave like lethal, relentless killing machines, even to the point of self-destruction.

Can you point out the places where traditional karate training develops the samurai virtues of mindless endurance and absolute obedience? Ask yourself these questions:

• Does our karate training require instant obedience?

• Does it require blind, unquestioning loyalty to the master?

[249] McCarthy, 1999b, p. 73.

[250] Van Wolferen, Karel, *The Enigma of Japanese Power: People and Politics in a Stateless Nation,* 1989, p. 250-251. These comments on Japanese values are mainly drawn from this very impressive dissection of Japanese society.

- Are we trained to "push through" pain and injury, to overcome fatigue, and never show weakness?

The blisters on our feet say "yes" to all three questions. This is the "good character" the Japanese masters expected karate to teach. It has nothing to do with courageous individual action, protecting the weak, or obeying your conscience. Good character in Japan means to be silent, to follow orders, to ignore your conscience, and *never* question your superiors no matter what they tell you to do. In peacetime, this makes Japanese society a model of harmonious cooperation, of which they are very proud. In wartime, however, the same values produce widespread atrocities and horrendous war crimes. That is a harsh judgement, but Japan's history bears it out.

"Karate-do" does not "perfect your character." It teaches you to act Japanese. From their point of view it is the same thing. We have to ask ourselves if these are the values we want our students to embrace.

The Self-Defense Myth

If karate doesn't perfect character, at least we can still teach people self-defense, can't we? Unfortunately, it would appear to not be the case.

Karate-do strengthens spirit and teaches some remarkable self-defense skills, but it isn't even close to a complete self-defense curriculum. The Shuri Crucible makes the reasons clear for the first time:

- **Shuri-te is a combat art perfected for a unique tactical situation that no longer exists.** Shuri-te policy and technique don't match the needs of our students.

- **Shuri-te is optimized for warriors.** Shuri-te does not offer techniques tailored to women and children who must fight off predatory men.

- **Shuri-te lacks entire categories of self-defense techniques.** Grappling skills, submission skills, night-fighting skills, and vital-point technique are missing from Shuri-te.

- **The *do* promotes the idea that the kata applications are really not important,** when it is the deadly applications that people come to us to learn.

- **The Shuri bodyguards were above the law. In modern terms, they had "a license to kill."** We are not at liberty to maim and kill our opponents.

- **Taking an opponent prisoner is not addressed in Shuri-te.** Our students want to know how to subdue an opponent and hold him for the police.

- **Playground fighting was irrelevant to Shuri.** The Shuri bodyguards were not little children, but many of our students are.

- **Shuri-te ignores weapons because of the Satsuma restrictions of the Shuri Crucible.** Weapons are absolutely essential when teaching practical self-defense.

Matsumura threw away many vital self-defense techniques because they didn't fit the Shuri Crucible. Itosu concealed the applications of the kata, withholding the fruits of decades of research when he created the *do*. The rules of sport karate have gradually outlawed the few practical techniques that remained. Modern karate classes teach only the least-effective residue of the system, not the deadly art of Shuri-te.[251] Modern karate has been neutered, declawed and defanged. It is not a practical combat skill anymore.

At least Shuri-te still offers us the powerful internal skills of linear karate. Well, does it really? Most Shuri lineages lost the internal skills when junior black belts, who had trained briefly in Okinawa or Japan, returned home and opened their own schools. After 50 years, half-trained junior teachers have generated large national organizations of half-trained junior teachers. In the end, we have created thousands of karate classes across America (and elsewhere) where even the *renshi's* and *kyoshi's* dance their way ineffectively through the bodyguard kata. They don't understand the mission. They don't understand the applications. Most of them haven't a clue about creating power. Their karate is shape without substance. We have produced thousands of black belts who cannot protect themselves or anyone else.

This is the reason 99 percent of our students quit. We offered them the one thing that we couldn't deliver: self-defense. Karate has failed them.

It is time that we delivered on that promise. It is fine to study the *do*, but karate must also be a *jutsu*. There is no reason it cannot be both. Traditional karate needs to come out of the Shuri reception hall and into the 21st century.

---

[251] The sport-karate mindset subtly limits all of our training. For instance, the most effective targets for self-defense students are the knees and testicles. The "anatomically-correct" Century "Body Opponent Bag (BOB)" pictured in Figure 9-34 contains no strikable surface below the waist. How are we supposed to practice self-defense when we can't practice on the knees, groin and feet?

Shuri II Self-Defense Standard

Earlier in this book we designed a hypothetical fighting art for the Shuri bodyguards. We analyzed the threat, defined goals and established missions. We made a list of required skills to match the missions. Then we started selecting jutsu applications to match the list. This is how you design a martial art.

Let us go do the same thing again: design a new version of Shuri-te to fit the self-defense needs of modern karate students. In this chapter we will propose a standard, describing the missions, goals and required skills of a 21st century self-defense art based on Shuri-te.

This standard needs a name. "Shuri II" may be appropriate. The standard applies to all of the Shuri-te styles. Shuri II is a list of goals we must meet, not a list of specific techniques. We need goals that match the real hazards our students face. We need to marshal techniques to satisfy the goals. The techniques have to match the abilities of the fighters.

Technique selection will be up to you, based on the suggested goals, your knowledge and your experience.

Shuri II Fighters

Men, women and children get into different kinds of trouble with different kinds of enemies. They have different attitudes toward combat. Potential rescuers respond to the three types of victims differently. Reach, strength, weight and mental toughness are all different.

One of the glaring flaws of the *do* is that we teach men, women and children exactly the same techniques and strategies—as if age, gender, size, strength and weight made no difference in actual combat. We tell the students to assume that their opponent is exactly the same size they are. Nothing could be farther from reality. The opponent is always larger and stronger than you are.

To achieve effective self-defense, the Shuri II standard must recognize that men, women and children will be in different kinds of fights, and need different self-defense techniques. The Shuri II standard must adapt flexibly to each category of fighter.

Shuri II Self-Defense Goals

The whole point of the Shuri II standard is to re-examine traditional karate and identify the places where the art doesn't meet the self-defense needs of the modern student. Then we need to extend traditional training to address the gaps.

Shuri II self-defense students don't need to extract the king from the crowd and block pursuit. With this in mind, what are the objectives?

- Resist simple assault
- Resist armed assault
- Resist rape
- Resist abduction
- Resist home invasion
- Perform an arrest
- Perform a rescue
- Fight as a team
- Attack vital points
- Use weapons
- Fight in the dark
- Fight on the ground
- Know the law
- Live by the rules

A student who can demonstrate the knowledge and skill to meet these goals has satisfied the requirements for a certificate in Shuri II self-defense.

Resist Simple Assault

Shuri II fighters are prepared to win a dominance fight.

The world is full of jerks who try to dominate our karate students through intimidation and pain. The students come to us to make it stop. It isn't enough to teach them to endure pain.

Men get into one-on-one dominance fights with other men, especially where alcohol, road rage, or women are involved. These fights are not usually lethal but can be very damaging. We need to teach the men how to end the fight abruptly without getting jailed or sued.

Women don't usually get into dominance fights except with their husbands or boyfriends, which we call "domestic abuse." The proper response to the first attack is an agonizing counterattack that teaches a permanent lesson.

Boys, and sometimes girls, confront bullies at school and on the streets. The unarmed schoolyard bully can be dealt with by defeating the first one very painfully. In my experience, our student needs to win only *one* such fight and then the problem goes away for years.

There are two levels of preparation for winning a dominance fight. The first is your underlying martial art, such as karate. Karate prepares you for the typical fistfight pretty well. The emphasis is on an effective block or evasion with a near-simultaneous, crippling counter-attack. Evade the first punch, take out his knee or collarbone or eardrum, and walk away. Don't get into a slugging match.

The second level is spirit preparation. Traditional karate fosters a powerful, indomitable spirit. This attitude alone can stop an attacker in his tracks. Bullies often get cold feet when the proposed victim isn't impressed by their blustering.

Resist Armed Assault

Shuri II fighters can resist armed assault—and armed assault usually means a robbery. First, let's emphasize common sense. Teach your students to avoid the situation. If they can't avoid it, teach them to give up the money. Maybe the robber will walk away. This is always the cheapest, safest and smartest course of action in every respect. Most robbers are not murderers. Give him $100 so you don't have to spend $10,000 in medical and/or legal fees later.

Unfortunately, some of the bad guys want more than money.

Men need to learn techniques for coping with a club, knife or gun. They need to experiment, to know what works and what doesn't. Otherwise they will fight when they shouldn't and get killed.

Ladies should give him the money and watch his eyes. If they don't like what he is thinking, it's time to jam that manicured nail through his eyeball and run.

Children usually don't have enough cash to attract adult robbers, although some kids have been robbed or even killed for their stylish shoes. Armed bullies are a matter for the law. Kids should be taught to disengage and report at the first sign of a weapon.

There are three aspects to the training. The first is to be firmly grounded in a traditional martial art. Fighting an armed opponent requires good judgment, timing, speed, power and a lethal mindset. Beginners can't do it. These are skills that come from years of practice. The second aspect is to teach specific disarming skills. Karate, self-defense, jujitsu and aikido all offer a selection of techniques for disarming a man with a knife or a gun. Some of these disarming

Figure 11-1: Adding weapons to *ippon kumite* (one-step fighting drills). One student is armed with a knife (1) and steps in to a thrust with the knife as the defender steps back and blocks (2). In this case the defender grabs the knife arm and strikes the attacker's head (3).

techniques actually work; others are dinglehoppers that will get you killed 10 out of 10 times.

It is easy to add disarming techniques to your normal kumite practice. In ippon kumite, give the attacker a rubber knife and have him hold it while attacking with a middle-level oi zuki. Have the defender evade the thrust and cripple the attacker's knees, break the arm, or otherwise dislodge the weapon. There are many options, depending on the art you choose. You will quickly discover what works and what doesn't.

The rare student will be able to disarm the opponent easily, just like in the movies. Most students need to be "killed" a few times to dispel their fantasies and teach them not to try this in real life. A man knowing his limitations is one of the most valuable self-defense lessons we can possibly teach.[252]

Train the few who can succeed; teach the rest to escalate to a better weapon.

Resist Rape

Shuri II fighters can stop a rapist.

Our female fighters have to be absolutely deadly. Anything less is not going to work for them. Tournament karate isn't good enough.

Due to body-size differences, women cannot realistically subdue a rapist bare-handed, but they can cripple him and escape, or they can "equalize" him with a weapon. Vital-point strikes, applied with conviction, can cut any man down to size.

The rape victim cannot overcome her attacker by main force. Rapists do not attack large, fit, muscular women. They attack women they can overpower. Moreover, the attacker chooses the time, the place and the method of attack.

It is important to emphasize the vulnerability of the testicles. I know of a student who was caught in a rape situation. She responded by fondling and stroking the rapist's genitals. When the time was ripe, she took one of his testicles between her thumb and forefinger and popped it like a grape. He did not follow her as she walked away, surviving by way of vital-point exploitation.[253]

---

[252] Callahan, Harry, "A man's got to know his limitations." *Magnum Force*, Warner Brothers, 1973.

[253] This story from Matthew Thomas, an old friend and Shotokan sensei who lives near San Francisco. The incident occurred in Boston about 20 years ago.

Resist Abduction

Shuri II fighters can escape a kidnapper.

The main reason parents bring their children to us is fear of abduction, even though the risk is extremely low. Children like Megan Kanka, Polly Klass, Elizabeth Smart, Juli Sund and Sylvina Pelosso haunt us out of proportion to their numbers.[254] The last two were abducted, tortured and killed within a few miles of my house. I took it personally.

Children cannot defeat a sexual predator, but we can teach them to be extremely slippery.

Young women and older children need to be told that "abduction" consists of a stranger trying to force them into his car. Tell them the

Figure 11-2: Learning to be slippery. Two male attackers take on a young lady (1). She sweeps the lead foot of the first boy (2) and then used a two-handed wrist release to break the second boy's grip (3). Separated from both attackers, she can now get away (4).

---

[254] The Polly Klass Foundation lists 10 to 20 child abductions per year. If you read between the lines, about half of them appear to be female teenage runaways on medication for depression, and some of the others are child-custody fights. See *www.pollyklass.org*.

classic abduction stories. For children, it's the man who is driving around looking for his lost dog. "Have you seen my dog? No? Well, then, would you get into the car and help me look for my dog?" Make them aware, but be careful how you explain the danger.

For older girls and young women, tell them about Ted Bundy. His technique was to put a fake cast on his arm, and then ask a pretty girl to help him load groceries into his van. When she leaned into the van with a box of groceries, he hit her over the head with the cast and bundled her into the van.

The key is the car. Don't get near a stranger's car for any reason! Even if he points a gun at you, you are better off shot and bleeding on the sidewalk.

We teach them karate, of course, so they can kick, block and dodge. In addition, I teach my students a wide variety of grappling releases. We drill on breaking wrist holds, clothing holds, arm locks, chokes, bear hugs, etc. The goal is to make the student hard to hold. This makes it much more difficult to drag the victim into the bushes or to the waiting van. You'll find many of these techniques in Chapter 9, and more in Mashiro's *Black Medicine*, Volume III.[255]

To teach slipperiness, you can make a contest out of dragging people across the room. Attackers try to drag victims across a line on one side of the room. Defenders try to break free and run to the safe zone at the other side of the room. Change partners and try again. That can get pretty lively.

Resist Home Invasion
Shuri II fighters can defend their homes.

The home invasion robbery/rape is relatively uncommon in America because many homes contain firearms. It is more of a problem in disarmed countries such as England and Australia. Home invasion of the elderly has been a major political issue in Australia recently, with attempts to make the burglary of an occupied home worthy of a life sentence—the same as murder.

Resisting home invasion should be a major focus for young women sharing an apartment. The inhabitants and the home should be

---

[255] Mashiro, N., *Black Medicine, Volume III, Low Blows,* Paladin Press, 1981.

prepared to repel invaders. Weapons should be identified. Tactics should be planned and rehearsed.

For this discussion, assume that children will not be involved in a home-invasion fight. For one thing, home invaders avoid homes with children. Parents will fight to the death for a child, and that isn't what the home invader wants. He picks a different home.

Home invasion is not a friendly tussle on the lawn. It begins with a vicious beating and is usually the prelude to rape or murder. How should Shuri II fighters prepare for it?

First, we again pay respect to a solid foundation in a traditional martial art. It takes a trained fighter to defeat a premeditated attack. Timing and power are everything.

The home invasion topic might be your opportunity to propose a private lesson in the student's home. That's really the best way to approach this subject. The student's home should be analyzed for potential weapons, and the fighter familiarized with the basic skills required by the weapon. There should be some suitable weapon within reach no matter what direction the victim flees. I don't mean guns and daggers, necessarily. Candlesticks, fire extinguishers, brooms, kitchen knives, and a grizzly-bear-sized canister of pepper spray can be distributed around the house so that *some* weapon is always within reach.

Perform an Arrest

Shuri II fighters can arrest an opponent of equal size.

The Shuri II standard does not require you to make a felony arrest on the highway, but students should be able to immobilize and hold people who are about the same size and weight as the student. The large males can use their height, weight and shoulder strength to immobilize an opponent for several minutes until the police arrive. Women and children can practice these techniques also, but they should not expect to subdue a grown man. Size *does* matter.

It is hard to imagine a situation where a child needs effective restraint techniques. On the other hand, playground fighting consists of counters to various hold-downs and joint locks. Perhaps if we teach the restraint technique *and* the counter, we will be serving the needs of the children.

In my shotokan classes, I have the men practice ippon kumite using counterattacks that trap the punch and twist the arm into a joint lock. They quickly become quite adept at capturing and locking the opponent's punching arm, and they enjoy it.

There are similar techniques for catching a kick and turning it into a devastating ankle or knee lock, or a spiral fracture of the tibia. It is sobering to have someone catch your foot, throw you on your face, and pin you in less than a second. It explains why there are so few kicks in our kata.

If your clientele is appropriate, you should teach them at least one effective choke. The carotid artery choke (the blood choke) is extremely effective and offers little chance of serious injury if the students are closely supervised. The technique quickly renders an opponent helpless, no matter how psyched, drugged, or just plain crazy he might be. (Get a judo teacher to show you the safety precautions before you try this in class.)

Finally, your students should be able to demonstrate how to secure an opponent. You can't assume that there are handcuffs available. Hand them a roll of glass-filament strapping tape or an extension

Figure 11-3: Catching and trapping the punching arm. In one-step fighting, let the students practice techniques that capture the punching arm (1, 2) and force the attacker to the floor (3, 4).

cord. Teach them to bind wrists behind the back, and bind the crossed ankles up behind the back, also.

Perform a Rescue

Shuri II fighters can rescue a victim of violence.

If a karate student needs to rescue a victim from a brutal attacker, we have a moral obligation. We know how to fight. We cannot simply watch as a helpless victim is beaten and brutalized.

It is my belief that a man must protect and defend all weaker persons from acts of violence. That is the biological role of the alpha male, a million years in the making. He needs to be equipped with techniques to interfere in a beating, abduction or rape.

Women need to be trained to come to the aid of other women. Practically any woman will try to rescue a child who is being beaten, but she usually doesn't know how. Teach her.

Children should be trained in rescue techniques for playground

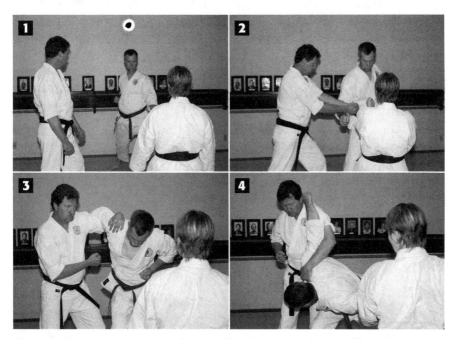

Figure 11-4: Practicing rescue techniques. How many times have you blocked a punch aimed at someone else's face? Here two students are practicing standard ippon kumite (1). A third student stands to the side. His assignment is to interfere with the punch and prevent it from connecting (2). In this instance, the third student blocks the strike and slips behind the attacker's right shoulder (3) to bring him down (4).

situations, but the primary rescue technique should be to run for help. Don't just stand there. Go get a teacher!

Performing a rescue means to perform self-defense on behalf of a third party without getting anyone killed in the process. The simplest solution, although not guaranteed, is simply to attack the perpetrator from behind. Make him abandon his victim in order to deal with you. Then, of course, you have to contend with the problem.

You can add rescue drills to your beginner kumite practice quite easily. For ippon kumite, for instance, add a third fighter to each group. The attacker steps in with *jodan oi-zuki* (face front punch). The defender steps back with the usual *age uke* (upward block). The rescuer has to block or disrupt the attack before the punch can land, beginning at various nearby positions. Place the rescuer to the left or right of the defender, and then move him around to other positions including directly behind the attacker. Challenge him to solve the problem.

For situations where the victim is being held or choked, practice the usual escape techniques and then break up into groups of three again. Have the rescuer determine the highest priority action (release the choke, usually) and then identify the attacker's greatest weakness. Follow the priorities of your martial art for this. In shotokan, the snap kick to the testicles from behind is a great rescue technique. You almost never see it taught in a class because it contradicts the competition mindset.

Fight as a Team
Shuri II fighters can fight as a team.

Fighting as a team was the *sine qua non* (essential ingredient) of ancient Shuri-te, yet modern karate classes usually don't go there. Team fighting is not a sport. It is a very deadly art intended to help two women overcome a rapist or home invader. Siblings who walk to school or wait at bus stops together should be trained to fight as a team, to help ward off an abductor or a bully. It also applies to elderly couples, and to siblings such as latchkey kids. If one karate student can be formidable, two of them working together are about 10 times as formidable.

The first goal is to create sensory overload. The attacker must be deluged by incoming blows, shouts and flying objects that disrupt his plan. The students have to take away control.

Figure 11-5: Fighting as a team. Alternating groin kicks from behind (1) and in front (2) are devastating to attackers.

The second goal is to trap the attacker *between* the team fighters, so he can't turn his full attention to one fighter without turning his back to the other. This is the key.

The third goal is to take him down decisively from the rear. The groin kick from behind is perfect. Explore the potential for grabbing his hair from behind and yanking his head back. That's the setup for the other fighter to apply the front groin kick. He can't see it coming while you are swinging from his ponytail.

Try some carefully-supervised two-against-one free fighting. It is good training for both sides as long as it doesn't get too wild.

Attack Vital Points

Shuri II fighters use vital point techniques.

Vital point "pecking" allows a smaller, weaker person to rob an opponent of his superior strength. This is a place where we can take a lesson from little Chotoku Kyan, whose vital-point technique was devastating.

Women should be trained and drilled constantly on the most vicious vital-point strikes, especially those directed to the eyes, ears, throat, testicles, knees, shins and feet. In addition, all escape techniques for women should begin with a vital-point strike that weakens the opponent's hands and arms. Teach them to hammer specific nerves, muscles and tendons as they struggle to break the grip.

On the other hand, men need to know which vital points to *avoid*.

Figure 11-6: The sharp edge of the sword. A woman's karate can't crush like a club; it must cut like a knife. Don't train her to punch the stomach in *ippon kumite*. She must literally go for the throat. This is *hiraken*, the lethal foreknuckle strike to the larynx.

Figure 11-7: Kicking the shin in ippon kumite. Children should use shin kicks as their routine counterattack in ippon kumite. This kick isn't dangerous when barefooted, but it can be devastating with shoes on. It anchors the opponent without serious consequences to either party.

I teach my students to avoid strikes to the neck or throat unless they intend to kill. Picture the judge saying, "You paralyzed this man for life because he spilled your beer?" You don't want to make that kind of mistake. Stay away from the neck and throat unless someone's life is in danger.

For children, vital-point strikes should be part of learning to be slippery. Teach them to hammer down on forearm nerves to break a wrist grip, for instance. Teaching children to attack eyes, ears and knees can be problematic because of rough play and having to hold back on the playground. In place of these targets, children can be instructed to kick shins. A good shin kick with the edge of the shoe can stop a bully in his tracks and anchor him to one spot without danger of permanent injury. Think of it as a "playground" vital point. The shin kick should be constantly emphasized in kumite drills for kids.

Figure 11-8: Vital points are essential for women. These ladies are warming up by jabbing their fingertips into a flying beanbag. They quickly develop the eye-hand coordination to strike an eyeball on the first try.

You can train your class in vital-point technique simply by prescribing specific counterattacks during basic fighting drills. Instead of doing gyaku zuki every time, have them spend one night doing *mawashi zuki* to the temple. Another night, use nukite to the eyes or throat. The next night use uraken to the temple. Spend enough time on each major vital point so they will remember it.

For precise vital-point attacks, the women need to practice lightning-fast pokes at a moving target. They can warm up by poking at a tethered beanbag. If female students can hit the flying beanbag with their fingertips, hitting an eye should be no problem.

You can find the complete atlas of vital points in Mashiro's *Black Medicine*, Volume I.[256]

Use Weapons

Shuri II fighters use every kind of weapon.

Shuri II students must deeply understand that using a weapon multiplies their chances of survival. Picture yourself in a blood fight against a larger, stronger opponent. Are you going to win? Now picture yourself in the same situation, holding a baseball bat. Do you notice any difference? A weapon multiplies your effectiveness by a factor of 10. When in danger, always reach for a weapon.

Kitchen kobudo is simply the self-defense skills of ancient *kobudo* applied to modern objects. If we are serious about teaching practical self-defense to beginners, kitchen kobudo is the key to immediate progress. It is also an important key to student retention.

In our daily lives, we move through a sea of lethal weapons. They are all around us. As a Shuri II teacher you need to be proficient in all of the kitchen kobudo weapons: pens, cell phones, spray weapons (including fire extinguishers), electric shock weapons, clubs (flashlights), flails (belts), shields (briefcases, books), staffs (brooms), light and heavy kitchen knives, swords (umbrellas), hatchets (and hammers), pistols, shotguns and rifles.[257] The firearms are on the list

---

[256] Mashiro, N., *Black Medicine, Volume I, The Vital Points of the Human Body in Close Combat*, Paladin Press, 1978.

[257] See Mashiro, N., *Black Medicine, Vol. IV, Equalizers*, Paladin Press, 1995, for the complete course in kitchen kobudo self-defense skills. You might also be interested in Vol. II of the same series, *Weapons at Hand*, which lists over 100 common household objects and how to use them as weapons.

because you might take one away from the attacker. If you don't know how to shoot, you'd better know how to *hit* him with it.

One naturally recoils from teaching weapons to children, but an armed child can defeat an unarmed man. The question is: Are you serious about teaching children effective self-defense or not? If a child is in actual danger from an adult, the patty-cake "tournament karate" we teach them is not going to help. You have to make your own decision here.

There is a political dimension to teaching children about weapons, of course. If you handle this badly, the local thought police will shut down your school. Therefore, the Shuri II standard requires that school children be taught how to use "non-lethal" weapons such as pens, flashlights, books, chairs, notebooks, lunchboxes and brooms to fend off an attack and escape. Don't teach the little kids or the teenage boys how to use knives. That's for teenage girls and women.

Hold up a cell phone and ask the students how to use it as a weapon. It is surprising how many people don't think of dialing 911.

Special emphasis is placed on kitchen knives as self-defense

Figure 11-9: "Kitchen kobudo" practice during beginner kata drills. Students should practice performing their kata using various household objects as weapons.

weapons because every kitchen in every house and every apartment in the world contains knives. Even walking down the street you can stop for a moment at a 24-hour mini-mart and walk out again with a butcher knife in a paper bag.

For karate students, the single-edged kitchen knife is easy to integrate with the techniques they already know. Hold the knife point-down, edge-forward, so that the back of the knife lies against the outer edge of the forearm. Now do an upblock, downblock or outside-forearm block, so that the knife is caught between the opponent's arm and yours, cutting him deeply. Using this technique, you can make a young woman shockingly formidable in just a few minutes.

Weapons training can be integrated with routine kata practice. About once a month I pass out common household objects (brooms, portable phones, flashlights) and chanbara weapons to the class, and then lead them through their beginner kata.[258] I challenge them to figure out what the kata teaches them about the weapon. This session is great fun, and is highly beneficial in terms of real self-defense skills. The students trade weapons after each kata.

Only use wooden or rubber knives in the dojo. *Never* let the students get near a real blade.

Use Tactics

Shuri II fighters have a tactical plan.

We all tell the students to break free and run away, but in what direction? When a Shuri II student breaks loose and starts to run, she isn't just fleeing. She's executing a plan.

The best tactic is to reduce the number of immediate assailants to one. Find a place to fight where the enemies have to line up and come in one at a time. Back into a hallway. Stand in a doorway. Get between two parked cars. Another tactical application is to set up your fighting stance next to a tree or telephone pole. Keep the pole against your left shoulder to interfere with those looping roundhouse techniques the naïve opponent wants to use. Use the environment to your advantage.

Don't just run blindly. Run toward weapons. Combining a simple weapon with the right tactical location can turn the tables completely.

---

[258] See http://www.samuraisports.com for padded kobudo weapons of all kinds. Enormous fun for all ages.

For children, tactics are oriented toward getting help. Make sure they know where to run for help. Go to neighbors. Dial 911. Hit a fire alarm. (School fire alarms get immediate response). Tell a teacher. Tell a shopkeeper. Flag down a motorist. Teach the children to attract attention.

Parked cars can be very useful. For example, climbing up on the roof of a car *really* attracts attention. Leaping from car to car across a parking lot sets off a lot of alarms and brings people running. Jumping into an unlocked car, locking the doors, and leaning on the horn is also a good tactic. Worming your way under a car, where an adult cannot easily follow, should at least be considered.

If two-against-one free-fighting is good training for team defense, then one-against-two free-fighting is good training against multiple attackers. Learn to use one attacker as a shield against the other. Hammer the first attacker to the ground and then play ring-around-the-rosie with the remaining opponent. Force him to jump across his fallen friend to reach you. When he does, meet him halfway and catch him in the air using sen no sen timing.

Have the students experiment with fighting in doorways, hallways, and between parked cars. Make a special lesson of fighting on a stairway. Make them aware of ways to make the environment limit the attacker's options.

For very young women, I teach a special response to a masher. It begins with an overhand slap to the face, using the heel of the hand against the nose/lips and the fingertips into the eyes. This is followed quickly by clapping the ears with the palms of the hands. The third move is a vicious kick to the shin. Then I teach the girls to run away… but to where? Run toward help. Run toward weapons. Run toward a stairway.

Note that the important part is to have a plan and execute it. Otherwise the student will just stand there like a deer in the headlights, frozen to the spot, until it is too late.

Night Fighting
Shuri II fighters can fight in the dark.

Our fighters must be adept at locating and devastating an opponent in pitch darkness. They also need to know how to use limited light to their advantage. Self-defense fighting often happens *at night*.

Men don't often have a pressing need to fight in total darkness, so let's talk about night on the street. There is a big advantage to making the opponent look into automobile headlights while he fights. This has a natural application in road-rage situations. Get your back to the headlights and make him look at them. ("Get your back to the moon!" cried Master Itosu.)

Then there is the scenario where the rapist creeps into the woman's house and leaps on her bed when she is asleep. This may be the only example of a true fight in pitch-black darkness. Use vital points. Get one finger into an eyeball and wiggle it around before you try to break free. Find the scrotum and twist it like a doorknob. Then yank on it and let it snap back. Find an ear and clap it with your palm. Attack him ruthlessly until he screams for mercy! Then kick your way loose and run for a weapon. With the weapon in hand, run to the neighbors for help. Let *them* dial 911.

Figure 11-10: "Sticky hands" for night fighting. The defender (right) keeps her hands in contact with the attacker's forearms and "rides" his punches in and out, guiding them away rom face and body targets (1a, 1b). In the second scenario (2a, 2b) the defender adds face, neck and throat strikes in time with the attacker's withdrawing hand. You can insert these strikes and still catch the attacker's arm again as it comes forward for the next punch. (Frame 2b shows a classic night-fighting strike from kanku dai, step 14.)

Children probably won't have as much need to fight in the dark, but we could place some emphasis on how to *hide* in the darkness. Playing hide-and-go-seek in a dark, shadowy environment would be good training if it can be done safely.

There is an easy way to introduce night fighting in a shotokan class. Kanku dai (kusanku) used to be a night-fighting kata before it was linearized by Itosu. The kata's author, Sakugawa, defeated a boatload of Chinese pirates in darkness. Now and then I turn down the lights in the dojo and we all fight "pirates" in the dark while performing kanku dai. Students love this exercise. The only substantial difference is that knife-hand blocks must be performed as "searching hand" techniques, as if sweeping the area for enemies we can't see.

Sound management is also important. You don't want to give away your position by thumping the floor each time you step or by breathing too loudly. Then, once you make contact with an enemy, you have to hold on to him until you can finish him with a vital-point strike. For practical self-defense in darkness, clutch the opponent, find his face, and jam a finger or thumb into his eye before breaking free.

Sticky-hands techniques are vital to night fighting, and are almost absent from Shuri-te. At the basic level they are very simple. Meet the opponent's punch with some type of inside block. Keep your wrist or hand in contact with his forearm as he pulls back for the next punch. Just keep light pressure and let his motions guide yours. Do the same thing on the other side. His attempts to punch automatically guide your hands into blocking position. Once students get the idea, they are very amused to discover that they can "ride" the opponent's punches even in total darkness.

Also, it is important to notice that the circular shuto-uchi chops to the neck in kanku dai are excellent for fighting a person you can touch but cannot see. You cannot say the same for linear strikes such as oi zuki or *mae geri keage* (front step kick). The long-range linear techniques require vision. Sweeping circular techniques are the natural weapon of night-fighters. They find the opponent and connect solidly.

First contact in the dark usually occurs at shoulder level. Have one student close his eyes while the other circles him. Have the second student grab the first one with one hand, somewhere on the shoulders or upper arms. Teach the "blind" student to press his shoulder into the opponent's hand, feeling how the enemy's body gives slightly in response to the pressure. From this slight cue, most students can turn directly toward the opponent and hit him with a reverse punch to the body.

There are many devastating arm and shoulder locks that begin with the opponent's hand on your shoulder. The techniques in this book for releasing a grip on your jacket are excellent for night fighting (See Chapter 9).

It isn't safe to let blindfolded students attempt jiyu kumite, but you might consider putting students in chanbara gear while blindfolded. Let them stumble around the floor trying to hit each other with the padded chanbara swords. This is kind of like swinging a club at a piñata, but the piñata gets to swing back!

The purpose of this drill is to teach the students to associate

Figure 11-11: Learning to fight in the dark. These two students are both blindfolded, simulating a fight in the dark. The first challenge is to locate the enemy. A student new to the game stands upright, using his weapon to sweep at shoulder level. The experienced student crouches near the floor, searching for the opponent's feet. This shot was taken about one second after contact. (For safety, we use chanbara weapons and helmets, plus close supervision.)

darkness with silence and swing a weapon horizontally when they can't see the opponent. The naïve opponent wanders around the room swinging his sword at shoulder level. After a little experience, the students learn to squat down and be silent, while gently probing a wide arc around them with their chanbara sword. When they touch an opponent's shin, they leap to the attack.

Once again, the real purpose of the training is to give the student a plan to execute. They must not just freeze in the face of danger.

Karate Ground Fighting
Shuri II fighters can fight on the ground.

The Shuri bodyguards didn't include ground fighting in their art because they were outnumbered so badly that hitting the ground was the same as dying. A modern self-defense class, however, must inlcude ground fighting in some fashion. Most dominance fights and most rapes eventually go to the ground.

Shuri II fighters need to understand, and be constantly reminded, that karate ground fighting isn't wrestling. When we lose our footing we keep right on punching, striking, kicking, kneeing, elbowing, eye-poking, groin-smashing, ear-slapping, and bone-breaking, just like we would if we were standing up. Stay with what you know. Don't try to wrestle.

There are three basic situations that you must address with your students. The first is the one where the student hits the ground but the opponent is still standing. This involves pivoting on the small of the back to keep your feet directed toward the enemy, so you can kick his shins, knees and groin when he reaches for you. Several foot-throws can be employed from this position.[259]

The second situation is the one where you and the opponent have hit the ground in a tangle of arms and legs, and the opponent starts trying to wrestle. The goal of the Shuri II student is to break free and regain his feet. In this situation, the opponent's grappling frame of mind leaves him unprepared for the vicious karate techniques we can inflict on him.

Put the students on the mat and encourage them to explore what knees can do to the back and kidneys; what elbows can do to ribs and face; what hammerfists can do to the collarbone, temples and groin;

---

[259] Mashiro, 1981, demonstrates these techniques.

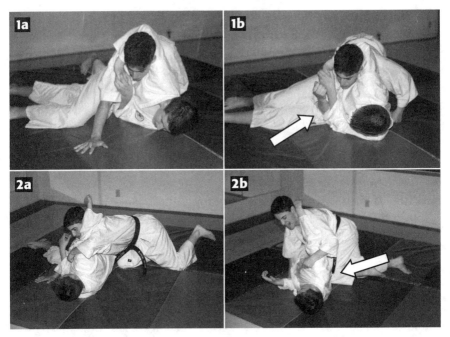

Figure 11-12: Karate ground fighting. Many fights wind up on the ground (1a). The elbow to the groin or bladder (1b), and the knee to the spine or kidney (2a, 2b), are very effective karate ground-fighting techniques.

what ippon ken can do to the chest and back muscles; what fingers can do to the eyes, nose and throat; and the advantages of grabbing the opponent's hair or genitals and yanking or twisting them. Even biting has its place. Ground fighting uses every tooth and claw.

The third situation is the classic playground holddown, where the opponent sits on your chest and holds down you arms or punches your face or tries to choke you with his hands. This is a position of extreme disadvantage, and yet the application of vital-point technique can turn the tables quickly. For instance, in the playground holddown it is often possible to just punch the attacker directly in the groin with your fist, slap his ears or strike his throat. My favorite technique is to use my left hand to grab his hair at the crown of his head and then stick my right thumb in his eye. By exploiting the hair and the eye, it is pretty easy to roll the opponent off to my left. He always rolls off with his knees spread, inviting a fast snap kick to the testicles.

Although ground fighting involves more than the techniques and options outlined here, the key is simple: *Fight, don't wrestle.*

Know the Law

Shuri II fighters know the law of self-defense.

The fist fight is only the first fight. First you fight the muggers; then you fight the lawyers. Which group do you think is more ruthless? How you conduct the first fight determines whether or not you survive the second one.

A Shuri II dojo educates men about how far they can go before self-defense turns into battery or mutual combat. The lawyers are always hovering in the background, filing their teeth into sharp points.

Our female students need to know their rights and the specific legal thresholds of the crimes visited upon women. When is it appropriate to start fighting? Again, the legal definition of self-defense is narrow, and our students must remain within it or pay the consequences later.

Children need to know in plain and simple language what is OK and what is not OK. The other guy can *say* whatever he wants. He can't *touch* you. Tell him to stop. If he won't stop, then *fight*. Kick him in the shin and run for help.

Never forget that trained Shuri II students are effective. They are going to inflict damage. It must be legally justifiable or we have done them no service.

I try to give my students an occasional exposure to an attorney as a guest lecturer. In addition, it is a good idea to require some outside reading before the brown belt test. The student should be able to answer a few questions about Mas Ayoob's *The Truth about Self-Protection*, for instance, or Carl Brown's *American Law and the Trained Fighter*.[260] Who says we can't ask them to *read*?

For children, self-defense law often means understanding local school-district policy about playground fights. My children's school district has adopted a "zero-tolerance policy" toward violence. This means if you are attacked by a bully on school grounds you are supposed to stand there with your hands in your pockets and let him knock your teeth out. If you defend yourself or come to the rescue of a friend, *you* will be suspended with a permanent impact on your grades. While this seems to be cowardly and unfair, it is their policy. Make sure they understand.[261]

---

[260] Ayoob, *The Truth about Self-Protection*, Police Bookshelf, 1985. Brown, Carl, *American Law and the Trained Fighter*, Ohara, 1983

[261] Children should be advised that (1) they have the right to defend themselves (even if school policy says otherwise) and (2) the sensei will expel any student who starts fights. (Funakoshi once severely scolded Nakayama over this very issue. See Hassell, 1995, p. 80.)

Live By the Rules

Shuri II students have rules to live by.
We can't just blindly assume that punching and kicking builds good character. Many of our students have no idea what "good character" means. We have to tell them.

Sakugawa wrote the first *dojo kun* (list of rules for karate students) about 200 years ago, which means his rules are somewhat out of date. Funakoshi's dojo kun are closer to the mark, but written in the wrong heritage for our students. We need a code of behavior that fits our Western heritage in ways Sakugawa and Funikoshi could not imagine. What I have in mind is something like this:

The Black Belt Oath

I wear the black belt. It means I have a special responsibility, because I carry life and death in my hands.

I do not hurt people. I protect the young, the weak and the helpless. If I see someone being hurt, I make it stop. I don't just look away.

I obey the law. When someone breaks the law, I tell the police, even if it is a friend. I do not just ignore a crime.

I tell the truth. I don't lie, not even when I might be punished. When someone is lying, I say so. I don't just pretend I didn't hear.

I win or lose by the rules. I do not cheat. When I see someone cheating, I say so. I won't let them steal a prize or a grade that they didn't earn.

I keep my promises. When I give you my word, I don't take it back. I expect others to do the same.

I follow my conscience. If something is wrong, I say so, even when all of my friends disagree. I will not be silent just to be safe or popular.

I swear on my honor to preserve rather than destroy; to avoid rather than confront; to confront rather than hurt; to hurt rather than maim; to maim rather than kill; to kill rather than die; and to die rather than dishonor my belt.

The ancient masters tell us that winning 100 victories in 100 battles is not the highest skill. The highest skill is to win without fighting. This will be my lifelong goal.

This is my oath, sworn on my sacred honor, and only death will break it.

This oath was written for a 12-year-old audience, but it makes an important point. After all, if a shotokan black belt can't stand up for what is good and true in the world, who can? I have this oath on the wall of my dojo. Now and then I look up and see one of the teenagers studying it with careful attention.

Make sure your students know the rules. Don't just train them to be mindless samurai. They need a code to follow.

Bringing Karate to Life

The Shuri II standard is not only a means of updating Shuri-te and making it more relevant to our students, it is also a way to revitalize their flagging interest in traditional karate. It brings karate back to life.

Traditional karate is dying because it is a difficult and painful hobby that isn't as exciting as it looks in the movies. For practical self-defense, the first year of karate isn't as effective as simply buying a canister of pepper spray. Many people live into their 80s these days, so the *do* doesn't provide remarkable longevity anymore. There are plenty of sports where you don't get cracked ribs, broken noses and blown knees. Why would anybody want to study karate?

You know the answer to that question, and *I* know, but it is one of those wordless messages that cannot be written in a book. We have to attract and keep students in order to show them. The Shuri II standard is a blueprint for revitalizing traditional karate by moving the emphasis back to effective, practical self-defense for men, women and children. Combined with our new knowledge of the devastating Shuri-te bunkai, we can use the Shuri II standard to *bring karate to life again*. We can do this without losing or changing any part of the art we love.

Chapter 12

Conclusion

This concludes my presentation of the Shuri Crucible theory. Our visit to 19th century Okinawa has led to a series of surprising discoveries.

What lessons have we learned?

- Hard-style karate didn't just happen. It was created to meet a unique historical challenge: the Shuri Crucible.

- Karate does not prepare you to fight a single attacker. It prepares you to fight a mob. Karate is the answer when there are too many opponents to count.

- Karate is designed to finish each opponent in two seconds or less. It is absolutely ruthless.

- Karate was never intended for self-defense; it was intended for defending someone else.

- The kata contain techniques for freeing yourself from restraint, attacking a mob, cutting directly through a crowd, and for kidnapping an enemy celebrity.

- The weapon-stealing techniques in the kata work equally well for *bo* staffs, katanas, sabers, pistols and rifles.

- Hard-style karate abandoned Chinese vital-point strikes because they took too long to apply. These skills were not "lost." They were deliberately discarded.

- Shuri-te karate gave its participants unnaturally long lives (compared to their contemporaries).

- The Shuri-te bunkai were not lost over time. Itosu left the applications behind when he converted the jutsu into the *do*.

- Many common self-defense situations are not addressed by karate because they were not appropriate to the Shuri Crucible.

- Modern karate needs to be augmented in specific ways with weapons, grappling and vital-point technique before it can meet the Shuri II self-defense standard.

Familiar Faces

When Commodore Perry invaded Shuri Castle, he ended the day by dining at the regent's house. During the festivities, several photos were taken. Figure 12-1 is a close-up view of the regent and his two grim-looking assistants at that dinner. As my theory of the Shuri bodyguards developed, the young man to the regent's left started to look familiar. The relaxed, wide-set eyes, broad forehead and casual posture reminded me of someone I had seen before.

The young man's age looks like early 20s. In the full lithograph the man holds something on a chain that might be a secretary's portable inkpot and brush, and could certainly be used with lethal effect as a flail. Who was he?

Could this be a picture of the 23-year-old Yasutsune Itosu, 25 years before Gichin Funakoshi took his first karate lesson? I think it is.

It certainly looks like Itosu. The general features and age are correct. The shape and proportions of the nose are an exact match to the sketch. The line of the jaw and shape of the lips are identical in

Figure 12-1: The regent of Okinawa, Sho Taimu, with two bodyguards.

both pictures. The broad, square forehead is there. The pronounced naso-labial folds of the sketch are just starting to show in the younger face. The round, Caucasian-looking eyes are startling in both the sketch and the lithograph! Allowing for the difference in age, the facial features are point-by-point identical. If Miyagi's sketch is accurate, this *must* be Itosu in the lithograph.

Now ask yourself this question: If Itosu is guarding the regent's left flank, who is the man on the regent's right?

On that day, 50 U.S. naval officers and two companies of Marines were loose in Shuri with two cannons. Perry was arrogant and bellicose. The regent was at the mercy of 250 armed enemies. Perry ordered Sho Taimu to submit to a photograph. The equipment was set up and the photo was taken.

If you had been Bushi Matsumura, where would you have been

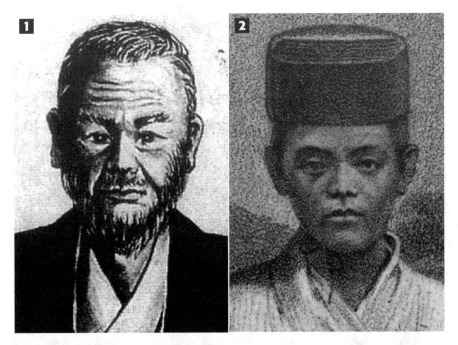

Figure 12-2: The Miyagi sketch of Itosu (1) compared to the face of the regent's younger bodyguard (2). Allowing for the difference in age, the facial features are point-by-point the same. (The lithograph image has been reversed left-to-right to correct for the daguerrortype mirror-image effect. When making daguerrotype portraits, Perry's photographers would reverse kimono closures, sword positions, etc., to make the final product visually accurate as a mirror-image. See http://www.blackshipsandsamurai.com/visualnarratives/panel_port02.htm for more details.)

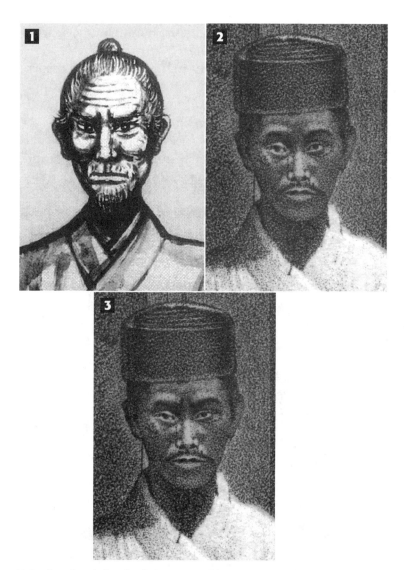

Figure 12-3: The Miyagi sketch of Matsumura (1) compared to Sho Taimu's senior bodyguard (2). The shape of the forehead, nose and jaw line is a perfect match. If you can't see the resemblance in the original images (1, 2), look at the bottom image (3). Image 3 has been morphed slightly to give the face the same intimidating expression as the sketch. Suddenly, the master's riveting gaze comes alive.[262]

---

[262] I used Adobe Photoshop Elements 2.0 to lower the eyebrows, narrow the eye openings, and add some tension to the lips, while leaving the bony structures strictly alone.

standing when that photo was taken? Shouldn't that be Matsumura behind the regent's right shoulder?

Do you recognize him? The face in the lithograph has surprisingly dark skin, but the features are familiar. The major features of the sketch line up exactly with the lithograph, particularly the long, straight, narrow nose, the sunken cheeks and the narrow jaw.

What about the special eyes? In Figure 12-4, the eyes are oddly and *unevenly* slanted in both the sketch and the lithograph, which would be a very unlikely coincidence. Remember that a lithograph is a tracing of a photo. It is true to life.

When I first examined the Miyagi sketch of Matsumura, I was struck by the angry, deeply-slanted eyes. I took this to be artistic exaggeration. I thought the artist had deliberately given Matsumura the eyes of a temple demon to express his fierce fighting spirit. Japanese art often portrays warrior demons in much the same way.[263]

When I compared the Matsumura sketch to the lithograph of the senior Shuri bodyguard, I suddenly realized that the extreme eyes were not an exaggeration. The demon eyes were drawn from life.

Figure 12-4: Unusual eyes. Matsumura's eyes are asymmetrical in both the Miyagi sketch (top) and the "Photoshopped" lithograph close-up (bottom). His right eye (on the left of the image) appears thickened and disfigured.

---

[263] See the cover photo of Funakoshi's *Karate-Do Kyohan*, Kodansha, 1973.

These are not simply Japanese/Chinese eyes. These eyes are steeply slanted compared to the eyes of the regent in the same picture. Also, the bodyguard's two eyes are slanted *differently*, and one eye has an unusual shape. This face has been distorted by a birth defect, an infection, or some impact injury early in life. I suspect that Matsumura was punched in the face as a boy and suffered a crushed cheekbone with accompanying sinus infections. This could have changed the appearance of the damaged eye in much the way we see in the lithograph.

This was a culture where uniformity was so important that you could divorce your wife for being left-handed. How would the keimochi children have treated a boy with a distorted eye? I think he might have been a miserable outcast.

Disfigured by a punch to the face? If so, no wonder Matsumura learned to use his fists.

As I said in the introduction, I never found a picture of Azato, but I came very close. I believe this is an unrecognized portrait of Sokon Matsumura and Yasutsune Itosu, grimly guarding the regent of Okinawa at the climax of the most alarming confrontation in Shuri's history.

Here we see two determined men facing many enemies. They are the creators of Shuri-te, and the leaders of the Shuri bodyguards. They will defend their principal against one opponent or against a thousand. The odds make no difference to them.

> *"I come to you with only karate, my empty hands. I have no weapons, but should I be forced to defend myself, my principals [sic], or my honor, then these are my weapons ... karate, my empty hands."*

Versions of this creed appear on a thousand shotokan Web sites. Most of these sites talk about defending their "principals," instead of their "principles." They don't know how correct they are. The picture of Matsumura and Itosu guarding their principal, Sho Taimu, is the very essence of the Shuri Crucible. *This is karate.*

Appendix: Karate Lineage Chart

This chart shows how the discoveries of Sokon Matsumura and Yasutsune Itosu have trickled down into the major styles of modern karate. I have also included the contributions of Chotoku Kyan, Kanryo Higaonna and Chojun Miyagi. These five men are the superstars of Okinawan karate. Everyone else is defined by his relationships to one or more of these famous men.

It is useless to depict all the relationships among these masters and their students, so I have simplified the chart by leaving out many famous names. Most of Matsumura's teachings come to us through Itosu. Most of Higaonna's teachings come to us through Miyagi. The knowledge did not pass cleanly from master to student, as diagrams like this would have you believe.

Still, it is useful to contemplate the paths of knowledge between Bushi Matsumura and the various karate styles we see today. One way or another, Matsumura touched every branch of modern karate except for the recent Chinese imports like kenpo, goju-ryu and uechi-ryu.

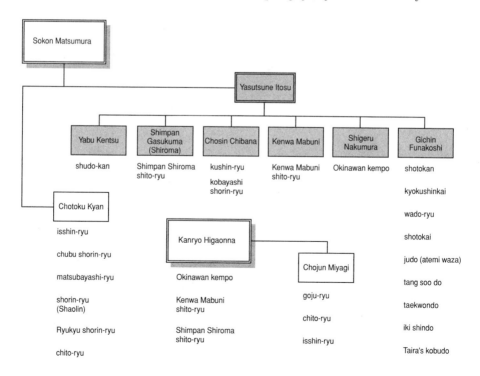

Glossary

age uke: upward block

alma mater: "nourishing mother" (Latin); a person's college or university

atemi waza: striking techniques of judo

awase: denotes using two hands at the same time

bo: a hardwood staff, usually five or six feet long

bona fide: "in good faith"(Latin); genuine, authentic

budo: "the way of the warrior"; used here to denote medieval Japanese warrior culture

bunkai: the fighting skills that the *kata* were designed to teach

bushi: "war man"; warrior

chanbara: sword fighting; used here to mean the soft, padded weapons that have recently appeared in the martial arts marketplace

chuan fa: Chinese unarmed fighting, popularly mislabeled "kung fu"

daimyo: a feudal lord of Japan—often brutal and despotic, like a count or an earl in medieval Europe

daisho: the traditional display of two samurai swords on a rack; the big sword (*katana*) is the *daito*, the short sword (*wakizashi*) is the *shoto*

de facto: in reality or fact, even if unofficial

dim mak: an elaborate Chinese theory of vital-point striking based on acupuncture meridians

dinglehopper: a kata application that is pathetically wrong

do: a constructive life path

dojo: training hall

dojo kun: a list of rules for karate students

eku (or ekubo): a wooden oar used in *kobudo* as a wooden sword

enbusen: "a line on the floor"; used to denote the "floor plan" of a kata

fumikomi: stamping kicks, as if to break the opponent's knee or crush the arch of his foot

gaijin: foreigner, with the connotation of "barbarian"; the *kanji* (Japanese writing) actually means "outsider"

gedan barai: lower level swinging down-block

gi: the white cotton karate uniform copied from Jigoro Kano's judo uniform by Funakoshi in the early 1920s and then adopted by all Okinawan karate styles after 1936

giri: the unbearable burden, the unpayable debt; the respect and obligation you owe to your teacher

gyaku zuki: *shotokan's* powerhouse reverse punch; punching with the arm that is opposite the forward leg, using hip rotation to generate power

hachimaki: turban or headband

hangetsu dachi: a fairly wide stance with the knees pulled inward in which the practitioner steps forward in crescent-shaped steps to keep the groin covered while hooking behind an opponent's leg

hanko: a signature seal, such as a Chinese chop

hara: belly; the center of gravity of the body, in the bowl of the pelvis (karate); the center of the spirit (as in the Japanese suicide method of *hara kiri* or "belly cutting")

harem: a sacred, forbidden place (Persian)

hikite: pullback hand

hiraken: striking with the fingers folded but not closed into a fist so that the contact is made with the second knuckles (usually against an opponent's throat)

hiza geri: knee kick, as in slamming one's knee into an opponent

hoari topcoats: the *keimochi* nobles of Shuri wore ankle-length kimono with wide, belled sleeves as the uniform of their upper-class status

honne: the real truth, what really happened, what people really think (contrast to *tatemae*)

ikken hisatsu: "one fist, certain death" (derived from a similar expression in Japanese fencing); the knock-down power that distinguishes hard-style from soft-style karate

ippon ken: one-point fist; a fist with one knuckle stuck out like a point on the front of the fist

ippon kumite: one-step fighting drills in which the attacker makes one attack and the defender makes one defense and one counterattack

jigen-ryu: a style of Japanese sword fighting popular among Satsuma samurai

jiyu kumite: free fighting, as in fighting for points instead of blood

jo: a short bo stick, about four feet in length (This is exactly the size of the handle of an Okinawan parasol. These parasols are often visible in Commodore Perry's lithographs, mainly carried by keimochi men.)

jodan: face or head level

judan: the 10th degree (highest rank) in shotokan karate.

juji uke: "X" block; a block using two hands with the wrists crossed with which it is relatively easy to catch an opponent's wrist or ankle

jujutsu: traditional Japanese unarmed combat arts, very different from karate; judo is the sport version

jukendo: the sport of bayonet fencing, using wooden rifles with padded ends

jiyu kumite: free fighting, as in tournaments

jutsu: skill or technique; something with a practical use

jutte: medieval Japanese nightstick, similar to a *sai* but with only one hook on the side

kage zuki: hook punch; a short punch that strikes sideways across the front of the body

kake-te: open-hand block, hooking block; often used to block a punch and then grasp the opponent's arm

kakiwake uke: wedge block used to break a front choke hold by bending and separating the opponent's elbows

kakushi-te: "hidden hands"; the term refers to the bad habit of explaining kata applications by making up additional moves that aren't in the kata

kamae: a posture of readiness; a fighting stance

kanji: Japanese pictographic writing in which each symbol stands for a word or idea

karateka: the group noun for people who study karate

karma: the determination of your destiny or fate as influenced by the sum total of all of your good and bad acts

kata garuma: shoulder wheel throw

katana: a Japanese samurai sword more than two feet in length, capable of transecting two or three human torsos at a single stroke

keimochi: the upper-class families of Okinawa who served as the bureaucrats of the Shuri government (also see *shizoku*)

Keiseimon: the southeast gate to Shuri Castle, behind the Seiden

kendo: the sport of sword fencing, using wooden or split bamboo swords

kenpo (or kempo): the Japanese reading of *chuan fa*; although called "karate" in Japan, *kenpo* is a Chinese art recently transplanted to the islands

kensai: an honorific title awarded after death meaning "sword saint" or "fist saint," depending on the recipient

ki: spiritual power or energy

kiai: "spirit battle"; a shout to focus energy into an opponent

kiba dachi: "horse stance" or "side stance"

kihon: basic techniques such as kicks, blocks, punches, strikes and stances

kime: focus; the basic principal that directs all energy into an opponent, accepting none of it back into one's own body

kizami zuki: to punch with the front hand; to jab

kobudo: the martial art that uses Okinawan farming and fishing implements as makeshift weapons

koshi: "hip," as in *koshi kamae*, a fighting stance with your fists stacked next to one hip

kumite: practice or contest fighting

kun or kun-yomi: the Japanese reading of a kanji symbol, which may have multiple *on* and *kun* readings

kung fu: principally an American term signifying Chinese martial arts in general

linear karate: karate characterized by high-impact, straight-ahead attacks; also known as hard-style karate

mae geri keage: front snap kick (*mae* is "front", *geri* is "kick", *keage* is "rising" or "snapping")

mae geri kekomi: front thrust kick (*kekomi* is "thrusting")

makiwara: punching post, originally wrapped in soft rope made of rice straw

manji uke: a blocking posture in shotokan kata where you have one arm raised up behind you and the other arm extended down in front of you, usually performed in back stance

mawashi zuki: roundhouse punch; a snappy, curving punch that connects with an opponent's temple

menkyo kaiden: the ultimate certificate of complete mastery of a martial art given to a new master by a previously-certified master

mokujyo: the wooden rifle/bayonet used in *jukendo* fencing

nami gaeshi: returning wave kick, wherein the foot sweeps up and across the body as if protecting the groin, then stamps back down; proceeds like a wave washing up on the beach and then running back into the ocean

nidan geri: double kick, specifically the flying double-front snap kick

nihon nukite: two-fingered poke at the eyes

ninja: a stealthy Japanese assassin, usually depicted in black pajamas

nukite: spear hand; a class of techniques that poke vital points with various numbers of fingertips

ochokui: the stairway behind the throne, inside the Seiden

oi-zuki: front punch (strictly speaking, "pursuing" punch); usually launched while stepping forward in *zenkutsu dachi*

on or on-yomi: the ancient Chinese reading of a kanji symbol, which may have multiple *on* and *kun* readings in Japanese

oshi uke: a swinging downblock with the palm up, striking with the thumb side of the forearm

otoshi empi uchi: downward elbow strike

Ouchibara: the Okinawan royal family's private domain behind the Seiden

oyo: applying bunkai to situations not strictly present in the kata

peichin: the title of an Okinawan noble employed by the Shuri government

regent: a government official temporarily executing the office of king, as when the real king is too young to take command

renzuki: multiple rapid punches

sai: a rather odd, blunt dagger shaped like a trident and used as a police nightstick in Okinawa

samurai: the feudal lords of Japan

sanchin dachi: hourglass stance; a very tight stance with the toes turned in and the knees pulling toward each other, as if trying to hold a soda can between the knees while stepping forward and backward

sankaku tobi: triangle leap; a formerly secret technique that lets one bypass an enemy by leaping past him

Seiden: the two-story building that was the seat of the Okinawan government; contains ShuriCastle's two throne rooms

seio otoshi: the kneeling shoulder throw seen at the beginning of *empi* kata

senpai: the assistant instructor or the senior student of the dojo

sensei: master, teacher, doctor, professor; the owner/leader of a school

sen no sen: timing in which you strike the opponent at the exact instant he decides to attack

seppuku: ritual suicide; also known as hara kiri ("belly cutting")

shiai: an arranged fight at full intensity with no rules; the loser can get hurt or killed, as can the winner

shinai: a practice sword made of split bamboo

Shinbyouden: the small mausoleum behind the royal living quarters at Shuri Castle

shizoku: the Japanese name for the dispossessed keimochi families following the Meiji restoration

shodan: first-degree black belt rank; sometimes used to mean "virgin"

shogun: military dictator of Japan

Shoreiji: the southern Shaolin Temple of China.

Shorinji: the Shaolin (young forest) Temple of China

shuriken: a small, sometimes star-shaped, throwing knife

shuto uke/uchi: knife-hand block/strike (*shuto* is "knife hand"; *uke* is "block"; *uchi* is "strike")

[sic]: "thus" or "so" (Latin); indicates that a surprising or paradoxical word is not a mistake and should read as it stands

sine qua non: "without which not" (Latin); the essential element

soto ude uke: outside forearm block (*soto* is "outside"; *ude* is "forearm"; uke is "block")

sutemi waza: sacrifice throws where both parties land on the ground together

tabi: socks split between the first and second toe, for wearing with *zori* sandals

tachi dori: stealing an opponent's weapon from him

tai sabaki: shifting out of the line of attack; sidestepping

Tamauden: the large mausoleum outside the Shuri Castle walls

tanto: a samurai sword less than one foot in length; a dagger

tatemae: the official (generally false) version of events (contrast to *honne*)

teisho uchi: to strike with the heel of the palm

tettsui: hammer fist; to strike with the little-finger side of the fist

tobi: "flying," usually applied to some form of jump kick

tode: "Chinese hand"; Okinawan word for fist-fighting prior to 1926

tonfa: the wooden handle of a rice-grinding millstone, used as a club in kobudo

tessen: an iron truncheon disguised as a folding fan; samurai gentlemen often carried fans in their belts

uchi: in the context of karate techniques, uchi can mean "inside" or "strike"

Uchinanchu: the Okinawan word meaning "the people of Okinawa"

Uchina guchi: the native language of Okinawa, which is neither Chinese nor Japanese

uraken: strike with the back side of the fist in a whipping motion

urasuka: the dais that elevates the throne of the Okinawan king

wa: the Japanese sense of communal well-being and harmony, the disturbance of which is the height of bad manners

wakizashi: a samurai sword between one and two feet in length

yama-zuki: "mountain punch" (yama means "mountain," referring to the "w"-like kanji character for "mountain"); when performing a mountain punch, the head and arms make a W-shaped pose

yoko tobi geri: side flying kick (*yoko* means "side"; tobi means "flying"; geri means "kick")

zenkutsu dachi: front stance

zori: sandals with a strap between the first and second toe; commonly called "thong sandals" or "flip-flops" in America

zuki: punch (with a fist) or thrust (with a sword); *zuki te* is "punching hand"

Bibliography

Abernethy, Iain, *Karate's Grappling Methods*. NETH Publishing in association with Summersdale Publishers LTD, England, 2000.

Alexander, George, *Okinawa: Island of Karate*. Yamazato Publications, 1991.

Alexander, George, *An Analysis of Medieval Japanese Warrior Culture and Samurai Thought as Applied to the Strategy and Dynamics of Japan's Twentieth Century Era of Warfare*. Doctoral dissertation, Western Pacific University, 2001.

Appleman, Roy, et al., *United States Army in World War II, The War in the Pacific, Okinawa: The Last Battle*. Center of Military History, United States Army, Washington, D.C., 2000.

Ayoob, *The Truth About Self-Protection*. Police Bookshelf, 1985.

Basic Field Manual, *Unarmed Defense for the American Soldier*. June 30, 1942, FM 21-150.

Bennett, Tony, *Early Japanese Images*. Tuttle, 1996.

Bishop, Mark, *Okinawan Karate, Teachers, Styles and Secret Techniques*. Tuttle, 1999.

Brown, Carl, *American Law and the Trained Fighter*. Ohara, 1983.

Caiden, Martin, *A Torch to the Enemy*. Ballantine, 1960.

Clavel, James, *Shogun*. Dell, 1976.

Cook, Harry, *Shotokan Karate: A Precise History*. (No publisher), 2001.

Cunningham, Don, *Secret Weapons of Jujutsu*. Tuttle, 2002.

De Mente, B. L., *Behind the Japanese Bow*. Passport Books, 1993.

Funakoshi, Gichin, *Karate-Do Kyohan*. Kodansha, 1973.

Funakoshi, Gichin, *Karate-Do, My Way of Life*. Kodansha, 1975.

Funakoshi, Gichin, *Karate-Do Nyumon*. Kodansha, 1988.

Funakoshi, Gichin (translated by Shingo Ichida), *To-Te Jutsu*. Masters Publication, 1994.

Haines, Bruce, *Karate's History and Traditions*. Tuttle, 1995.

Henshall, Kenneth, *A History of Japan from Stone Age to Superpower*. St. Martin's Press, 1999.

Hokama, Tetsuhiro, *History and Traditions of Okinawan Karate*. Masters Publications, 2000.

Johnson, Nathan, *Zen Shaolin Karate*. Charles E. Tuttle Co., 1994.

Johnson, Nathan, *Barefoot Zen*. Samuel Weiser Inc., 2000.

Kerr, George, *Okinawa: The History of an Island People*. Tuttle, 2000.

Kim, Richard, *The Weaponless Warriors*. Ohara, 1974.

Martinez, Javier, *Isshinryu Chinto Kata Secrets Revealed*. San Juan, 1998.

Martinez, Javier, *Isshinryu Kusanku Kata Secrets Revealed*. San Juan, 1998.

Martinez, Javier, *Isshinryu Naihanchi Kata Secrets Revealed*. San Juan, 1999.

Mashiro, N., *Black Medicine, Vol. I-IV*. Paladin, 1978-1995.

McCarthy, Patrick, *Classical Kata of Okinawan Karate*. Ohara, 1987.

McCarthy, Patrick, *Ancient Okinawan Martial Arts: Korryu Uchinadi, Volume 1*. Tuttle, 1999a.

McCarthy, Patrick, *Ancient Okinawan Martial Arts: Korryu Uchinadi, Volume 2*. Tuttle, 1999b.

Nagamine, Shoshin, *The Essence of Okinawan Karate-Do*. Tuttle, 1976.

Nagamine, Shoshin, *Tales of Okinawa's Great Masters*. Tuttle, 2000.

Nakasone, Genwa, et al, *Karate Do Dai Kan*. Tosho Inc., 1938.

Nakayama, Masatoshi, *Best Karate: Jitte, Hangetsu, Empi*. Kodansha, 1981.

Nicol, C.W., *Moving Zen*. William Morrow & Co., 1975.

Perry, M.C., *Narrative of the Expedition to the China Seas and Japan, 1852-1854*, reprinted by Dover Press, 2000.

Perry, M.C., *The Japan Expedition 1852-1854: The Personal Journal of Commodore Matthew C. Perry* (edited by Roger Pineau, with an introduction by Samuel Elliot Morrison). The Smithsonian Press, Washington D.C., 1968.

Sells, John, *Unante, The Secrets of Karate*. 2nd Edition, W.M. Hawley, 2000.

Shotokan Karate Applications, Vol. 1-3. Ertl/Bendickson Productions, 1998. http://www.karatevid.com.

Silvan, Jim, "Oral Traditions of Okinawan Karate," *Journal of Asian Martial Arts*. Vol. 7, No. 3, 1998, p. 73.

Sugiyama, Shojiro. *25 Shoto-kan Kata*. Privately published by author, 1989.

Spahn, Mark and Wolfgang Hadamitzky, *The Kanji Dictionary*. Tuttle, 1996.

Tegner, Bruce, *Complete Book of Jujitsu*. Thor, 1978.

U.S. Army Field Manual 7-8, *Infantry Rifle Platoon and Squad*. Department of the Army, 1992.

Van Wolferen, Karel, *The Enigma of Japanese Power*. MacMillan, 1989.

Index

Demura, Fumio, 16, 108

dinglehopper, 176, 203, 214

empi kata, 60, 69, 172
  renamed from *wansu*, 104
  step 1, 194, 196
  steps 7-8, 189
  steps 35-36, 215, 230

Ertl, Joel, 153, 155, 157, 159, 183

Fang, Chi-Niang, 34, 265
  fighting a stork, 34

Fitzpatrick, Jerry, iii, v

Florentine, Issac, 153

Funakoshi, Gichin (Shoto), 14, 55, 96, 97, 98–106
  compensating for height, 58
  feud with Motobu, 59, 105, 240
  kobudo kata, 108
  meaning of Shoto, 106
  photo, 99
  poverty, 100
  starving in Japan, 103
  struggling with bunkai, 240
  To-Te Jutsu, 54
  training with Azato, 63, 100
  training with Itosu, 58, 245
  training with Kiyuna, 72

Funakoshi, Gigo, 67, 103

Funakoshi, Kenneth, 153

gankaku kata, 36, 51, 154
  comparison to chinto, 159–64
  renamed from chinto, 104
  stairway fighting, 162
  step 7, 201
  steps 15-17, 210
  steps 18-24, 234

Gillespie, Toshiaki, 153

goju-ryu style, 96, 153
  Buddhist origin, 50
  founded by Miyagi, 94
  kata, 153
  sanchin kata, 164

gojushiho kata, 51, 59

Gushi, Shinyu, 153

Gusukuma, Shimpan, 17
  1936 meeting, 105
  training with Higaonna, 94

hakutsuru kata, 164

hangetsu kata, 51
  renamed from *seisan*, 104
  step 1, 194
  steps 13-21, 202
  steps 7-9, 193

Harrison, John, 21

heian godan kata
  stealing weapons, 221
  steps 9-12, 221
  step 15, 180
  step 22, 224
  steps 22-23, 223, 227
  steps 22-25, 208
  steps 23-26, 214
  steps 25-26, 224

heian kata, 39, 59, 172
  authored by Itosu, 60
  renamed from pinan, 104
  tactics, 114, 170–72

heian nidan kata
  authored by Matsumura, 51
  steps 1-3, 199
  step 2, 203
  step 7, 182, 183
  steps 8-11, 201
  steps 8-15, 204

heian sandan kata
  step 1, 178
  steps 2-3, 178
  step 9, 187
  steps 12-16, 204, 205
  steps 13-15, 210
  step 16, 206
  steps 19-20, 215
  steps 19-21, 191
  steps 19-22, 192
  steps 20-21, 196